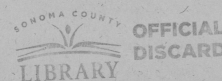

MEXICO
BEHIND
THE
MASK

MEXICO BEHIND THE MASK

A NARRATIVE, PAST AND PRESENT

Beldon Butterfield

Potomac Books
Washington, D.C.

Library of Congress Cataloging-in-Publication Data

Butterfield, Beldon, 1935–
    Mexico behind the mask : a narrative, past and present / Beldon Butterfield.—1st ed.
      p. cm.
    Includes bibliographical references and index.
    ISBN 978-1-61234-426-3 (hardcover : alk. paper)
    ISBN 978-1-61234-427-0 (electronic)
1. Mexico—History. I. Title.
    F1226.B965 2013
    972—dc23

                                  2012034676

Printed in the United States of America on acid-free paper that meets the American National Standards Institute Z39-48 Standard.

Potomac Books
22841 Quicksilver Drive
Dulles, Virginia 20166

First Edition

10 9 8 7 6 5 4 3 2 1

To my wife, Kate,
for her patience and understanding

Study the past if you would divine the future.

CONFUCIUS

◆ ◆ ◆

Contents

Acknowledgments

I WANT TO THANK MY WIFE, KATE, for her support in this three-year endeavor. She never doubted this manuscript would find a publisher. This book would never have been possible without the help of Gastón Moreno who knows more about Mexican history than anyone I know. As in the past, Veronica Byrnes helped editorially, while senior editor Elizabeth Demers at Potomac Books was invaluable, not only for her excellent editing, but also her knowledge of Mexican history. A special appreciation to Patricia García Arreola for her assistance on the index. Thanks also to Amanda Irle for her guidance and research in the editing process. Alfonso Cortina, whose career includes being director of the *Economist* magazine's Peer Forum in Mexico, put me in contact with people who were beyond my reach, while in the United States Stephen "Rennie" Spaulding, the international banker with endless contacts, and Dan Serby, with his many years in the State Department, did likewise. Special thanks to all those members of the Club Deportivo Mundet in Mexico City who urged me on with many hidden aspects of Mexico's past—thus the book title *Mexico Behind the Mask*. Our many discussions on our day outings in Yautepec, Morelos, and Villa Inquieta in Acapulco, of Mexico's unique political past and present have been incorporated into this book. To all those friends who urged me not to give up— *Viva México*.

Preface

THE IDEA FOR THIS BOOK STARTED back in 1967 when I was invited to lunch at the University Club in Mexico City by Victor Agather, an "old Mexico hand." Agather was more than that. He was one of the many American entrepreneurs who helped modernize Mexico's industrial base after World War II.

Like so many American pioneers in Mexico's road to industrial maturity, Victor Agather was a man with a colorful past. During World War II he was one of the U.S. Army Air Force pilots who belonged to the 509 Composite Group, the air crews trained in secret to launch the first A-bomb attack on Japan from Tinian Island. He retired with the rank of colonel. Years later he rebuilt a B-29 Superfortress from scrap available in aircraft graveyards and named it *Fifi* after his wife. It became the last plane of its kind to fly and can now be found in the Commemorative Air Force museum in Midland, Texas.

The gist of our conversation at lunch that day was Agather's concern that many of those Americans who had been responsible for turning Mexico into a modern industrialized state would be forgotten. His belief was that the following generations were somehow obligated to keep their story alive. The Mexicans had always considered the mantra "We need the gringos, but never thank them" etched in stone; in other words, never credit the Americans with anything but exploitation of the military and economic kind.

Decades after my meeting with Agather, the writer Clifford Irving, who spent many years in Mexico before moving to Colorado, insisted I write a book based on my experiences in Mexico—one that told the story of a nation that Americans could reach out and get to know, as one should, their next-door neighbor. Once I decided to embark on writing this book, I was obliged to give more than a cursory look at the possible consequences.

I was aware that Mexicans are not appreciative of foreigners writing about their past and present unless one follows the historical paradigms in which they have come to believe. Writing a different version required a more than passing consideration, having concluded Mexican historians were expert revisionists, or at best chose to skirt some of the serious issues that have caused Mexico so many problems throughout the nation's past. For example: "You have to understand that we are a poor country. . .," and what follows in support of that premise. "Not true. . . . Mexico is a rich country."

When I was getting my degree in history at Washington and Lee University, I took a course on looking at countries based on their geographic location and natural resources. Mexico ranked as one of the richest countries in the world, not only because of the favorable geographic location, but also the immense wealth above and below the surface of its landmass. So what went wrong? That was the problem that needed answering. If I could shed some light on this question, maybe some of these errors might be corrected. I admit that could be wishful thinking on my part, but there is no harm in trying.

In my defense, I'm obligated to state the obvious. I have lived in Mexico since 1962, first in Mexico City, then in Guadalajara, and now in San Miguel de Allende. I love this country and its people; otherwise I would have left a long time ago. If in the course of this book these feelings toward my adopted country come into question, the reader should keep in mind the purpose of this undertaking is to reach out to Americans so they might better understand their southern neighbor, which throughout history has stoically accepted bullying and benign neglect by one of its close allies. Inevitably, this narrative also led to targeting the mistakes Mexico itself has made in the past while at the same time making a concerted effort to keep these hidden from the rest of the world. *Mexico Behind The Mask* is an attempt to shed light on what Mexico and its people are hiding from themselves and the rest of the world.

Eventually, those who most encouraged me to put this narrative on paper were my Mexican friends, who constantly made suggestions as if they understood that revealing secrets had a salutary effect on the subconscious mind. Naturally, nobody wanted to be quoted by name. If someone was going to take the heat, let it be the gringo. In the end, criticisms of the point of views I have expressed will inevitably be based on not the truth behind the written word, but the guilty author. Ridiculing the messenger is always easier than attacking the message.

At the same time, there is no greater truism than that the United States and Mexico are joined together like Siamese twins; the heads may disagree, but the bodies have to learn to live with and depend on each other. Sometimes what makes us different also brings us together. That is undoubtedly one of the lessons I have tried to impart to those who honor me by buying this book.

Prologue:
History, Legend, and Lore

MOST MEXICAN SCHOLARS WILL AGREE that Octavio Paz Lozano, the 1990 Nobel Prize winner in literature, is one of the leading authorities on the psyche of the Mexican people. In his 1950 Spanish-language work *The Labyrinth of Solitude*, Paz writes, "Mexicans instinctively regard the world around them as dangerous. This reaction is justifiable if we consider what Mexican history has been and the society Mexicans have created." Speaking of masks, he continues, "The impression Mexicans create is like the Orientals, hermetic and indecipherable." What are they hiding and why? The answer is not that easy. Bad karma has always been an unwelcome companion and, much like fleas on a dog, hard to get rid of.

There is another equally insidious aspect of Mexico's past that constantly surfaces in reference to some of the negatives in their hidden national character. The unique Mexican word *malinchismo** imposes its presence throughout the nation's history; it is a word that restricts Mexicans from looking beyond their borders for new ideas and solutions for fear of being thought a traitor to the nation's extreme xenophobic interpretation of loyalty and nationalism. Those leaders who dared venture beyond this myopic vision are eventually branded as traitors and will inevitably pay for their transgressions. We will see the importance of *malinchismo* and *malinchista* as we delve into our story of Mexico's past and present. The words' importance cannot be emphasized enough.

The overall question Americans should ask themselves is this: is their southern neighbor, a nation most people know little to nothing about, important?

---

* Taken from a woman named La Malinche, an Aztec who showed the Spaniard Hernán Cortés the weak points of the Aztec Empire. Because of this treacherous act, her name signifies "traitor."

The United States and Mexico share a two-thousand-mile border, yet the divide that exists between both people seems wider than that. This rift becomes clearer when looking at recent events such as North American Free Trade Agreement (NAFTA), immigration issues, and the mounting violence between Mexican drug cartels and the Mexican government. These three issues are what I refer to as the "Troika of American Foreign Policy."*

◆

This book is a narrative of Mexico based on reflections of the past and present and on my personal experiences over a period of nearly a half century, emphasizing where possible the relationship and participation of the United States. Some of this story deals with established historical fact intertwined with legend and lore. My views will differ considerably from the hundreds of thousands of words that Mexican historians have written about their country. Their mission has always been an attempt to turn defeat into victory, failure into success, dictatorship into democracy, and corruption into acceptable behavior. As these distortions become a false reality, they stand on their head, as in a funhouse mirror reflecting objects upside down. If this sounds surreal, so be it, for Mexico is undoubtedly the home of the bizarre, strange, odd, and, at times, absurd.

What country can claim to have had the same president for eleven non-consecutive terms? His name was Gen. Antonio López de Santa Anna y Pérez de Lebrón. His entire time in office barely exceeded three years. More absurd was that during the Texas Revolution, according to legend, he lost the critical Battle of San Jacinto against the army of Sam Houston because he was being sexually entertained by an American mulatto indentured servant named Emily Morgan. Legend remembers her as "The Yellow Rose of Texas" in appreciation of the key part she played in the fight for Texas Independence in 1836. This battle, which lasted a mere eighteen minutes, eventually ended in the largest land grab in U.S. history and cost Mexico half of its territory.

Of course, that is no more absurd and bizarre than a man, having lost a close election, insisting that he is the legitimate president. Would-be president

---

* I first heard this description of American foriegn policy at a lecture given by ambassador to Mexico Jeffrey Davidow (1998–2001).

Andrés Manuel López Obrador, known as AMLO, and his followers placed a large tent in the middle of the Zócalo, the central square in Mexico City similar to the National Mall in Washington, D.C., for the sole purpose of receiving his constituents. On occasions when the true president of Mexico, Felipe de Jesús Calderón Hinojosa (2006–2012), attends official functions, such as national holidays or presentations in front of Congress, the usurper wears the tricolor sash representative of the president's office. The make-believe president López Obrador also uses these occasions to hold his unofficial meetings where he acts out the role of being the legitimately elected president. This is the same man who took fourteen years to earn a degree in social sciences from the Universidad Nacional Autónoma de México (National Autonomous University of Mexico, UNAM), the breeding ground of Mexican leftist radicals and future political leaders.

In September 2008, Mexico's Teachers Union leader Elba Esther Gordillo Morales bought fifty-nine fully equipped 2009 Hummers as presents for local teacher union members, leading to the following observation by a leading Mexican newsletter: "This is a national embarrassment in a country with so many shortcomings in education. We must find out where the resources to buy these Hummers came from and review how they were purchased."

Naturally, these words were never acted on. As is normal in matters dealing with politicians, "It's business as usual." This also brings up another popular Mexican saying: "To my friends the full protection of the law, to my enemies the full enforcement of the law."

Unfortunately Mexicans have come to accept this kind of behavior, and the nation resists any change to the status quo. After all, the people have long known their country has for decades come to accept institutionalized corruption. In an article that appeared on April 17, 2007, in *El Financiero* (the *Wall Street Journal* of Mexico), the government reported that Mexicans spent $2.58 billion yearly on bribes, roughly 8 percent of their total income. This statistic surprised no one. Mexicans know that most politicians and government officials are corrupt. If they are honest they might find themselves in jail as a menace to society, or in an insane asylum for having lost their sense of reality.

More recently, the World Economic Forum 2010 stated that corruption was the second largest problem with doing business in Mexico. That was followed by a report that appeared in April 2010 from the president of El Centro de

Estudios Económicos del Sector Privado (Center of Economic Studies of the Private Sector), which said that companies in Mexico spent 10 percent of their income, roughly between 7 and 9 percent of the GDP, on bribes.

The business of corruption was clearly stated by an ex-governor of the state of Mexico, the right honorable Carlos Hank González: "Show me a politician who is poor and I will show you a poor politician." The prevailing belief is that if you are not stealing, then you are cheating yourself.

◆

Mexico is divided into three separate nations. The north is politically moderate, industrialized, with a large middle class, and is the primary beneficiary of NAFTA due to the proximity to the United States. The Agrarian Reform* resulting from the Mexican Revolution of 1910 turned agriculture into a disaster. Despite that general statement, it is the north that can lay claim to a partially developed agricultural industry. It is the north that can also boast of low unemployment, a public and private educational infrastructure, and a proliferation of universities. In his book *Cuentos Chinos*, Andrés Oppenheimer, a syndicated columnist for the *Miami Herald* and an expert on Latin America, had this to say about Mexico: "When we talk about the new cultural model, the most decisive influence is that of the northern part of the country."

The south, on the other hand, is poor, lacking in infrastructure, politically on the extreme left, uneducated, devoid of industry, and is still holding on to the disastrous sacred cows of the Mexican Revolution, including the defunct ideals of agrarian reform centered on the distribution of land into communes known as *ejidos*.† It is the home of various guerilla groups such as the Ejército Zapatista de Liberación Nacional (The Zapatista Army of Liberation, EZLN) in the state of Chiapas, and the Ejército Popular Revolucionario (Popular Revolutionary Army, EPR) in the state of Oaxaca. Many political observers also include the Asamblea Popular de los Pueblos de Oaxaca (Popular Assembly of Towns in the State of Oaxaca, APPO), which is responsible for the teachers' strikes that tied up the capital city of Oaxaca and brought education and the tourism industry to their knees. The last of these events occurred as recently as February 2011, in

---

* See appendix 5, "The History of Land Reform: 1910–1934."

† An *ejido* is a plot of land not to exceed 10 hectares (22 acres) leased to the peasant as part of the government's program of land distribution.

protest to President Calderón's planned visit to the city of Oaxaca. The Mexico-bashing U.S. media widely reported the event as just one more example of Mexico's lawless behavior.

The south also has a large population of indigenous people who are, for the most part, nearly illiterate and not integrated into modern Mexico. Vast areas of the south, such as the states of Chiapas and Oaxaca, demographically and culturally are more like Guatemala. The south has yet to join even the third world, while the north is clearly a modern emerging nation.

Between these two imaginary nations is that sprawling urban stain of 22 million people called the Valley of Mexico, which includes the Federal District/Mexico City, the nation's capital. Many Mexicans refer to this great metropolitan area as the third Mexico. In this book I will describe it as "the spider in the web." This term appeared in the *Economist* magazine's "Annual Report on Mexico" in its November 2006 edition. The description simply means that all roads lead to the power centralized in Mexico City, a curse that I will refer to throughout this book. As with the Roman Empire, having control over the capital is having control over the entire country.

Divided Mexico does not end there. There is a widening gap between urban and rural Mexico. Mexico is an urban society that has, for all intents and purposes, neglected the rural division of the country. The rural areas are largely dominated by peasants, known as campesinos.

Sociologist Oscar Lewis wrote extensively about the Mexican peasant, which he described as living in a "culture of poverty." He wrote, "These people have a strong feeling of marginality, of helplessness, of dependency, of not belonging. They are like aliens in their own country, convinced that the existing institutions do not serve their interests and needs."

The real progress of Mexico is the emphasis on industrial development; the jewel in the crown being NAFTA. While this treaty between the United States, Canada, and Mexico benefits Mexico's industrial base, there are no benefits for the sagging agricultural economy. While urban Mexico marches steadily into the first world, most of rural Mexico finds itself mired in stagnation and antiquated methods of farming. Slash and burn practices have also taken their toll. Large areas of rural Mexico have been turned into a wasteland. With no cohesive plan to better the agriculture industry of Mexico, the divide between urban and rural grows more protracted. For many living in rural Mexico, the response is to migrate to the major cities only to find they have joined the underemployed while increasing the numbers of those living in the belts of poverty. To date the only real opportunity for work is to cross the border into the United States illegally as an undocumented alien.

But there is also another aspect of Mexico that bears studying for Americans. What is little known is the important role the United States and its people have played in the past as far back as the U.S. Declaration of Independence. When the United States declared its independence, the official currency of that new nation was the "Mexican silver peso." In 1795 the United States created its own currency, "the dollar" or "greenback." The par value was based on the Mexican silver peso. From 1795 until 1857, the United States had two official currencies: the greenback and the Mexican silver peso.

It is impossible to tell the story of Mexico without discussing the cultural divide between the two countries. By not understanding these cultural differences, Mexicans and Americans have a stereotyped view of each other, usually resulting from Hollywood films. But the differences go far beyond mere stereotyping, and by understanding them and acting accordingly we can narrow the gap. Even though this book does not deal with cross-border culture, I would be remiss to not give the reader at least a taste. Mexicans traditionally are different from Americans, despite the fact that with the advent of NAFTA some of that is changing. Both countries are not only involved in "production sharing"* and trade, but many of the cultural barriers are breaking down despite a lingering resistance on both sides of the border—a border that Mexicans cannot forget symbolizes the scar of an unjust war and that Americans resent when millions of Mexicans cross illegally as undocumented immigrants and workers.

Much of Mexico's past is like a tangled rope that seems impossible to undo. But, when the rope is finally straightened the truth emerges, and the complexities become mundane.

I have based my account on what I've seen and experienced and on historical facts that can't be tampered with, despite hundreds of different interpretations. The Aztecs did arrive in the valley of Mexico in 1325 AD. Hernán Cortés de Monroy y Pizarro did conquer the Aztec Empire in 1521. Mexico did gain its independence from Spain in 1821. The Republic of Texas was created

---

* Two countries agree to share in manufacturing and assembly.

in 1836 from territory belonging to Mexico. The United States did go to war with Mexico in 1846, resulting in a 50 percent loss of Mexican territory to its northern neighbor. The French did invade in 1862. There was a Mexican Revolution in 1910, followed by the disastrous Agrarian Reform laws. The Partido Revolucionario Institucional (PRI) did evolve into the party that governed Mexico through a series of self-proclaimed presidents from 1929 to 2000. Mexico did isolate itself from the outside world until *la apertura*, the opening of the economy, in the middle of the 1980s. The system of presidential successions and the non-reelection clause in the Constitution of 1917 did keep the internal political peace, but at a terrible cost to a nation led by broken promises, government mismanagement, and greed. NAFTA did become a reality in 1994, followed immediately by the Zapatista uprising in Chiapas, led by the mysterious, and always masked, *subcomandante* Marcos. Shortly after Marcos's emergence, Mexico suffered through the assassination of the PRI presidential candidate Luis Donaldo Colosio Murrietta, which caused a financial crisis that brought the country to the verge of chaos and eventually spread to the rest of Latin America as the "Tequila Effect." Mexico, after years of insisting that it was a democracy *a la mexicana*, did hold open primaries and a subsequent free election for the office of president in 2000; a historic election without the heavy-handed intervention of the ruling party.

However, many aspects of Mexico's past and present are not part of this chronology. I have tried being selective on what I believe the American reader will find interesting and relevant to these two nations that share a peaceful two-thousand-mile border, even if at times they seem barely tolerant of each other.

There is so much more we can agree on. The problem is the interpretation of these events, and others not mentioned, explaining how Mexico went from one of the richest countries on earth to joining the third world. Mexico proved incapable of taking care of millions of its own people but somehow managed to blame as many others as possible for these mistakes. Conveniently, outside of Mexico the United States became the major culprit. "When the United States sneezes, Mexico has pneumonia," goes the refrain. What could better exemplify this attitude than that wonderful Mexican saying attributed to President José de la Cruz Porfirio Díaz Mori (1876–1910), the ruler who became the catalyst of the Mexican Revolution of 1910: "Poor Mexico, so far from God and so close to the United States."

The good news is that Mexico is going through major changes, regardless of the resistance of political dinosaurs who want to continue their unchecked power of the past. At times these changes have come at a terrible price to the nation and its citizens.

Introducing Mexico

I have spent fifty years living between Mexico City, Guadalajara, and, more recently, San Miguel de Allende, a Spanish/Mexican colonial town in the state of Guanajuato, located on the high plateau of Central Mexico. San Miguel de Allende has become a magnet for Americans looking for a seasonal residence or a permanent home. I sometimes give lectures to newly arrived foreigners, mostly Americans, interested in learning about this country. What I have found is that the majority of Americans I have met here in Mexico, regardless of age, gender, or formal education, know little about their own country's history and even less about Mexico's. In his book, *The Cycles of American History*, Arthur Schlesinger Jr. referred to Americans as a "history-less people." He did not mean that the United States did not have a rich history, just that most Americans did not know it.

The first thing I teach my audience is that if you want to learn about Mexico, start by looking around your new environment, and ask yourself what makes it different. Many of the qualities that attract Americans to Mexico also provide the clues to the country's long and complex past. The first question I pose, since it is the most obvious when walking the streets near the central plaza of any Mexican town, is, "Why do Mexican homes have walls around them?"

By the time I finish my three-day lectures I expect them to know the answer. But there are other questions I hope they can resolve on their own from observing the stately buildings and churches in Mexican towns and cities, taking a close look at the topography, and experiencing activities in the surrounding countryside. Much of Mexico's past can be observed in these different venues if one takes the time to look. Training our mind's eye to give meaning to what we see will enrich our lives and extend the experience of being in a country so unlike the United States far beyond the scope of the standard tourist's guidebook, which makes sure you see only the obvious.

I am a firm believer that the micros tell us more about a place than the macros, which inevitably have to be broken down into their individual parts if we want to understand a statement like "Mexico is a poor country because 40 percent of its people live below the poverty level." Let's assume for a moment that that's true, but what does it tell us about the nation? Not much, since we can use similar statistics to describe numerous countries around the globe.

I'm also convinced that what seems irrelevant often becomes relevant if we take a few minutes to analyze what we have just observed. I have selected a few examples.

- You are driving down the highway when your wife says, "Stop the car! Look! There's a perfect Kodak moment." What she has just seen is a farmer cultivating a field with a wooden plow drawn by a mule. Once the zoom lens has done its job, the couple drives off. Having observed the use of farming technology that dates as far back as the Old Testament should make someone a little curious as to what is going on.

- While driving through Mexico you arrive at a quaint Mexican village and decide to spend the night. The next morning you go out to your car, which is now covered in a thin film of dust. You think nothing of this because next to your car there is a young boy waiting to wash it, as well as every other car parked in front of your hotel. Had you taken the time to investigate the origins of this dust, you might have noticed a clear blue sky. There is also no factory within at least a hundred miles that would have produced such dust. Since it's fairly early in the morning, your curiosity is awakened as you observe that up and down the street women are watering and scrubbing down the sidewalks in front of their walled-in homes. This is obviously a daily routine, but what are they scrubbing off, and where is it coming from?

- A well-known saying is *ni modo*—"who cares?"—usually accompanied by a shrug of the shoulders. What does this saying really mean?

- If you travel throughout Mexico, you will soon realize that the highway system north of Mexico City is at least four lanes to all the major border checkpoints into the United States. Not so toward the south and the border checkpoints leading into Guatemala and Belize.

- When someone answers the phone in Mexico they say *bueno*, which every Spanish dictionary will tell you means good. In the rest of Latin America they answer the phone and say *hola*, which means hello.

- One cannot be in this country very long before someone, maybe just a waiter, will say *un momentito,* followed by raising his arm and making a space between his thumb and forefinger indicating his intentions with words that literally mean, in a tiny moment. It is up to you to interpret the actual time interval represented between thumb and forefinger.

- Mexican men show their affection for each other with the *abrazo*, which is something like a bear hug between two underweight sumo wrestlers. When we see Mexican President Felipe Calderón (2006–2012), embracing Andrés López Obrador, the interloper who has dedicated his life to claiming he is the legitimate president and Calderón merely a usurper who stole the last election, the sumo wrestler analogy becomes clearer. They absolutely hate each other. Why then is an abrazo supposed to represent a sign of affection?

Despite what the reader may think, these anecdotes can be seen as colored tiles arranged in their proper place to form a mosaic that will eventually say, "This is Mexico."

Most of us have heard the old saying "You can't see the forest for the trees." I like to be more specific. You have seen just seen some of the leaves that connect to a branch that connects to the trunk that connects to a tree that eventually becomes a forest. Understand these connections, and you will have an insight in understanding Mexico.

Here are some answers to the questions posed earlier:

- Why do Mexican homes have walls around them? Because they only trust themselves when their own security is at risk. There is a Mexican saying that goes like this: "Please, God, protect this home from doctors and the law." Relying on the legal system for justice is a concept that only applies in other countries. "*Mejor un mal arreglo que un buen pleito*," or "Better a bad deal than a legal battle." Law enforcement is never to be relied on, in the belief that the police are behind most of the crimes. As Octavio Paz writes, "Mexicans instinctively regard the world around them as dangerous." The roots of this fear are found in Mexico's past.

- The Kodak moment with the campesino and his wooden plow tells the story of Agrarian Reform, one of the failures of the Mexican Revolution of 1910. The revolution went a long way towards ruining the agricultural base of Mexico. We will see how this affects Mexico's development and forces a segment of the population to look for work elsewhere, the best option being on the other side of the border.

- The thin coat of dust on the car is the result of slash-and-burn farming practices that send the topsoil into the atmosphere with the slightest breeze. The residue eventually lands on your car and on the streets and sidewalks of most rural towns. If you multiply this dust by decades of peasant farming under the Agrarian Reform, you will understand where Mexico's topsoil went and why a rich agriculture country became poor, with subsequent dire consequences.

- *Ni modo*, accompanied with a shrug of the shoulders, is a sign of resignation meaning, "so what? It can't be helped," or "there's nothing we can do about it"; a stoic trait that runs through people in most walks of Mexican life.

- The difference in the highways in the north and south, separated by Mexico City, is about NAFTA in the north, which in Mexico translates into thousands of trailers daily crossing the border, representing trade between the three countries. There is nothing much going on in the south, except a lot of discontent and poverty, resulting in the theory of the three different Mexico's: north, south, and central, the last being Mexico City— the political, financial, and cultural hub of the country.

- The use of the word "bueno" instead of "hola" when answering the phone relates to the past: The person answering merely wanted to know if the phone worked. This is a metaphor for Mexico, especially when we look at the mismanagement of state-owned companies and the government.

- *Un momentito*, that wonderful use of the concept of time, generally means "*Oigo, pero no cumplo*," which literally means "I hear you, but I don't obey." For a country that lived under the dictatorial rule of the PRI from 1929 until 2000, the use or misuse of a time frame as an obligation became one of the ways to rebel. The space between the thumb and forefinger is a reflection of time that has absolutely no meaning and it is left up to the viewer to make a calculated guess. It could cover time intervals from five seconds to whatever that person is predisposed to grant.

- The abrazo, the familiar way Mexicans greet each other, also has a deeper meaning. Andrés Oppenheimer in his 1994 book *Bordering on Chaos* says it best: "As far as historians can remember, double talk and deceit have been part of Mexico's national character. The abrazo is said to be a by-product of Mexico's culture of deceit. Of course, a good number of abrazos—at least nowadays—are legitimate shows of affection, but quite often hard to tell the hardy ones from the fake ones." During the Mexican Revolution the abrazo, and the patting down that accompanied the ritual, was a cover for one man checking the other for weapons.

Understanding the hidden meaning behind the everyday use of many words, popular sayings, and practices tells the observer more about a country than reading a book outlining historical events.

As a long time resident of Mexico City, I know there are certain elements of my life and way of thinking that have changed since I lived in the United States. Here are some examples:

- I believe a shot of tequila cures almost every ailment and illness. I have learned to enjoy eating *tacos*, *enchiladas*, *carnitas*, *chicharrón*, *morcilla*, and *moronga* at street taco stands, but I believe eating at McDonald's is an unhealthy import responsible for turning the country into a mass of obese waddling geese.

- There are more prescription drugs in my briefcase than in CVS, and I don't have an actual prescription for a single one.

- I blame crime on the poor and on law enforcement, which most everyone knows is corrupt. I blame the government for almost everything else. What's left over I blame on the gringos, having forgotten that a good part of me is still one of them.

- Sometimes I eat lunch and dinner with business acquaintances and friends on the same day, many times at the same restaurant.

- When I married a Mexican woman, I became a firm believer in the Mexican marriage vows as officially outlined by the marriage epistle according to Melchor Ocampo:

  > The man, who is the principal source of courage and strength, should and will give the woman protection, nourishment and direction. He should treat her always as the more delicate and sensitive partner, and generously offer his strength in her time of need.
  >
  > The woman, whose principal talents are self-sacrifice, beauty, compassion, keen insight and tenderness should, and will, give her husband obedience, pleasure, assistance, consolation and advice. She should always treat him with a delicacy and with the respect due to the one who supports and defends her.

- On the religious side, I never accompany my wife to mass, but I never fail to set up an altar at home on the Day of the Dead. This altar includes two skulls, three candles, food, my wife's rosary, and pictures of the deceased in both families. I hope they will appreciate the gesture from the hereafter. I have a hard time accepting that the dead are to be more revered than the living, except on Mother's Day.

- I absolutely refuse to host an open house for her family, reminding her that we don't live in a hotel. The one time I broke down I got the feeling I'd been attacked by a swarm of locusts. Fortunately, these soirees always have countless volunteers ready to step up and play host. Not only do family members attend, but also include the extended family, usually those people who can provide key contacts in the government, and jobs for the black sheep of the family. If you want dozens of in-laws on your doorstep, marry a Mexican. They may be a pain at times, but when the going gets tough they come to the rescue.

- Finally, I'm always convinced the next *sexenio*, the six-year presidential term, will be better than the last one. I can't accept this is never the case.

Actually, I haven't gone entirely native. I only slightly cheat on my taxes, compared to my Mexican friends who have turned this into the national sport. Professional soccer is boring. I much prefer watching U.S. pro football and college basketball. I don't cheer for Mexico in the Olympic Games. What's to cheer for? They rarely win. Mexico's history also seems like one big justification of losses, territorial and otherwise.

What I really find offensive is that every time I'm forced to enter an office manned by bureaucrats the wait is interminable, even for the simplest transaction. When one finally gets an audience the paperwork that inevitably follows suit is accompanied by these bureaucrats sage words: "This is not the United States. Unfortunately this is Mexico, where everything is more backward and in much need of reform. The government has assured us these reforms are imminent." Going into the twenty-first century changes do seem to be taking place. I suspect the bureaucrats have run out of places to store all the paperwork.

I despise Americans who trash their own country in front of Mexicans. It's hard enough to get a Mexican to respect a gringo considering past events between both countries, only to have some know-it-all voice an unsolicited opinion, such as "NAFTA is just an excuse for American companies to exploit the Mexican worker." Mexico seems to draw an inordinate number of Joe Bidens.

To many Americans, Mexico is a fairly unknown country made up mostly of stereotypes appearing in western films: unshaven faces under dirty sombreros, ill-fitting clothes that seem to smell even through the screen, crossed bandoliers, pistols, rifles, and a propensity to bite the dust at the hands of the gringo gunslinger.

There was, of course, the more sophisticated version of the next-door neighbor as described in a cover story titled "The Domino Player" that appeared in *Time* magazine on September 14, 1953: "Mexico, the old picturesque land of the eagle and the serpent, of barefoot peasants drowsing in the plazas and well shod politicians browsing the treasury."

Five years later, on December 8, 1958, the thinking at *Time* magazine had evolved. "Though Mexico is next door to the U.S., the country south of the border is still mostly a colorful legend. It is, to many Americans, unsanitary and exotic. It is violent: The plump *señora* in the cartoon scolds her *sombreroed* husband as he cleans his pistol, saying 'Oh Pablo, you're not going back into politics!'"

To best understand Mexico's many problems leading up to the present, it is important to go back to the beginning to try and see what happened, and why it happened. A good place to start is in the year 1325.

THE SPIDER IN THE WEB
(1325–1810)

J ULIUS CAESAR, UPON CONQUERING GAUL in 47 BC, made the memorable
statement, "*Veni, Vidi, Vici.*" In 1519 the Spanish conquistador Hernán
Cortés must have thought something similar when he arrived just north of the
present-day city of Veracruz, Mexico. Winston Churchill might have said it a
little differently: "Never in the history of human conflict has such a small force
conquered such a large region, with such massive wealth."

To understand Mexico and its people, it is essential to understand the first
two conquests of Mexico, first by the Aztecs in 1325, then by Hernán Cortés
from 1519 to 1521. In the aftermath of the Spanish conquest came the Spanish
colonial period, which lasted from 1521 to 1810.

It is impossible to tell the story of this segment of the Mexican narrative
without reference to two female figures, La Malinche and the Virgin of Guadalupe, Patron Saint of the Americas. Some might say they are the very essence
of the future nation.

It was the conquest and the continued centralization of power, first by the Aztecs and then the Spaniards, that brought Mexico to its knees, whether through civil war, revolution, foreign intervention, or exploitation. As a result of the conquest, Mexico City became the spider in the web, the very center of power, military might, and culture of New Spain. It has been Mexico's strength and her inevitable weakness. The conquest foisted the Roman Catholic Church on the Mexican people, and the Spaniard's subsequent lust for wealth had no bounds. It also established the *mestisaje*, the crossing of Spanish and Indian bloodlines. The conquest gave birth to the Mexican caste system. The conquest created the campesino, the peasant, who throughout Mexico's history has been a noose around the nation's neck. And it was the conquest that unveiled the enormous hidden mineral treasures below the surface of New Spain. Understand the conquest of Mexico and its consequences, and you have the basic knowledge for understanding Mexico.

1

The First Two Conquests
(1325, 1519)

◆

IF WE WANT TO UNDERSTAND NORTH AMERICA, it is essential that we begin by knowing that the origins of Mexico totally differ from those of the United States or Canada. Mexico's early history is one of conquest, first by the Aztecs and then by the Spaniards, who did not come with the intention of colonizing these newly discovered lands (that came later). The Spaniards' intent was to plunder for themselves and the Spanish empire they served. Extracting the mineral wealth of Mexico was always the priority on their agenda.

In the case of the United States, colonization was the overriding reason the original settlers emigrated from Great Britain. These new arrivals were more interested in religious freedom, commerce, land ownership, farming, and bringing up a family. Another major difference, aside from language and religion—Catholic versus Protestant—is that Mexico created a complicated caste system with the European Spaniard in control.

The conquistador Hernán Cortés took less than a dozen years in the sixteenth century to occupy all the territory of present-day Mexico and Guatemala. The American colonies had barely moved inland from the eastern seaboard in the hundred years since arriving at Jamestown in 1607. By that time Mexico was a well-developed Spanish colony. If one imagines the vastness of the Midwestern plains and the snow-covered mountain ranges that daunted the future expansion of the United States in the latter part of the eighteenth century, it's hard to believe that beyond the Rocky Mountains the Spaniards/Mexicans had already created colonies in the future states of New Mexico and California.

Mexicans like to think they are descendants of two great civilizations, the Maya and the Aztec. Truth be told, the Maya abandoned their cities in the southern Maya lowlands of Mesoamerica around 900 AD, although they continued to exist in the northern Yucatán. They were long gone as a major Meso-American civilization when the Aztecs discovered the future Mexico in 1325 AD. A blood-thirsty lot dedicated to conquest and the collection of tribute paid by the Indian nations and people they subjugated, the Aztecs would be destroyed by the Spaniards after a dictatorial rule of less than two hundred years.

Asserting descendance from the Mayans is a historic stretch. However, nobody can seriously question the Aztecs being the forefather of the Mexican people. From the interracial mixing of Aztec and the conquering Spaniard, the Mexican was born. Known as the mestizo, today they make up the overwhelming majority of the population of Mexico.

The enigma is why are the Aztecs so admired in Mexico? Why are there so many monuments and murals in national palaces depicting their greatness and that of Cuauhtémoc and Cuitláhuac, two of their emperors? The Spanish conquerors led by Hernán Cortés are all but forgotten; not a single bust or statue of the conquistador can be found in the entire country.

One of the great statues in Mexico City, a gift from Spain, commemorates Emperor Charles IV astride a mighty steed. The Mexicans renamed it El Caballito (The Pony). This bizarre attitude toward the Spaniards raises the question of why Mexicans still consider Spain the mother country? Maybe the answer is that the confrontation between Aztecs and Spaniards was a clash of two imperial, morally corrupt societies that eventually melded into the fore-runner of modern Mexico. That still does not answer the question of why the Aztecs are so revered. With a culture based on human sacrifice and cannibal-ism they were definitely worse than the Spanish. Possibly the answer is that there are few vestiges of the Aztecs while the Spanish presence is everywhere with churches and majestic buildings littering the Mexican landscape.

The Spider In The Web

In the year 1325, a group of nomads, known as the Náhuatl, moved into what today is known as the Valley of Mexico. Where did they come from? Nobody really knows. To attempt to explain the mystery, the keepers of legend and lore invented the mythical place Aztlán.* They created the idea that there were seven inhab-ited caves somewhere near the west coast of Mexico.† From these caves people

---

* *Aztecatl* in Náhuatl translates to "People of Aztlán." The original location of this legendary city is still contested, but most scholars agree that it is definitely somewhere in the north of Mexico.

† Known as the seven caves of Chicomoztoc.

trekked in a southerly direction, eventually arriving where Mexico City is today. Some Mexican historians suggested the original settlers in the Valley of Mexico were Chichimeca Indians from the central state of Guanajuato to the north.

Anthropologists, however, have taken a different view. They generally agree that Aztlán is in reality many separate places that probably included the Southwest of the present-day United States and possibly extended as far north as the Bering Straits that once connected Alaska with Russia. As farfetched as it may seem, the Pueblo Indians, in the southwest of the United States, were known to have abandoned their villages around the year 1300, as a result of a protracted twenty-five years of drought. They headed south in search of more fertile lands. Some may even have gotten as far as the Valley of Mexico in 1325. Regardless of their origin, these nomads became known as the Aztecs.

The wandering Aztecs searched for a sign that would tell them where to settle. The sign turned out to be an eagle with a snake in its beak, standing atop a cactus. That symbol now appears on the Mexican flag, government buildings, and on all official stationery. Unfortunately, the sign came to the Aztecs in the middle of five lakes. Not to be dissuaded, the people built their city on these lakes by creating floating plots of land called *chinampas*. Canals and causeways connected the man-made small islands that led to the Plaza Mayor (Central Square), the center of the newly founded city they named Tenochtitlan. Once settled, they branched out and conquered the Indian nations around them, including the Toltecs, Zapotecs, Mixtecs, and Coatzacoalcans on the Gulf of Mexico. It was the Toltecs who were largely responsible for designing and building the temples in the great city of Tenochtitlan, capital of the Aztec One World.

To tell a Mexican that the Aztecs were foreign invaders can be considered offensive. It's like punching a hole in their historic balloon, especially since no one has ever found the mythical seven caves of Chicomoztoc. The Chichimeca Indian version has never been proven. Even if this were true, it does not excuse them from being invaders. They were not native to the lands they eventually conquered. What else could one call them?

Many foreign visitors to Mexico confuse the Aztecs with the builders of the pyramids on the outskirts of Mexico City. Those pyramids belong to the Teotihuacán civilization that, at the height of its power, ruled Meso-America. This pyramid city was already a five-hundred-year-old archeological site when the Aztecs arrived in the Valley of Mexico in 1325. Unfortunately, when one looks for the remnants of the Aztec civilization, there is little left. The Spaniards made sure of that.

—◆—

By the early sixteenth century the Aztecs had accumulated enormous wealth, a large part of which was on display in Tenochtitlan, renamed Mexico City under Spanish rule. Following in the footsteps of the Aztecs, Mexico City became the capital and center of power of New Spain. As with the Aztecs, the centralization of power became the Achilles' heel of Mexico throughout history; this combined with the great mineral wealth beneath the surface of the land cursed the nation for centuries to come.

The first major curse came from the Spaniards, who during the early fifteen hundreds were already trading up and down the coast of the Gulf of Mexico. They heard rumors that far away to the west and beyond the mountains, there was a city of gold. These coastal Indians had never been to the "city of gold,"* but they assured the Spaniards the gold was there. Talking about gold to Spaniards was similar to inciting a school of sharks into a feeding frenzy.

In the year 1519, the adventurer and visionary Hernán Cortés appeared with his band of six hundred gold-hungry thugs, whose last known addresses were the dungeons of some of the worst prisons in Spain. The Spaniards also counted on twenty horses that strategically functioned as mobile armor, which managed to keep the mighty Aztec army at bay in awe of creatures they had never seen before.† At first, they believed man and horse were but one creature bound together into a formidable fighting machine. To this terror, add ten cannon that must have had a serious effect on an Aztec warrior's composure in battle, not to mention his eardrums. Had the Aztecs known the words "weapons of mass destruction," the horse and the cannon would surely have fit their description.

With the desire to conquer hidden behind the pretext of bringing Christianity to those who had never been so fortunate as to see the light, the Spaniard's cry as they plundered their way to Tenochtitlan must have sounded something like, "First, as Christians, our duty is to take care of the Lord's business; then we can take care of our real business—gold."

---

* For the Spanish, the mythical city of gold was known as El Dorado.

† The conquest of Mexico introduced the modern horse to the North American continent. These horses eventually became the mustangs of the southwest.

When the Spaniards landed just north of the city of Veracruz and came in contact with the coastal Indians, they asked what the people called themselves. The answer sounded like the word *mexica*, pronounced *me-shee-ka*. The word *mexica* sounded to the Spaniards like *México*, which eventually became the word Mexico in English.

There is no question that the Spaniards were awed by what they saw upon their arrival to this great Aztec capital. Bernal Díaz del Castillo, author of *Historia verdadera de la conquista de la Nueva España* (*The Conquest of New Spain*) was a witness to these events. He provides a vivid description of the Spanish entrance into Tenochtitlan:

> During the morning we arrived at a broad causeway and continued our march towards Iztapalapa, and when we saw so many cities and villages built on the water and other great towns on dry land and that straight and level causeway going towards the center of their world, we were amazed and said it was like the enchantments they tell of in the legend of Amadis,* on account of the great towers and temples and buildings rising from the water, and built of masonry. And some of the soldiers even asked whether the things that we saw were not a dream.

Outwardly the differences between the Aztecs and the Spaniards were their language, the color of their skin, and how they dressed. Unmask their inner souls and they were much alike. No wonder Cortés and Montezuma II, the Emperor of the Aztec One World, got along. Díaz narrates that Montezuma enjoyed playing an Aztec game with pebbles. He tells us that Montezuma caught Pedro de Alvarado y Contreras, one of the Spanish captains who went on to conquer what is today Guatemala, cheating at keeping score. When Montezuma learned to play cards, Díaz points out, he honored his Spanish hosts by also learning to cheat.

Montezuma took Cortés and his men on a tour of the city. When they eventually reached the Templo Mayor, Díaz gives us the following description.

> When we arrived at the great temple [Templo Mayor] and before we had climbed a single step, the great Moctezuma [Montezuma in English] sent

---

* *Amadis de Gaula*: Fourteenth-century tales of knight-errantry written by Garci Rodríguez de Montalvo. From one of his books we learn of the mythical place named California.

six *papas* [priests] and two chieftains down from the top to escort our
Captain [Cortés]. The top of the *cue* [temple] formed an open square,
something like a platform, and it was here that the great stones stood on
which they placed the poor Indians for sacrifice. Here also was a massive
image like a dragon, and other hideous figures, and a great deal of blood
that had been spilled that day.

The last reference was to the Aztec practice of human sacrifice: "They strike
open the wretched Indian's chest with flint knives and hastily tear out the palpi-
tating heart, which, with the blood, they present to their idols. Then they cut off
the arms, thighs and head, eating the arms and thighs at their ceremonial ban-
quets." Bernal Díaz also tells us they ate them in a sauce of peppers and toma-
toes, surely the precursor of *salsa mexicana*, sometimes known as pico de gallo.

Díaz continues: "I cannot omit to mention the cages of stout wooden bars that
we found in the city, full of men and boys who were being fattened for the sacrifice at which their flesh would be eaten." This same fate befell many a Spaniard,
with the added touch, "They flayed their faces, which they afterwards prepared
like gloved leather, with their beards on, and kept for their drunken festivals."

From the top of the Templo Mayor, while the priests temporarily stopped
their grisly business, Montezuma gave Cortés and his entourage a visual tour of
the city. The Spaniards marveled at the splendor of causeways and canals, rich
flower gardens, and a giant aviary with more exotic birds that any European
had ever seen before, as well as the cleanliness of a city beyond anything known
in Europe. They were shown a functioning zoo, a modern freshwater aqueduct
system, and a giant market of fresh produce and goods from around the Aztec
world. If Mexico was to become known as the land of extreme contrasts, this
is where the description probably started.

While the Spaniards got more gold than they could get their greedy hands
on, the Aztecs probably got what they surely deserved—defeat, humiliation,
and eventual near extinction. Smallpox and other diseases imported from
Europe became the Spaniards' most effective secret weapon, much like the bio-
logical weapons of today.

Historians and archeologists believed the main temple of the Aztecs, the
Templo Mayor, was on the site where the National Cathedral now stands in
the main plaza of Mexico City, known as the Zócalo. They were wrong, as

proven when the city was building Line 1 of the subway system in 1969, and workers literally drilled one of the tunnels into a stone wall. They had just found the Templo Mayor, just behind and to the right of the cathedral.

Even though Cortés destroyed most of Tenochtitlan, one can still relive the glory days of the Aztecs by visiting the National Museum of Anthropology in Mexico City, across from Chapultepec Park, and the more recent restoration of sections of the Templo Mayor. A museum adjoining the temple opened in 1987 and has been much improved through the years. And of course, a visit to Pre-Colombian Mexico should include at least a half-day trip to the Pyramids of Teotihuacan.

Without a doubt a must-see for visitors to Mexico City is a half-day tour to the floating gardens of Xochimilco. Here are the remnants of what Tenochtitlan must have looked and felt like. From any number of embarcaderos (piers), visitors can board a *trajinera*, a flat-bottom vessel similar to the giant canoes used by the Aztecs as they traveled along the canals of their ancient capital. Every time I visit these floating gardens, I'm amazed how easily one's imagination can regress to the days when Tenochtitlan was truly the center of "the one world."

Once the Spaniards gained control over Tenochtitlan, they changed the name to Ciudad de México. They also moved quickly, taking immense amounts of territory in their own version of Manifest Destiny.

In 1541, Hernando De Soto was the first European to see the Mississippi River. In 1540, Francisco Vásquez de Coronado y Luján and his band were the first to set eyes on the Grand Canyon in northern Arizona. He wintered in what is today Santa Fe, New Mexico. In the spring of 1541, he crossed the Great Plains of northern Texas. Pánfilo de Narváez trekked across Florida, getting as far as Tampa Bay where, after being attacked by the natives and all sorts of swamp creatures, he got fed up and declared, "Spain ends here," and then set sail for Mexico. He never made it. Juan Cabrillo, a Portuguese explorer who was part of the Cortés expedition, sailed up the western coast of Mexico to discover California.* He landed in the Bay of San Diego in 1542. His subsequent discoveries included Santa Catalina Island, Santa Barbara Channel, Monterey Bay, and San Miguel Island. None of these left any kind of settlement that future generations could point at and say, "The Spaniards were here," but there were some exceptions.

---

* This refers to the California that belongs to the United States. Baja California was discovered earlier.

In 1609, Pedro de Peralta settled in Santa Fe and turned it into a small colonial town. One hundred years later the Spaniards settled in Albuquerque, named after el Duque de Aburquerque, one of the many titles of the Spanish viceroy Don Francisco Fernández de la Cueva (1653–1660). On June 13, 1691, the feast day of St. Anthony of Padua in Italy, a group of Spanish missionaries settled next to a river, today in the state of Texas, and named it San Antonio in his honor.

All three of these towns became reminders of Spain when the Americans started to migrate west. This is as far as Mexico's expansion went in an effort to colonize the northern territories. As we will see, the exception turned out to be California, largely due to the efforts of an extraordinary Franciscan missionary, Padre Junípero Serra. The inability to colonize much of the northern frontiers came at a terrible cost to Mexico a century and a half later when it lost half of its territory to the expansionist United States.

The courage, strength, and fortitude of these early arrivals to Mexico must be admired. They were extraordinary men.

Mexico remembers the defeat of the bloodthirsty Aztecs as the conquest of a mighty and noble people. Well into the future, celebrating defeat will turn into a Mexican trait. The exception turned out to be Montezuma, whom many Mexicans revile as a traitor because he allowed a mere six hundred Spaniards to conquer his empire. As noted, Hernán Cortés and the men that came with him did not fare so well; not a single statue in Mexico carries their names. But the story of Cortés does not end there. The Spanish Empire thought he was getting too powerful and decided to have him marginalized.

In 1541, utterly neglected by the Spanish court, the conqueror of the Aztec Empire and New Spain forced his way through a crowd and approached the carriage of Charles V, King of Castile and Emperor of the Holy Roman Empire.

"Who is this man who has the audacity to approach me?" the astounded emperor asked.

"I am a man," replied Cortés proudly, "who has given you more provinces than your ancestors left you cities."

Few traces of the Aztec civilization survive compared to the greatness of the Maya and the Teotihuacans. The latter disappeared around 750 AD, but their pyramids still stand majestically outside Mexico City. Adding to these archeo-logical sites are the Spanish colonial government buildings, cathedrals, churches, and municipal palaces, standing like timeless sentinels heralding a grandiose past. There are the stately homes, parks, roads, bridges, mines, aque-ducts, and more—the list is endless—all built by the historically maligned Spaniards.

Remnants of the Aztec Empire are seen mostly in murals, codices, statues, and museums, while the other great civilizations that flourished in what today is Mexico left behind a wealth of spectacular pyramids and buildings and a legacy for all to see and admire. But all was not lost. The real story of the Conquest of Mexico survives in the story of two women, whose lives and leg-ends defined Mexico for centuries to come.

2

The Mothers of Mexico and the Caste System

◆

Throughout history women have played an important part in the creation of nations. Mexico is no exception.

The Secular Mother of the Mestizo Nation

She was born into an Aztec family of royal blood and sold into slavery when her father died and her mother went to live with another man. Or so the story goes. But regardless of the facts, we know she was an Aztec from a family of certain rank, and we know she became a slave in the Coatzacoalcan nation that bordered the Gulf of Mexico. Her Indian name was Malineli Tenepatl, sometimes known as Malentzín. Many historians will simply refer to her as Malineli. One of several slave girls given to the Spanish as a gift from the conquered nation, she was soon able to converse in their language as well as her native language and the language of the Coatzacoalcan nation.

When Hernán Cortés arrived on Mexican shores, one of the things he most needed was a translator, and Malineli fulfilled all the requirements. What caught the attention of Cortés was the fact that this woman, in addition to the local dialects, could speak Náhuatl, the language of the Aztecs. Not only that, but she also understood the ways of the Aztecs, against whom she harbored a deep hatred for having sold her into slavery. As the translator for Cortés, she would help him conquer her own people.

Bernal Díaz del Castillo, in his chronicle, *The Conquest of New Spain*, tells us she was so valued that the Spanish baptized her into the Catholic Church, giving her the name Doña Marina. Castillo dedicates a chapter under her Spanish name, concluding, "This was the great beginning of our conquest, and thus, praise be to God, all things prospered with us. I have made a point of telling this story, because without Doña Marina we could not have understood the language of New Spain and Mexico."

When Cortés arrived at Montezuma's palace and took him prisoner, the two exchanged long dialogues. Cortés wanted to talk about gold, while Montezuma was trying to decide whether his guest was the feathered serpent god Quetzalcoatl,* who in legend had promised to return around the time that the conquistador arrived on the gulf coast of Mexico. In one of the myths dealing with his disappearance, Quetzalcoatl was last seen going east off the shores of Mexico.†

In one of the Aztec codices, Montezuma is shown talking to the Spanish conqueror, with Doña Marina standing behind them. Montezuma referred to Cortés as Malinche, loosely translated in Náhuatl as "captain," and since Doña Marina was always standing with them translating, the Aztecs called her "La Malinche," the captain's woman.

As time passed, La Malinche bore Cortés a son. Symbolically he became known as the origin of the mestisaje, or mestizo nation of mixed Indian and European bloodlines. Octavio Paz, in his book *The Labyrinth of Solitude*, refers to the Mexican people as "The Sons of La Malinche."

But La Malinche is also remembered for something else. From her we get the Mexican words malinchismo and malinchista. The simplest interpretation of the word is "traitor." Due to her hatred of her own people who betrayed her, she exacted revenge by counseling Cortés on how they could be conquered. She pointed him in the direction of the Tlaxcalan nation where she assured him he would find an ally to help him conquer her people. And so this inside information came to be. Just as La Malinche predicted, the Tlaxcalans joined the Spanish and became an important military force in the final defeat of the Aztec Empire.

But there is a more subtle meaning to these two words. The person who covets foreign ideas and possessions is also a traitor. So if Mexicans prefer to shop in New York, or go to Houston for medical attention, they are considered malinchistas.

Mexicans like to think of themselves as a nationalistic people. Throughout much of its history the country has made a concerted effort to isolate itself from

---

* In Náhuatl, *Quetzal* (feather), *Coatl* (serpent). He was the patron god of the Aztec priesthood of learning and knowledge.

† Cortés took advantage of this myth, which made Montezuma suspect he might indeed be the only other god, aside from himself. Many believe that Montezuma wanted Cortés alive and allowed himself to be taken prisoner with very little resistance.

the rest of the world. With this isolationism in mind, it is easy to understand why the craving for foreign ideas and products implies treachery by the upper class. A simple example is the preference of the wealthy for scotch over tequila. Mexicans always considered tequila a drink for the masses, until it became popular in the United States and then spread to the rest of the world. When choosing wines, it is totally unfashionable to order anything from a Mexican vineyard. It is much more chic to order an expensive, but bad, French wine.

But it is in the political arena where the words malinchista and malinchismo have their greatest effect. Those presidents who could claim they were true nationalists, regardless of their record in office, were assured a free pass in retirement. They did not need to fear any kind of political backlash, such as banishment or standing trial for their disastrous policies and other nefarious activities. The politicians who were tainted by malinchismo were guaranteed a more difficult path to retirement. Some were forced into exile; others were accused of the offense of last resort: "self-enrichment by illicit means."

The constant battle between nationalistic fervor and the desire to adopt foreign ideas and material possessions is an internal battle the Mexican people have had to contend with throughout their history. It is never a good idea to remind Mexicans of this bipolar national characteristic, unless they themselves bring it up.

The Religious Mother of the Mestizo Nation

From the time that Christopher Columbus established the first European colony on the island of Hispaniola and called the natives *indios*, after mistakenly thinking he had arrived in India, an enormous controversy arose in the Catholic Church that brought together the best secular and religious intellectual elites of Spain. The question on all their minds was: "Are these indios animals, or are they humans?"

If Descartes had said, "I think, therefore I am," the Catholic equivalent was, "I have a soul, therefore I am." Did these Indians have a soul? The question would soon be solved by what some consider a miracle, and skeptics consider a hoax, that converted the Indians of Mexico to the Catholic faith, and at the same time brought them under the control of the church and Spanish rule.

On December 9, 1531, an Indian named Juan Diego climbed the hill of the Tepeyac outside of Mexico City, and on the exact spot where the Aztecs had built their temple to Tonantzín, the goddess of fertility, the Virgin Mary appeared to him. Juan Diego shared his vision with a priest, who insisted he needed proof of such an extraordinary event. According to legend, on December 12 the Virgin appeared again and ordered Juan Diego to gather Castilian roses, place them in his *tilma*, a poncho-like protective cloak, and present them to the priest. When Juan Diego opened the cloak in front of the priest, the Virgin's image appeared.

What made Juan Diego's vision unique was that the Virgin Mary spoke to him in Náhuatl, the language of the Aztecs. She instructed Juan Diego to build a church on the same site where she appeared, the site of the temple to the Aztec goddess of fertility, so that the indigenous people of Mexico, whom she considered her children, could be baptized into the Catholic Church.

She was also dark skinned. The Mexican poor know her as La Vírgen Morena, the brown skinned Virgin, but she is better known as Nuestra Señora de Guadalupe, Our Lady of Guadalupe, Patroness of the Americas. For the believers, this miracle was a clear mandate from God. Carlos Fuentes, the internationally acclaimed Mexican writer, said it best: "One may no longer consider himself a Christian, but you can't truly be considered a Mexican unless you believe in the Virgin of Guadalupe." Octavio Paz, with tongue in cheek, agreed. "The Mexican people, after more than two centuries of experiments, have faith in the Virgin of Guadalupe and the National Lottery."

She is also known as the religious mother of the mestizo nation now known as Mexico. The leading authorities on this icon will tell you that in the manner she appears there is little doubt that she is pregnant. Around her waist there is a black sash with a bow in front. During the Aztec period, pregnant women announced their delicate condition by wearing this telltale black sash with a bow in front. The issue of her pregnancy can have one going down a slippery slope if you don't know whom you are talking to, as I found out the hard way. A strict Catholic believer was outraged when I brought up the subject at a luncheon.

"Atheists should never talk about religious matters," he screamed, reminding me, "Only Roman Catholics can consider themselves Christians."

A visit to the Basílica de Guadalupe in Mexico City will undoubtedly convince a visitor of the importance of the Virgin to the people of Mexico. There are yearly pilgrimages by tens of thousands of campesinos from all over the country who come to pray to her image. This is especially true on December 12, the day she appeared imprinted in Juan Diego's tilma. Though not an official state holiday, most Mexicans take the day off anyway.

The debate among scholars concerning the Virgin of Guadalupe has always been between the religious conviction that her appearance was indeed a miracle, and the secular interpretation that the tale was a ruse to persuade the indios to join the Catholic religion and bring them under the control of the Church and Spain. Nevertheless, she is a powerful figure among the indigenous people, and some would say she is the very symbol of Mexico itself.

And so we have the convergence of the secular and the religious into one people who will become the overwhelming majority of Mexicans. The union of La Malinche and Hernán Cortés symbolically created the mestisaje, while the Virgin of Guadalupe brought them under control of the Catholic Church. The influence of these two women also established the Mexican caste system; a social structure that continued for more than three centuries. I can honestly say that these two women personify the foundation that Mexico is built on.

The Caste System

Mexico is not a country of immigrants made up of diverse religions, cultures, and race. Unlike the other two countries in North America—the United States and Canada—it is a country built on the mestizo, a human byproduct of conquest from which a caste culture arose.

At the top of this caste system were the *españoles*, the Spain-born Spanish, who from the beginning of the Spanish colonial period were known as *gachupínes* and *peninsulares*, named after the Iberian Peninsula. The former means *el que alza las espuelas*, loosely translated as, "the man who wears the spurs," the first thing the indios saw when they approached a Spaniard on horseback.

Next in line were the *criollos*, those Spaniards born in Mexico. Their relationship to the gachupínes was somewhat similar to the American colonials and the British. Despite being of European descent, they had nowhere near the power reserved for the Spanish born.

The mestizo, the cross between a Spaniard and an indigenous person, came next in this hierarchy. Though not allowed to own property, this group was not as expendable as the next in line.

At the bottom of the caste system was the *indígena* or Indian. They became slaves in all but name and, like the blacks and indentured servants in the United States, performed the backbreaking work of building a nation. As slaves, the well-being of this group was irrelevant.

In time, the strict rules pertaining to the caste system became more flexible, especially after Mexico attained its independence in 1821.

One might conclude that this system prevented the people at the bottom from reaching the top. This is not the case. Benito Juárez García, one of the five "Liberators of the Americas," was a full-blooded Zapotec Indian from the state of Oaxaca. He was the architect of the Constitution of 1857, which separated church and state and stripped the Catholic Church of its property. He was also president of Mexico from 1858 to 1872. Although Mexico was under French rule from 1862 until 1867, he continued acting as president from the city that bears his name—Ciudad Juárez.

José de la Cruz Porfirio Díaz Mori was the president/dictator of Mexico for the next thirty-five years. His autocratic rule terminated with the start of the 1910 Mexican Revolution. His mother was a Mixtec Indian and his father a mestizo.

There have also been countless Mexican presidents who were mestizos. At least two presidents were criollos—Miguel de la Madrid Hurtado and José López Portillo y Pacheco. These examples are just an indication of how fluid the movement up the political ladder can be, but there is another side to the Mexican caste system.

Lighter skin is better, from the perspective of Mexican society. When someone in Mexico says, "*Álguien le hizo el favor* (Somebody did her the favor)," they are indicating that the child is lighter skinned than the mother. If someone says, "*Está mejorando la raza* (She is bettering the race)," there is no confusion behind the meaning. Lighter is righter in Mexico. One thing I have learned is to never question a Mexican about this, for unless they are a close friend, total denial will be the answer.

When my daughter was born, the first thing her Mexican godmother said to me was, "I hope she was born with blue eyes." She already knew my daughter was white due to my British ancestry and her mother being a criolla of Spanish descent. I found this question totally off-the-wall at the time, but I have since learned that in certain quarters the caste system is very much alive.

3

The Spanish El Dorado
(1521–1810)

◆

HAVING CONQUERED THE AZTECS, the Spaniard's first mandate was to destroy Tenochtitlan and from the rubble build a magnificent copy of a Spanish city. This the Spaniards did, constructing their new city with the same stones of the Aztec temples they destroyed. They built their churches and *cabildo** on the site of what was once the Templo Mayor of the Aztecs. The new boys had arrived, and they quickly made sure there would be little left to remind them of the old guard. When it came to an indestructible giant pyramid like the one at Cholula, south of Mexico City, the Spaniards built a church on top to remind their soon-to-become slaves that any attempt on their part to retain the customs and beliefs of their past civilization was totally futile. Returning to the past would be dealt with harshly, torture and death being the best options.

The Spaniards soon moved into the interior of Mexico, which they referred to as *la provincia*, or the boonies. Until recently, any place outside of Mexico City fell into this outback category.

What most residents of Mexico City, known as *chilangos*,[†] have discovered is that once they relocate out of the capital the lifestyle is surprisingly better than expected. Many kept their Mexico City homes with the full intent of returning sometime in the future. This mind-set of Mexico City being the center of the Mexican universe points us once more to a country centered on that spider in the web.

Thomas Gage, a British visitor to Mexico City in the seventeenth century, observed:

---

* *Cabildo* refers to the government building surrounding the main plaza or zócalo.

† *Chilango* is a complex word that people from Mexico City use with pride and those in la provincia use in a derogatory reference to people from el D.F. (Distrito Federal).

Their buildings are built of stone and brick, very strong, but not very high, by reason of the many earthquakes, which endangered their houses if they were above three stories high. The streets are very broad, in the narrowest of them three coaches may go, and in the broader six may go in the breadth of them, which makes the city seem a great deal bigger than it is.

In my time it was thought to be of between 30 and 40,000 inhabitant Spaniards, who are so proud and rich that half the city was judged to keep coaches, for it was a most credible report that in Mexico in my time there were about 15,000 coaches. It is a by-word that in Mexico there are four things fair, that is to say, the women, the apparel, the horses, and the streets. I may add the beauty of some of the coaches and the gentry, which do exceed in cost the best of the Court of Madrid and other parts of Christendom: for here they spare no silver, nor gold, nor precious stones, nor cloth of gold, nor the best silks from China to enrich them.

There is an old Mexican saying that goes something like this: "God looked down on a land and endowed it with great riches. When he realized his folly, he created the Mexicans."

If this is true, then it behooves us to understand what Mexicans mean by "endowed it with great riches." Looking at the rapid expansion of this new Spanish colony, one can appreciate the sentiment. The Spaniards misnamed the landmass that became known as Mexico. They should have called it El Dorado, after the mystical City of Gold, or many cities of gold, to be found on this new continent. The development of Mexico came the closest to fulfilling this Spanish pipe dream. Gold adorned the plumed headdresses of the Aztec princes and was even embedded in their sandals and clothes.

A heads-up entrepreneur could become an instant success manufacturing and selling picks, shovels, wheelbarrows, and any other equipment pertaining to mining. Nearly all the major cities of Mexico were built around mining the vast metallurgical wealth of these newly discovered lands.

For three centuries the city of Guanajuato, now the capital of the state bearing the same name, produced one-fifth of the silver mined in the entire world. During the eighteenth and nineteenth centuries various silver coins—known generically as *águilas* after the Mexican symbol containing the eagle, serpent, and cactus—were considered the most reliable currency in world trade, so much so that the United States adopted it as its official currency after gaining independence from Great Britain.

Taxco, in the state of Guerrero, opened its mines in 1522. Since the 1940s, thanks to a New York jewelry designer by the name of William Spratling, Taxco can take great pride in being one of the world's centers of handmade silver jewelry. In recognition of Spratling's contribution he is remembered as "The Father of Mexican Silver Jewelry." Taxco silversmiths produce jewelry for such well-established stores as Tiffany's in New York City.

In 1544 the Spaniards found silver and copper in most of the major cities of northern Mexico. From the city of Chihuahua, Mexico's main copper mines stretch northward through the area known as *la región de la Cananéa* to the towns of Bisbee and Douglas along the Arizona border. By the end of the nineteenth century the area was being mined by none other than William Randolph Hearst and other American adventurers and entrepreneurs.

This great wealth was to be found mostly in the northern part of the country. That disparity carries over into the present with the poverty of the south.

The Spanish rule that commenced with the first viceroy, Antonio de Mendoza, had many positive developments, especially once mining became the economic mainstay of the new colony. The construction of colonial towns, roads, and bridges for commerce, as well as harbors to connect the colony with the rest of the world, soon followed. The Spanish built schools and universities under the administration of the Catholic Church to the extent that a large segment of the educated population belonged to the clergy. These universities were founded a century before The College of William and Mary and Harvard University, the oldest institutions of higher learning in the United States. At the same time, they made sure to eliminate most of the pagan rituals of the Aztecs still practiced by much of the indio population. The Spaniards also promoted literature, art, and music along with European customs and traditions.

With these new towns came the Spanish colonial government and architecture that is so admired by visitors from around the world. Churches and cathedrals rose across the landscape, many taking more than a century to build. The construction of the National Cathedral in Mexico City began in 1573 and was finally completed in 1813.

Architects can point out the different styles used over such long periods of time in the construction of many churches, including Churrigueresque,

Renaissance, Neoclassical, Gothic, and what became known as Mexican Baroque. Add to this the administrative and municipal government buildings sometimes referred to as *palacios*, so-called because they truly looked like palaces. Most were built around central plazas that combined gardens with sculptured fountains and walls made of limestone, known as *cantera*.*

The Spanish Crown encouraged the wealthy miners to build churches that promoted the cause of the Roman Catholic evangelization of Mexico, in return for being excused from paying the tax of the royal fifth to Spain. Two of the best examples are popular tourist attractions today—the Mexican Baroque masterpiece of Santa Prisca in Taxco and San Cayetano next to the La Valenciana mine in Guanajuato. Santa Prisca was built by Don José de la Borda, owner of the Borda silver mines. He imported much of the interiors from Europe, some say to have a grandiose church resembling a cathedral to celebrate the marriage of his children and the future generations of Bordas. San Cayetano was built by El Conde de Valenciana in appreciation to God for the good fortune produced by that richest of all silver mines in Mexico, La Valenciana, which began mining back in 1558.

One-fifth of all this Spanish colonial plunder went to enrich the coffers of Spain. There is no question that Mexico's mining wealth was a bounty beyond Spain's wildest expectations. It is important to keep in mind that this preponderance of wealth preceded the discovery of oil in the late nineteenth century.

The questions one must ask is—what went wrong?

◆

Certain features of colonial rule were quite progressive, but these could not conceal the dark side of human abuse. Unfortunately, the good the Spaniards did was offset by the established caste system, which led to practices that seeded discontent and in turn fostered the War of Independence of 1810.

The peninsulares and the gachupínes reserved the highest positions of power and ownership for themselves, and to a lesser extent the criollos. The mestizos and the indios, their traditions and cultural heritage totally destroyed in the name of Christianity, became a broken people with no national identity. Their inability to resist colonization soon reduced them to a state of total dependence and compliance. In addition, both groups were excluded from owning land.

---

* The Mexican *cantera* stone-cutters are famous throughout Mexico and the American southwest.

By 1810, only 2 percent of the population owned the worthwhile real estate. Ownership of land largely comprised gachupínes, criollos, and the Catholic Church.

But this paled compared to the cruelties suffered by the indio population, especially those that worked in the mines. To prevent stealing, the Indian slaves were lowered naked into the mineshafts. They were overworked, poorly fed, and unable to breathe properly in the unventilated shafts, to name but a few examples of the suffering they endured, and most died at an early age. At times the Spaniards gave the impression that they liked the idea of seeing the indigenous population eventually exterminated, but they were also aware that they needed a continuous supply of Indian replacements to keep the mines producing. They were so mesmerized by the metal wealth they were reaping, they forgot about the humans doing the work. This kind of inhumane treatment might explain the Mexicans wanting to brush over the Spanish colonial period in their history books, while still looking upon Spain as the mother country. Sometimes this duality of feeling that differentiates between the Spanish conquest and Spain itself is not the easiest relationship to understand. Perhaps the heavy-handed Spanish rule became the harbinger of Mexico's reluctance in the future to open its borders to the outside world. Extreme nationalism was already on the march.

Despite the cruelties levied on the indios and mestizos, there is no better example of Spanish excesses than the arrival of the Mexican Inquisition in 1571, the last known victim of which was recorded in 1817.

The Mexican Inquisition (1571–1817)

Not much is known about how active the Inquisition was in Mexico. Neither Spanish nor Mexican historians paid much attention to this form of cruel punishment until, by one of those quirks of history, a collection of yellowed documents was discovered, shedding some light on the subject. Acquired at a book fair in California in 1996, these papers were authenticated and are presently to be found in the Bancroft Collection at the University of California at Berkeley. These documents describe the fate of forty-eight men, eleven women, and twenty members of the clergy at the hands of the inquisitors. The crimes dealt with were heresy, blasphemy, bigamy, and sexual solicitation, especially among the clergy. History tends to repeat itself, and the Catholic Church and its record of corruption was no exception, especially when it came to the clergy's sexual proclivities.

While many of the cases were not serious enough to warrant the death penalty, records indicate that those who suffered most were Jews. They had, hypothetically, under pressure from the Catholic Church, converted to Christianity and were known as *converses* (converts). Despite their supposed conversion, many continued to celebrate Jewish rites and traditions in the privacy of their homes. One such family, with the last name of Carabajal, lost two of their family members, who were strangled with an iron collar. The patriarch, Luis de Carabajal y Cueva, had become governor of the state of Nuevo León in 1579 and, despite his high government position, was burned alive with his mother and five sisters. They had been found guilty of secretly practicing the Jewish faith.

Legend has it that many victims of the Inquisition were wealthy, so the Church offered them the choice of being burned with dry wood if they were willing to make a contribution to the Church, or the much more painful slow burning green wood if they refused. The historic propensity for cruelty was shared not only by Catholics, but by religions across the ages that applied methods like garroting, burning at the stake, stoning, hanging, beheading, dismembering, blinding, and all sorts of creative torture, the purpose of which was to elicit confessions of religious misdeeds through excruciating pain and death.

The anti-Semitism of the Mexican Inquisition is still present today in Mexico City, which has a sizable community of largely Orthodox Jews. Most live in expensive highrises in places like the upscale Polanco and Herradura neighborhoods in the city. They keep to themselves and don't mingle with the non-Jewish population. While there are no private club bylaws that exclude Jews from membership, the unseen "not welcome" sign is ever present.

Behind their backs, many Mexicans refer to Jews as *judases*, alluding to Judas Iscariot, the traitor who snitched on Jesus Christ. They see nothing wrong in attaching labels to people who are different, unlike in the politically correct United States where pointing out differences is unacceptable. Anti-Semitism in Mexico also has its bizarre side, as I found out from a tennis friend who belonged to my Jewish-free sports club—with one exception.

One day my friend was ranting against the Jews when I intervened, "If you hate the Jews so much, how come I always see you playing mixed doubles with our mutual American friend?"

"What are you telling me?" he asked, looking rather perplexed.

"Don't you know she's Jewish?"

He shook his head. "That's not the same. She's an American Jew. Surely you know the difference?"

"Enlighten me."

"Don't you know that American Jews can't stand Mexican Jews?"

"I didn't know."

"They hate them more than I do."

Despite this strong feeling of anti-Semitism, anti-Jewish graffiti, public outbursts, and attacks against Jews are unheard of. If most crimes in Mexico City only receive superficial attention, this is not the case with crimes committed against Jews. Most of these crimes are solved in short order. I am told this is due to financial pressure from the Jewish community.

4

The Two Californias

◆

IN THE BEGINNING, CALIFORNIA, IN TERMS of Spanish influence, stretched roughly from the Russian River north of San Francisco to Cabos San Lucas on the southern tip of the Baja California peninsula. The territory north of the Russian River to the Oregon border, while claimed by Spanish colonial Mexico, had no Spanish presence and was dominated by a series of Russian forts. These forts served as centers where trappers could sell their furs and resupply before venturing back into the wilderness. The furs were then shipped by sea to Russia.

In the fourteenth century, Garci Ordóñez de Montalvo wrote a novel, *The Exploits of the Very Powerful Cavalier Esplandian, Son of the Excellent King Amadis of Gaul*, where he described an exotic island he called California. "There ruled on that island of California, a queen great of body, very beautiful for her race, at a flourishing age, desirous in her thoughts of achieving great things, valiant in strength, cunning in her brave heart, more than any other who had ruled that kingdom before her—Queen Calafia."

An expedition led by Francisco de Ulloa, under orders from Hernán Cortés to explore the mysterious coastline that became known as Baja California, arrived in the Bay of La Paz in 1535. The Spaniards did not stay long after coming face-to-face with the indigenous population, whom they called the Guaycura. The Guaycura were tall, fierce, and wanted nothing to do with their newfound visitors.

The Spaniards were convinced they had stumbled on that mythical island ruled by Queen Calafia. They named this new discovery California in her honor. In addition, the wine country in the north of Baja California, which is an extension of the San Fernando Valley in Southern California, is known as El Valle de Calafia. The Guaycura are also remembered for creating the Damiana Licor from the damiana plant. The people who drink it swear that it is an aphrodisiac.

Juan Cabrillo, a Portuguese navigator who served in the army of Cortés, discovered Alta California in 1542. His Portuguese name was Joâo Rodrígues Cabrilho. He first landed in what is today the San Diego Bay. Despite a museum bearing his name on Point Loma at the entrance of the bay, not many California residents seem to have heard of him, even though there is hardly a Californian who can claim not to have traveled the scenic coastal Hwy 1, also known as the Cabrillo Highway.

In 1601 the conde de Monterey, the Spanish viceroy to Mexico, ordered Sebastián Vizcaíno to map the California coastline discovered by Cabrillo. Sailing up the coastline he named many of its prominent features such as Carmel Valley, Sierra Point, Coyote Point, and Monterey Bay after his *patrón,* the Spanish viceroy. Missionaries soon followed.

The Franciscan Order founded the Upper California missions, while those in the lower part belonged to the Dominicans. In 1804, the Spanish decided that California should be divided into Alta California (Franciscan), and Baja California (Dominican), sometimes referred to as Nueva (Upper) California and Vieja (Lower) California. Had this not been the case, in all probability what is today Baja California could have been included in the Treaty of Guadalupe/Hidalgo (1848), which ended the Mexican War and annexed California, the Republic of Texas, and what became known as the New Mexico Territories to the United States.

Considering that Baja California is connected to the United States and totally isolated from the Mexican mainland, Mexico can be grateful the nation just lost Alta California. Baja California would remain the forgotten land well into the twentieth century. From the Mexican perspective, Baja California hardly existed, one more curse resulting from the spider in the web. Had it been annexed to the United States, the contrast between the two California's might not be so evident. To the delight of nature lovers, sports fisherman, and outward-bound sailors, hikers, and kayakers, Baja California was left nearly abandoned, except for some isolated communities. The Americans gave it some life by developing the southern tip into a tourism mecca, while Mexico eventually connected the peninsula from north to south with the building of the Transpeninsular Highway in 1974.

Alta California

Californians know very little about the Spanish colonial period. In 1769, Gaspar de Portolá i Rivera and a contingent of scouts came up from Monterey by land

and discovered the Bay of San Francisco. He probably named most everything he set his eyes on like Alcatraz Island and the town of Sausalito.

Just north is Bodega Bay. Lt. Juan Francisco de la Bodega owned it from 1775 to 1821. Other names that can be traced back to Mexico, include Vallejo, Petaluma, the Napa and Sonoma valleys (now famous for California wines), and countless others in the Bay Area and surrounding countryside. Spanish names are numerous throughout the entire state. But of all the Spaniards Californians should remember, unquestionably the most important was Father Junípero Serra.

On one of my many visits to San Francisco I stopped off at El Embarcadero, from where most of the ferries leave to connect with places like Tiburon across the bay. I sat down to talk with a fellow passenger as we waited for our departure.

"Are you from California?"

"Yes. . . . Anything I can help you with?"

"What do you know about Junípero Serra?"

Long pause followed. "I think he played third base for the Giants."

"Really?"

He nodded his head. "Yeah. . . . I'm sure."

Born in Mallorca, Spain, Junípero Serra joined the Franciscan order in 1730. In 1749 he came to Mexico. Soon after he was sent by the Church to convert the indigenous tribes of the Sierra Gorda Mountains, in the highlands of the state of Querétaro, located in the geographic center of Mexico. As part of his evangelical contribution he helped in the founding and construction of five missions. The government of the state of Querétaro has recently taken great pains to restore these missions to their original splendor. All of them are known as UNESCO World Heritage Sites.

In 1767 Junípero Serra was put in charge of establishing missions in Alta California. Father Serra took his responsibilities seriously, and from his previous experience in Querétaro he understood that building missions was the primary instrument of converting the indios to the Catholic faith. He founded missions in San Diego, San Buenaventura (Los Angeles and Ventura), San Gabriel, San Luis Obispo, San Juan Capistrano, San Carlos Borroméo (Carmel), Santa Clara, Monterey, San Francisco, and elsewhere.

In the nineteenth century, Jane Stanford, a Protestant and wife of Leland Stanford, the founder of Stanford University in Palo Alto, had a granite monument erected in Junípero Serra's memory in Monterey. He is also remembered by a bronze statue of heroic size in Golden Gate Park in San Francisco. In towns and cities all over California, schools, parks, buildings, and streets are named after him.

On September 25, 1988, Serra was beatified by Pope Paul II. This recognition moved Serra one step closer to becoming an American saint, although it created a great deal of controversy.

The Mexican Catholic Church was outraged because the work Father Junípero had done converting the indios in the Sierra Gorda of Querétaro hardly qualified him as being from the United States. Additionally, when Junípero Serra did his evangelical work in California the soon-to-be colony officially belonged to Spain. Last, but not least, Serra himself was Spanish.

As far as Californians are concerned, Junípero Serra's most important contribution was introducing the grape vine. Legend has it that when the ships supplying San Francisco were delayed and the priesthood ran out of wine for communion, Father Serra sent for grape cuttings to guarantee a local source of wine.

Baja California

Baja California's history is a story of pirates, rogues, and adventurers. With the beginning of the Manila Galleon Route between the Philippines and the ports of Manzanillo and Acapulco on the west coast of Mexico, the first landfall for these galleons, called *naos*, was today's beach resort of Cabo San Lucas. This became fertile territory for pirates and privateers who, from a hilltop known as La Sentinela (The Sentinel) on the southernmost tip of the peninsula, could spot these lumbering vessels en route to the mainland.

From bays along the Sea of Cortés, the pirates could intercept their prey. Just north of Cabo San Lucas is the Bahía del Chileno, once home to a Chilean pirate and now a booming resort. Further north, a cove in the giant Bay of La Paz called Pichilingue, is a well-protected anchorage for English and Dutch pirates. Pichilingue was the name given to those who could not speak Spanish. One of the two ferries that today arrive from Mazatlán on the Mexican mainland is called *El Coromuel*, in honor of the Coromuel wind that blows in the Sea of Cortés. This wind, a cool westerly breeze, was named after a British pirate by the name of Cromwell who supposedly discovered this wind and used it to speed him along to his rendezvous with the lumbering, richly laden naos.

Before there was commercial air service from the mainland to La Paz, and before the trans-peninsular highway opened up Baja California from north to south in 1974, the La Paz telephone directory was overloaded with English surnames. The most common of these was Fitch. The British pirates seemed to have interacted far better with the natives than the Dutch.

Another fascinating aspect of Baja California is the *pinturas rupestres* (rock paintings) that are found in the Sierra de San Francisco mountain range, which divides the peninsula from north to south. Fascinating, because these paintings depict the existence of human and animal life that can only signify the presence of fresh water. Today, the peninsula is totally dry, with the exception of a few green areas mostly found in the Valle de Calafia wine country in the north.

Sailing along the western coastline inside the Sea of Cortés, still referred to as the Gulf of California on some maps, is an experience few will ever forget. There are places that look like an oasis, where water seems to flow out of nowhere. The uninhabited shoreline outlines a bare mountain range beyond, suddenly interrupted by an estuary of pure green vegetation and palm trees surrounded by a rocky and arid landscape where only a few desert creatures can survive. Rivers appear as if an artist, fed up with the stark brown and dusty landscape indiscriminately decided on a splash of green and blue to break the monotony, a reminder of a more verdant past.

Apparently, both Alta and Baja California at one time were equally habitable. One got developed; the other was left nearly abandoned.

In 1853, William Walker, an American adventurer, captured La Paz, the capital of Baja California. He proclaimed himself president of the Republic of Lower California. His term of office was short before the locals threw him out. In 1856, he went on to become the sixth president of Nicaragua, but with no better luck.

An American whaler and writer, Capt. Charles Scammon (1825–1911) discovered a lagoon on the west coast of Baja California near the town of Guerrero Negro (Black Warrior), named after a Japanese whaler who dressed in black sealskins. The lagoon, which became known as Scammon's Lagoon, today renamed Laguna Ojo de Liebre, was a natural sanctuary for gray whales on their southerly migration. Scammon proceeded to slaughter them to the point that these giant mammals nearly disappeared.

On the east coast of the peninsula, the French copper mining town of Santa Rosalía became famous for its prefabricated iron-beamed church designed by Gustave Eiffel, of Eiffel Tower fame, and shipped in its entirety from France. A state prison was built in the oasis town of Mulegé. The prisoners roamed free during the day, usually performing chores for local residents. No need to keep them locked up; the surrounding desert and unforgiving sun served as nature's harsh jailer. Where could one go in this sparsely populated peninsula, bound by the vastness of an ocean on one side and a sea on the other?

The Sea of Cortés is a unique place on this planet. Located between Baja California and the Mexican mainland, *National Geographic* called it "the fish trap of the world" because it serves as a spawning ground for hundreds of different species. Overly rich in plankton, the lower end of sea life ascends the food chain through a variety of saltwater residents, ever increasing in size, culminating with the return of the migratory gray whale from as far north as Alaska.

Sailing in the Sea of Cortés, you never lack the company of sleek dolphins arching through the water as they hug the sides of your boat like lookouts in search of some unseen danger. And suddenly, out of nowhere, a gray outline in a blue swell behind the transom of your boat appears—the whale that made these waters famous. Pirates must have loved them when they were not plundering the rich booty of the Spanish naos.

Considering the importance of the Sea of Cortés, recognized as one giant fishery, commercial fishing could have been one of the solutions for developing Baja California. While fishing fleets from the mainland ports of Mazatlán and Guaymas can be seen up and down the Baja California coastline, there is no fishing fleet based on the peninsula itself. Even if these fleets were allowed to deposit their catches in places like La Paz and other bays that could have been turned into ports, what could one do with the fish, considering that there was no air service between the mainland and the peninsula to speak of? The same could be said for roads.

A narrow, two-lane Transpeninsular Highway covering 1,060 miles from Tijuana to Cabo San Lucas was finally operational in 1974. With the exception of a scattering of isolated communities, most of Baja California had lain dormant for more than four hundred years after Francisco de Ulloa first set foot on its shores.

If Mexico had not lost Alta California to the United States back in 1848, one has to assume present-day California might have ended up looking very similar to Baja California. In other words, just another forgotten and neglected outback with untapped economic potential. Somewhere in the 1970s Mexico might have gotten around to building the first trans-California highway as an extension of the 1974 Transpeninsular Highway that bisects Baja. Maybe if it had gone the other way and the United States had acquired Baja California back in 1848, the Pacific and Sea of Cortés coastlines might have looked somewhat like the Southern California of today. One can only speculate.

The present-day rapid growth in Baja California—the future and present residence of thousands of Americans who are converting destinations like Cabo San Lucas on the southern end of this peninsula into one gigantic Mexican Palm Springs—is worth noting.

Shortly after World War II, W. Matt Parr and ex–U.S. Air Force pilot Luis Coppola Bonillas were just some of the more important Americans who set the stage for future development. John Wayne, Bing Crosby, Phil Harris, Desi Arnaz, and other "who's who" of the then–Hollywood crowd were the magnet that eventually turned Cabo into a tourist paradise.

This is just some of the history, legend, and lore associated with this unusual and bizarre peninsula called Baja California. The resorts of Cabo San Lucas, Los Cabos, and Loreto to the north, and the Mexican government's proposal to build eleven marinas in the Sea of Cortés, will soon change this pristine desert paradise forever. Most of these modifications will be made in the name of progress. Those of us who marveled at Baja California's wilderness and rugged beauty will have to share in memory the experience of those brilliant orange sunsets, symbolic of what was and will never be again.

MEXICAN INDEPENDENCE AND FOREIGN INTERVENTION (1810–1867)

M EXICAN HISTORIANS USE A LOT OF INK on the importance of Mexico's independence from Spain. The War of Independence, which lasted from 1810 to 1821, was nowhere near as momentous a historic event as the American Revolution. That war was not only preceded by a document known as the Declaration of Independence, but also followed by a constitution that still stands today. These documents live on as two of the most important in the history of western civilization.

In the case of Mexico, the War of Independence merely replaced the Spanish flag with the Mexican flag. Mexico's Constitution of 1824 was soon voided by Gen. Antonio López de Santa Anna. It was eventually replaced by the Constitution of 1857, which in turn made way for the Constitution of 1917—a result of the Mexican Revolution of 1910.

During this period, between Mexican independence in 1810 and the beginning of the Porfirian Era in 1876, Mexico was in a state of chaos. That is not to say the country made no progress, but whenever Mexico took one step forward, it inevitably took two steps back in its attempt to emerge as a modern functioning nation. Had that not been the case, there would have been no need for the revolution of 1910 that followed.

It is also during this period that we see the emergence of the United States as a major player in Mexico's history. It started when, under the banner of expansionism, the United States invaded Mexican territory. In 1836, Mexico lost a part of a territory called Tejas, which then became the Republic of Texas. The loss of Tejas was followed by the loss of California, then the New Mexico Territories, and the annexation of Texas to the United States in a disastrous war that lasted from 1846 to 1848. If that were not enough, the French invaded Mexico in 1862 and stayed until 1867.

This period also includes the story of Benito Juárez, one of the five Liberators of the Americas, a controversial figure who, through La Reforma, tried to bring hope to the poor and downtrodden. More important, because of the lasting effect it had on Mexico, La Reforma stripped the Catholic Church of its properties and its all-encompassing power over all walks of Mexican life. Yet, many also consider Juárez a traitor in the malinchista context.

5

Independence (1821) and the Texas Republic (1836)

◆

THE WAR OF INDEPENDENCE FROM SPAIN left Mexico vulnerable to foreign intervention. The first to take advantage of this new reality were American immigrants, largely from the Southern states. They settled in a territory known in Mexico as Coahuila y Tejas. By 1836 they were demanding their independence and the creation of a new nation.

The Mexican War of Independence, 1810–1821

Officially, the War of Independence started at 2 a.m. on September 16, 1810, when Father Miguel Hidalgo y Costilla rang the bell of freedom from the main church in what today is the city of Dolores Hidalgo, since named after him. Capt. Ignacio Allende y Unzaga, who soon became a general, joined him.

From the beginning the war did not go well. Within six months both of these gentlemen had their severed heads publicly exhibited in cages on two corners of the Alhóndiga de Granaditas, the main granary in the city of Guanajuato, a mere twenty miles from where the War of Independence had started. This was an inauspicious beginning on the road to independence. Nevertheless, Mexican historians have raised Hidalgo and Allende to the level of lay sainthood, whether deserved or not.

Two important leaders who continued the fight were José María Morelos y Pavón and Vicente Guerrero Saldaña. However, from a military standpoint, these two leaders had limited success. By 1821 the spider in the web was still occupied by the Spaniards, proving once again that the power that governs Mexico City controls the nation.

A most unlikely individual came to the rescue. Agustín de Iturbide y Arámburu, a criollo and a royalist who had initially fought against the forces of independence, stepped in and worked out a compromise with the Spanish viceroy. By this time Spain was worn out by the loss of lives and the financial burden of the insurrection. The viceroy agreed with Iturbide that Mexico could become independent as a limited monarchy dependent on Spain. The country officially remained Roman Catholic, and the criollos could have the same rights and social status as the Spanish peninsulares and gachupínes. Soon after, the viceroy, accompanied by his entourage and the Spanish military presence, withdrew, leaving Mexico unprepared to form any kind of stable government.

Gaining independence was one thing; governing was another. The inability to provide a viable government became a plague that spread throughout Mexican history. Forward planning was clearly not in the Mexican playbook. To the contrary, Mexico's future seemed largely based on visceral decisions and personal ambitions that never attended to the needs of the country.

Despite broad opposition, Iturbide, the antithesis of a revolutionary figure and a Spanish hidalgo at heart, declared himself emperor. He called himself Augustus I, constitutional emperor of Mexico. A copy of his throne can be seen in the Museum of Foreign Interventions housed in the Old Convent of Churubusco in Mexico City. That it should be found in a museum dedicated to foreign interventions by the Americans and the French is another of the curiosities that surround this nation. There are many others. The throne and its location could be interpreted as symbolic of a man Mexicans consider a traitor to the cause of independence.

Predictably, Iturbide's reign lasted a little over a year before Guadalupe Victoria, who became the first president of Mexico, dethroned him. There is an interesting footnote to Iturbide's short term as the head of state. Mexico's official national flag was constitutionally adopted in 1968. That flag is the one designed by Agustín de Iturbide.

From 1821 until the Revolution of 1910, Mexican politics became divided between the conservatives, who insisted that power be centralized in Mexico City, and the liberals, who understood that power had to be decentralized to include the entire nation. The liberals lost the argument. This had terrible consequences that, to a certain extent, continue to this day. The War of Independence did nothing to dislodge the concentration of power from Mexico City.

If we look at any city, state, or country map of Mexico, we immediately notice the prominence of such heroes of independence as Hidalgo, Allende, Morelos,

Guerrero, and Victoria, to mention a few. States, cities, schools, plazas, streets, and statues bear their names, yet Iturbide, who played such an important part in the final stage of independence, is, like Hernán Cortés, the forgotten man. He was officially declared a nonperson during the Luis Echeverría presidency (1970–1976) and literally written out of the official history books used by the Ministry of Education. He has never been forgiven for crowning himself emperor. Only his home in Mexico City, known as the Palace of Iturbide, commemorates him. It houses an excellent art collection owned by Banamex, one of the largest banks in Mexico.

Another answer to Iturbide's disappearance from revisionist Mexican history can possibly be traced to malinchismo. If there was ever a historical figure in Mexico who embraced foreign ideas, Agustín de Iturbide is the quintessential example. Regardless, in the end a malinchista was responsible for the final phase of the War of Mexican Independence, wedging a thorn in Mexicans' view of their history. Future historians needed to find a way to discredit Iturbide's real contribution to Mexican independence. Naming himself emperor and his allegiance to Spain became that convenient excuse.

Today, Mexico celebrates El Día de la Independencia (Independence Day) on September 15 and 16, marking Miguel Hidalgo's ringing the bell of freedom in 1810. In another odd twist of history, Emperor Maximilian, the Austrian Hapsburg prince who ruled Mexico from 1864 to 1867 during the French Intervention, officially established the holiday celebrating Mexico's independence from Spain.

For Americans, the more interesting story is the potential conflict in a far-off territory known as the state of Coahuila y Tejas. The United States was already starting its march across the North American continent. These new arrivals in Coahuila y Tejas were soon to become known as *los anglos* by the sparse Spanish/Mexican population. Most were from U.S. Southern states and were proponents of slavery, a fact that would not go unnoticed by the central government in Mexico City and future Mexican historians.

Texas

Before entering into this bitter aspect of Mexican history, which became the foundation for Mexicans' suspicions and distrust of the United States, it is essential to have a clear view of the conditions that existed in both countries at the end of the Mexican War of Independence in 1821.

From as early as the conclusion of the American Revolution, most Americans believed that lands from the Atlantic to the Pacific Oceans should be part of the United States. This epic undertaking commenced with the Louisiana Purchase from the French in 1803, followed by Florida, bought from Spain in 1819. As people moved West and South to occupy these newly acquired territories, this migration found itself bordering Mexican territory that went as far north as the present state of Utah and south to Arizona, known as the New Mexico Territories,* and an area adjoining the Louisiana Purchase known as Tejas. Then there was Alta California and Oregon that had to be dealt with if the United States territory was to reach the Pacific Ocean. In the 1840s, the march westward became known as the doctrine of Manifest Destiny.†

The idea of Manifest Destiny became popular under President Andrew Jackson (1829–1837), in what became known as Jacksonian Democracy. In the doctrine's simplest interpretation, the democratic principles of the United States embodied in its Constitution should benefit all adult males and not a select few who were landowners. Native Americans were excluded.

These ideas were a perfect justification for expanding westward and eventually decimating the Native Americans. Thus, it was hardly a surprise when the Americans started moving into Mexican territory as settlers. No resistance was expected from a weakened, newly established Mexican government. The only living obstacles to contend with were the small, warlike, nomadic Indian tribes that populated most of these territories, including the fierce Comanches, considered one of the most aggressive Indian tribes on the North American continent.

In 1821 the Spanish/Mexicans had only settled in the southern end of the territory of Tejas. Their influence barely extended beyond what are today the cities of San Antonio and Corpus Christi. Few in numbers, the Tejanos, mostly criollos, were not prepared to face off against the Indians, especially the savage Comanche.

Our narrative starts in 1824, when Mexico signed its first constitution amidst utter chaos—a weakened military, and political factions that could not agree on the nation's future—while continuing the disastrous policy of a cen-

---

* New Mexico Territories is a name given by the United States when Mexico ceded this territory after the Mexican War (1846–1848). It includes present-day west Texas, New Mexico, Arizona, and parts of Colorado and Utah.

† Manifest Destiny states that the United States was destined to expand across the continent. This became the overriding excuse for the Mexican War (1846–1848).

tralized government. It was unrealistic to think Mexico City could successfully govern a sparsely populated territory as far away as Tejas, or what eventually became known as the New Mexico Territories and California.

The U.S. immigrants into Tejas were referred to as *anglos* by the Mexicans. The anglos were known as Texians. Their Mexican counterparts were called Texacans, or Tejanos. Because of growing alarm at unrestricted anglo invasion, the Mexican government issued an edict in 1830 that no further immigration would be allowed into these lands.

Stephen F. Austin, a leader of the Texians, was sent to Mexico City in 1834 to try and get the government to repeal this 1830 edict. For his efforts, Austin was imprisoned for three months while the new government decided what to do with him.

The Texas War of Independence—1836 and Beyond

Austin was released from his Mexico City prison on the understanding that the Texians abide by the Mexican Constitution of 1824. Specifically, since Mexico had been officially declared a Roman Catholic country, the Texians were to convert, and renounce what Mexico feared was a growing trend towards Freemasonry. The second proviso dealt with slavery, which had been abolished in 1810, at the commencement of the War of Independence, and declared constitutionally illegal in 1828.

Austin, in representation of the Texians, agreed to Mexico's demands. To agree was one thing; to enforce these agreements was impossible. The Texians did not convert and, in keeping with their largely Southern background, brought their slaves with them when they immigrated into Tejas. In 1836 the Texians and the Tejanos declared their independence and established the Republic of Texas.

The Mexicans' first contact with the American anglos therefore resulted in two broken promises. Other unkept promises and agreements followed. Josefina Vázquez Mota Zoraida a Mexican historian, wrote a book for the Ministry of Education called *La Historia De México* (The history of Mexico). In the chapter "The First Confrontations," written for the standard history book for Mexican sixth graders, she had this to say:

> The faith in the American Constitution as a formula for perfect government would provide a justification for expansionism through the slogan

'extending the area of liberty,' [manifest destiny] that is to say, extending American institutions [the U.S. Constitution and the Bill of Rights] in order to save those poor souls who did not know them and were bound to the chains of tyranny. In the case of Texas, the extension of the area of liberty was also the extension of the area of slavery.

This cynical, but accurate, view of American expansion can leave no doubt as to where Mexico stands on the issue of Texas. From the Mexican point of view the slavery issue made a total sham of the ideals and promises of the American Constitution and the Bill of Rights.

President Antonio López de Santa Anna, also known behind his back as Quince Uñas (Fifteen Nails) due to his loss of a leg, raised an army and attacked San Antonio, then went on to defeat the Texas militia at the battles of Goliad and the Alamo. The Alamo is a mission on the outskirts of San Antonio where three legendary American heroes* died in the thirteen-day siege, as did all those who participated.

Two weeks after the fall of the Alamo, Gen. Sam Houston engaged Santa Anna's army at the Battle of San Jacinto and after a mere eighteen minutes the Mexicans, who completely outnumbered Houston's militia, were roundly defeated.

The next day, Santa Anna suffered the additional indignity of being taken prisoner disguised in a corporal's uniform while hiding behind a tree. Legend has it that when the Texans surrounded the remnants of his army, his troops kept referring to him as El Presidente when they asked him what they should do. When asked to drop his pants, he was wearing the silk underwear that made him famous with the ladies.

To negotiate his release, Santa Anna accepted the establishment of the Republic of Texas with a clear border between both countries marked by the Nueces River. Acting Texas president David Burnet and Santa Anna signed the Treaty of Velasco, and "in his official character as chief of the Mexican nation, he [Santa Anna] acknowledged the full, entire, and perfect Independence of the Republic of Texas." In exchange, Burnet and the Texas government guaranteed Santa Anna's life and transport to Veracruz. Back in Mexico City, however, a

---

* William B. Travis, James Bowie, and Davy Crockett. The battle has been immortalized in various Hollywood films.

new government declared that Santa Anna was no longer president and that the treaty with Texas was null and void.

Tracing the Nueces River from north to south, there is no question that more than half of present-day Texas was still in territory claimed by Mexico. The Texans called the remaining part the Disputed Territories. The Rio Grande did not become the border until it became the U.S. excuse to start the Mexican War (1846–1848).

But why end our story there without at least mentioning Emily Morgan, immortalized in the song "The Yellow Rose of Texas"? She was a striking mulatto, whom some say was a slave and others say was a servant indentured to a Colonel Morgan who fought side by side with Sam Houston before and during the battle of San Jacinto. Texas historians believe this mysterious figure, captured by Santa Anna's army, was also a spy who for a short time became the general's mistress. Santa Anna had a reputation as a ladies man, his silk underpants being one of his calling cards. Whatever her attributes, legend has it she was largely responsible for the Mexican defeat at the Battle of San Jacinto. In 1842, William Bollaert, a historian, wrote in his memoirs the following account:

> The Battle of San Jacinto was probably lost to the Mexicans, owing to the influence of a Mulatto Girl [Emily] belonging to Colonel Morgan, closeted in General Santa Anna's tent at the time the cry was made "The enemy! They come! They come!" and detained Santa Anna so long, that order could not be restored readily again.

More than a hundred years later John L. Davis, a historian at the University of Texas, wrote an essay, "The Yellow Rose of Texas," and was not so kind:

> The most prurient version places her at the plain of Saint Hyacinth in the general's tent on the afternoon of April 21, delaying him in a setting of champagne, chocolates, silver and crystal place settings, and few clothes—while the Texians started their charge, which ended in the bloody slaughter of Santa Anna's forces.

The plain truth is the Santa Anna officer corps awaited orders from their presidente to counterattack. The well-entertained Santa Anna never gave the order; the American attack turned into a rout. Having been trained to await orders from the jefe, Santa Anna's forces failed to rally on their own and were defeated. This was hardly the same army that fought so valiantly at the Battle of the Alamo.

Today a hotel in downtown San Antonio also bears the Emily Morgan name. The hotel is an official historic site literally across the street from the Alamo, the site of the famous battle that bears its name. If there is any real truth to this Texas Mata Hari, we will never really know. But for a true Texan, she is a myth become reality. Like the two women in the founding of Mexico after the Spanish conquest, Emily Morgan is one of the anchors of independence. If the story is true, she would have been one of the linchpins leading to Mexico's loss of half of her territory.

6

Intervention (1846–1848)

◆

My participation in The Mexican War was the
most dishonorable act in my career.
ULYSSES S. GRANT

IN 1844 JAMES K. POLK WAS ELECTED the eleventh president of the United States. An ardent supporter of the Doctrine of Manifest Destiny and Jacksonian Democracy, he ran for the presidency on the campaign promise of annexing the Republic of Texas, California, and the Oregon Territories; the latter was a shared claim with Great Britain. The British claim to Oregon was eventually settled in cash. Polk obviously forgot to mention all the territory in between claimed by Mexico.

As far as the United States was concerned, the lands between California and the Louisiana Purchase belonged to no one and were inhabited solely by savages, neglecting to take into account the Mexican settlements in Albuquerque and Santa Fe.

Polk lived up to each one of his campaign promises, including the annexation of what became known as the New Mexico Territories, making him one of the nation's most successful presidents. Despite these accomplishments, history has relegated him to relative obscurity. Could this be because even U.S. historians feel that his land grab through an unjust war went too far, or because he was unable to stop the expansion of slavery?

◆

Three days prior to leaving office, President John Tyler unilaterally declared the annexation of the Republic of Texas to the United States, to the delight of the incoming president. In one of his first executive acts, Polk sent a diplomat by the name of John Slidell to Mexico to get that country to accept the annexation.

An additional problem arose when the historic maps of the day showed that the Republic of Texas's border with Mexico was the Nueces River and not the Rio Grande—the latter being the border presented by Slidell. The Nueces River divides present-day Texas into nearly two halves from north to south; the smaller eastern pertained to the Republic of Texas that had been established in 1836. Slidell further stunned the Mexicans by offering to buy California for 40 million dollars.

When Slidell reported his diplomatic failure, Polk ordered Gen. Zachary Taylor to take charge of the disputed territory between these two rivers. Simultaneously, Mexico sent Gen. Mariano Arista north with the same purpose. He clashed with one of Taylor's patrols. This was the excuse that Polk needed to declare war and invade Mexico; well aware that Mexico was ill-prepared to defend her territory. What the United States called the Mexican War, the Mexicans have always referred to as a "foreign intervention."

Not everyone in the U.S. Congress favored war with Mexico. One of the most strident voices in opposition was Congressman Abraham Lincoln. He demanded the military provide the names of the dead American soldiers that had clashed with the Mexicans under the command of General Arista. The army was unable to do so.

Gen. Stephen Kearny had no problem overrunning the small criollo enclaves in Santa Fe and Albuquerque, nor did the combined forces of Cdre. Robert Stockton coming in from the sea and Capt. John Fremont from land face any real resistance occupying Alta California. The military campaign to capture Mexico City was another matter.

Gen. Zachary Taylor invaded Mexico through Monterrey, the capital of the northern state of Nuevo León. A fleet under the command of Cdre. Matthew Perry landed troops in Veracruz. (Perry was also the man who opened Japan to U.S. trade in 1852–1853 at a time when Japan, under the Tokugawa Shoganate, was closed to foreigners and any kind of outside influence.)

From Perry's fleet, Gen. Winfield Scott landed in Veracruz and moved his army of marines inland towards Mexico City. The last Mexican resistance took place at the military academy on top of the hill where Chapultepec Castle now stands. Mexican history records that the defenders were six military cadets known as Los Niños Héroes (The Boy Heroes). When ordered to retreat, the six cadets held their ground. The last one to give up his life was Juan Escutia, who, wrapped in the Mexican flag, threw himself from the parapets of the military academy atop Chapultepec Hill. Cynics say that he tripped over the flag, inadvertently sending himself to a glorious death.

Commemorations to Los Niños Héroes can be found in most of the large cities of Mexico. The most impressive of these is located at the entrance to Chapultepec Park, the Central Park of Mexico City. There are six marble statues, each topped with an eagle with folded wings. This tragedy reminds one of another Mexican saying: "Remember, the history of Mexico is a series of heroic measures ending in defeat."

The military academy was refurbished during the French occupation (1862–1867) and became the home of Emperor Maximilian and his wife Carlota, and of every Mexican president until 1934.

The Americans only stayed in Mexico for one year. Mexicans never forget that the American flag flew over the National Palace during that time. Even today I get e-mails from my Mexican friends reminding me of the Americans' perfidious behavior. Sometimes the e-mail is accompanied by a painting of the national palace, off Mexico City's central plaza, with the American flag flying overhead.

The Treaty of Guadalupe/Hidalgo (1848) put an end to the American occupation. The treaty stipulated that Mexico receive $15 million for California, reduced from the original offer of $40 million. The lands between California and Texas, which included the present day states of New Mexico, Arizona, Colorado, and parts of Utah and Nevada, became part of the United States. Mexico also agreed to the annexation of the Republic of Texas announced by President Polk in 1845.

What is surprising is the Catholic Church covertly supported the United States' intervention, as did much of the wealthy conservative class of Mexicans. They believed Mexico's primary need was a stable government. There was ample proof that Mexico was incapable of creating such a government after gaining independence in 1821.

Mexican historians, while railing against the Americans, are also extremely critical of the Mexican traitors who backed the invaders. Malinchismo had once more reared its ugly head.

In 1853, when Santa Anna returned once more to proclaim himself president, he sold the United States a territory that included the Mesilla Valley, just south of Las Cruces, New Mexico, and parts of southern Arizona. The territorial expanse was approximately the size of the state of Pennsylvania. The agreed price was 10 million dollars. This treaty became known in the United States as the Gadsden Purchase, and as the Tratado de Mesillas in Mexico. What Santa Anna did with this money is unknown, but the goals set forth in the doctrine of Manifest Destiny were now a reality.

From Mexicans I have talked to over the years, I've always been surprised that they don't seem to begrudge the losses of California and the New Mexico Territories as much as their deep resentment over the loss of Texas. Mexicans choose to ignore that most of the lost territory was sparsely inhabited except for the Indian population. Many people also choose to forget that these territories only became Mexican in 1821.

The establishment of the Republic of Texas covered a mere fifteen years, from 1821 to 1836, hardly enough time to create governmental control over a territory eight hundred miles from Mexico City. Nevertheless, in the eyes of the Mexican people this reasoning hardly matters. The underlying resentments, aside from the loss of territory, are because the United States broke so many agreements with Mexico over Texas and, in a country that had already abolished slavery, the Americans expanded this practice via the Texian immigration. This enormous hypocrisy has earned the United States Mexico's everlasting suspicion and mistrust.

For the United States the issue was simple. Coauthors Robert A. Pastor and Jorge Castañeda summarize this matter in the book *Limits of Friendship*: "The Texas war of independence and the war against Mexico are not seen within the context of U.S. Mexican relations. In the U.S., Mexico is viewed as a way station on the purposeful trek [Manifest Destiny] of the United States across the continent."

There are others points of view. Francisco Martín Moreno, a popular Mexican historian, spares no words in his bestseller dedicated to the history of the American intervention, first in Texas and later in the Mexican War. In his book *México Mutilado* (Mexico mutilated) he states, "When Mexico refused to sell its lands, the American envoy abandoned the country opening the door so that it could be occupied by an army comprised of real professionals trained in the extermination of human beings, the only creature in nature that uses reason as a means of collective slaughter." To this he added, "We ask ourselves why President Polk refused to annex all of Mexico according to the opinions of his closest advisors and only kept California, the New Mexico Territories and the Republic of Texas? . . . Because the North Americans only wanted those sparsely occupied lands they could freely control with a superior race, their own, those Anglo Saxons who would not be contaminated by a lower class of people, the Mexicans." According to Moreno, he claims President Polk was known to have said, "Will I have to exterminate six million Mexican aborigines who are slothful and stupid, as well as totally useless like our own redskin population?"

Mexico's animosity towards the loss of Texas can best be described by a historian from Dallas, Texas, whom I had had the opportunity to talk with. He was a member of a historic society that had a particular interest in the Battle of the Alamo. What follows is a summary of his story.

"Over the years, in acts of goodwill, the United States has returned to Mexico the Mexican battle flags from the defeats the Mexicans suffered in the Texas War of Independence and the Mexican War that followed. However, there is one battle flag Texans wanted in return. It is the flag of the Texians defending the Alamo, which was captured by the army of Santa Anna. We first officially contacted the Mexican government and asked them if they would return our flag as an act of reciprocity to our returning their battle flags," my friend said, shaking his head.

"I guess it didn't work."

"They didn't even answer us."

"So then what?"

"We then asked them if they might lend us the flag so we could put it on exhibition throughout Texas."

"Still no answer?"

"Oh no, they answered alright. No way, is what they told us."

"Then what did you do?"

He smiled. "We actually went to Mexico City." My friend again shook his head. "In desperation, we asked the Mexicans if they might just let us photograph the flag."

"I think I know the answer."

"They just smiled, then told us, 'We don't even know where it's being kept.'"

Anecdotes of the Mexican War

The first line of the Marine battle song, "From the Halls of Montezuma," refers to the Battle of Chapultepec in Mexico City. Four American officers who participated in this war became presidents: Ulysses S. Grant, Millard Fillmore, Zachary Taylor, and Jefferson Davis, who became president of the Confederacy during the Civil War. Most of the officer corps from this war went on to participate in the Civil War, including Robert E. Lee and Stonewall Jackson. But probably what most people don't know is the legend of the word gringo and the Old West saying, "a Mexican standoff."

The word gringo in English and Spanish is a sixteenth-century word from the reign of Charles V, Holy Roman Emperor and King of Spain. The word meant those people in the Spanish Empire who could not speak Spanish. The reference was to those citizens who lived in the lowlands of Europe, now Holland, Belgium, and parts of France. This description appears in *El Diccionario de la Real Academia de la Lengua Española* (The dictionary of the Royal Academy of the Spanish Language). The root of the word is *griego*, or Greek, as in "You are speaking to me in Greek. I don't understand you."

Mexico has its own meaning for the word gringo. There is a positive version when a Mexican says something like, "I want to introduce you to my gringo friend," being a sign of friendship. The negative version could be a statement by a Mexican such as, "I can't stand the sight of that gringo," intended as an insult. As far as Mexicans are concerned this double meaning can be traced back to the Mexican War.

Historically, the most important battle in the taking of Mexico City was not the storming of the hill in Chapultepec Park, but the Battle of Churubusco fought at the Old Convent of Churubusco, located on the south side of present day Mexico City. The defenders were in this convent, which straddled the only road impeding the entrance of Gen. Winfield Scott's army to the capital.

In the convent were three Mexican battalions. There was a fourth, known as El Batallón de San Patricio (Saint Patrick's Battalion), composed of Irish American Catholic defectors from Winfield Scott's army. They joined the Mexican forces in open rebellion against Irish American Catholic troops, fighting fellow Mexican Catholics.

This Irish American contingent is much beloved in Mexico. Their names can be found on various memorials, as well as celebrated on Saint Patrick's Day. There are marches with Irish bagpipers. Churches are decorated with green ribbons, and priests dress in green cassocks. There is also a memorial listing their names on the inside walls of the convent, which, the symbolic meaning not withstanding, houses El Museo de las Intervenciones (The Museum of Foreign Interventions). This museum displays the relics and written history of the U.S. interventions in Mexico of 1846–1848, 1914, and 1916. The history of the French intervention of 1862–1867 and its memorabilia are also on display.

Here is where legend takes over. The battle song of Saint Patrick's Battalion was "Green Grow the Rushes Oh," or, as pronounced by the Mexican troops, "*gringo de roshes-o.*" I have taken the liberty to suggest this is the positive use of the word gringo.

Legend also has it that at this battle the Mexicans yelled down from the parapets of the convent what sounded like, "*gringo go-ome,*" the Mexican version of, "Green coat go home." This was in reference to the green jackets worn by Winfield Scott's marines as part of their uniform. This could be interpreted as the negative use of the word.

According to the Mexican version of this battle, it was only won by Scott's troops because the Mexicans fought to the last bullet. This differs from the U.S. version that both contingents had totally spent their ammunition, turning the battle into a standoff with both sides unable to continue. It was at this point that the American commander decided to bluff his way to victory under a flag of truce. He demanded that the Mexicans surrender and turn over their ammunition. The Mexican commander is said to have answered, "If I had any ammunition left you would not be standing there." He then surrendered to the Americans.

As we know, the use of the phrase Mexican Standoff indicates a stalemate between two forces. I have a gun at your head, you have a gun at my head, and the first one to blink loses. Whether this is true or not, it's a good story.

7

The Mexican Lincoln and
the Austrian Prince

◆

HE WAS A PURE BLOODED ZAPOTEC indio, born into the bottom of the well-entrenched Spanish colonial caste system. He was brought up in total poverty in the high sierras of the southern Mexican state of Oaxaca. With no schooling available and a future that promised a lifelong bleak horizon of tilling the soil for survival, the boy migrated to the city of Oaxaca, capital of the state. He worked as a servant in a household that already employed his older sister as a cook.

Unable to read or write, it was unthinkable that this boy could not only become the president of Mexico, but also lead his country through a momentous period known as La Reforma, as well as one of its most difficult times, the French Occupation (1862–1867). Probably his greatest accomplishment was liberating his countrymen from the yoke of the Catholic Church. In time this resulted in dire consequences known as La Rebellión Cristero (the Christer Rebellion), which pitted the church against the state and lasted from 1926 to 1929.

Abraham Lincoln admired him to the point that the United States knew him as the Mexican Lincoln. Others referred to him as the Mexican Washington. His fame spread to Europe where two Italian socialists, one named Andrea, a teacher, and her husband Amilcari, a carpenter, with the last name of Mussolini, named their son after him; the man who ruled Italy and became known as Il Duce.

The Colombian government honored him with the title of Bemérito de las Américas, the highest order of merit in the Americas. He was also known as one of the five "Liberators of the Americas," in the company of Simón Bolívar, José de San Martín, José Martí Pérez, and George Washington. In 1939 Hollywood produced a biographical film about him starring Paul Muni and Bette Davis.

In Mexico there are streets, avenues, parks, schools, airports, buildings, and cities named after him, and even the United States recognizes his greatness with statues in New York City, Chicago, New Orleans, and Washington, D.C.

Probably, what describes him best is the Colombian government's decree in 1865 that his portrait be hung in the National Library with the inscription:

Benito Juárez, Mexican Citizen

The Congress of 1865 dedicates, in the name of the Colombian people, this homage attesting to his fortitude in defending the freedom and independence of Mexico.

In the same time frame a citizen speaking in front of the Colombian Senate made the following observation, a clear harbinger of future events: "Benito Juárez is the upright statesman who makes a clear contrast with one too many traitors and betrayers; the man of good faith that chooses misery and death to shame, because the word duty is more flattering to him than the insignia of Great Marshall; he is the genius that will scare away the horrifying tempest that has blown so recently upon the New World."

And then there's even the larger question: why do many Mexicans consider Juárez to be a traitor, much in the mold of a malinchista?

◆

The owner of the home where he worked as a houseboy sent Benito Pablo Juárez García to a Franciscan seminary. He decided not to become a priest, but to study law instead. Seminaries were the only schools where a mestizo or indígena could receive a decent education.

Through hard work he was elected governor of the state of Oaxaca from 1847 to 1853. In 1853 he decided on a self-imposed exile to protest the corrupt military dictatorship of Gen. Antonio López de Santa Anna.

Juárez spent this period of his life in New Orleans working in a cigar factory, living in near-total poverty. In recognition of this time spent in exile, the city later built a memorial to him on Basin Street, near the site where he worked. After two years he returned to Mexico, where he was instrumental in the creation of the Mexican Constitution of 1857, which led to the civil war known as La Guerra de La Reforma (1857–1860), once again pitting the conservatives against the liberals, led by Juárez. He was named interim president in 1858, thus initiating the Era of Juárez that lasted until the time of his death in 1872.

The most innovative aspect of this constitution was the separation of church and state, which greatly curtailed the power of the Catholic Church. Despite being educated by the priesthood, Juárez became disillusioned with the church and went as far as becoming, like George Washington before him, a Freemason.

In 1859 Juárez acted on the anticleric provisions of the new constitution by taking the extraordinary step of disenfranchising the bishops, priests, nuns, and lay brothers. In conjunction with this decree he expropriated all church properties, in the future to be owned by the state. His anti-Catholicism was made quite clear when he told one of his followers, "Mexicans need a religion that will make them read instead of wasting their savings on candles for the saints."

Until the early 1990s, when the anti-clerical laws established under Article 27 of the Mexican Constitution of 1917 were liberalized, a keen observer visiting Mexico might have taken note that the Catholic clergy and nuns weren't wearing their cassocks and habits in public. They were banned from doing so. The separation of church and state went to such extremes that when the daughter or son of a high-ranking politico had a church wedding, the father was expected to refuse to set foot inside. Today, visitors to Mexico will notice that many of the churches, parishes and cathedrals are in dire need of repair. They belong to the state. It is the government's responsibility to see to their upkeep, which until recently has never been a priority.

Ever since the government became more tolerant towards the Church's participation in the social and political life of the country and clerics once again could wear their cassocks in public, Mexico has undergone a program of restoring these buildings of worship and other historic monuments from the time of the Spanish colonial period under a program known as Pueblos Mágicos. Those towns qualifying for this designation receive funds from the federal government, the state and the municipality. Many have now been declared UNESCO World Heritage Sites.

The French Occupation (1862–1867)

The War of La Reforma left the treasury totally depleted, forcing the government to take a drastic measure. The McLane-Ocampo Treaty, also known as the Treaty of Transit and Commerce, became the reason why many in the Mexican intelligentsia consider Juárez to be a traitor to the nation.

This agreement between the United States and Mexico, signed in Veracruz on December 14, 1859, during the U.S. presidency of James Buchanan, sold the perpetual right of transit across the Isthmus of Tehuantepec to the United States for four million dollars. The U.S. transit rights would be free of any charge or duty, both for military and commercial use. The treaty also obligated Mexican troops to assist in the enforcement of rights permanently given to the United States.

The treaty also granted the U.S. right of passage through two strips of Mexican territory. The first was from the port of Guaymas on the Sea of Cortés in the northern state of Sonora to the city of Nogales on the border with Arizona, south of Tucson. The second strip was from the western port of Mazatlán, in the state of Sinaloa, eastward to the Gulf of Mexico just south of Brownsville, Texas.

The treaty was never ratified because of the concern of the northern United States that it might only increase the power of the slave states. Had it been ratified, Mexico would effectively have been under the control of the United States. In all probability there would be no Panama Canal, but a similar canal across the Isthmus of Tehuantepec where the Mexican landmass is at its narrowest, connecting the Pacific Ocean with the Gulf of Mexico.

The question has always been, why was Juárez willing to do this in exchange for a mere four million dollars? Many historians believe he needed the money to fight the conservatives who were screaming for his ouster, largely due to the country being unable to pay its foreign debt. He also needed a strong ally. That seems somewhat farfetched, considering that in this treaty Mexico sacrificed much of its sovereignty to the United States. Those who do not share the world's adulation of Juárez as a great leader and benefactor to a struggling nation are convinced he believed that Mexico's progress could not be left in the hands of Mexicans. To these people Juárez is the epitome of a malinchista.

In 1861 President Juárez, unable to raise the funds due to the refusal of the U.S. Senate to ratify the McLane-Ocampo Treaty, took the fateful step of calling for a moratorium on Mexico's foreign debt, largely owed to Britain, Spain, and France. The government was able to negotiate an agreement with the British and the Spanish, but the French, with encouragement from the conservatives in opposition to the Juárez government, decided this was the excuse they needed to get a foothold on the American continent. Much like a repeat of the Mexican War, behind the scenes the Mexican conservatives supported foreign intervention as a solution to bringing political order to a government they deemed incapable of ruling. Malinchismo, in a country supposedly steeped in nationalism, was once more coming out of the closet.

In 1862 the French occupied the port of Veracruz with the intention of imposing French rule in Mexico. Napoleon III was counting on the United States, involved in its own civil war, not having the military resources or the determination to impose the Monroe Doctrine of no European intervention on the American continent. Had that not been the case, it is nearly impossible to conceive of the French intervention.

The French believed that once they gained a foothold on the American continent, they inevitably became the dominant force and culture in the Americas. They coined the phrase "Latin America" or, as they saw it, Roman Catholic America. They believed in what might be called the French version of Manifest Destiny. France, a Catholic country and in its own eyes the most enlightened nation on earth backed by the strongest military in Europe, was convinced its destiny was to spread the French culture to the Catholic countries in this hemisphere.

As the French advanced towards Mexico City, the first major battle between the Mexicans and the French took place on May 5, 1862. It became known as the Battle of Puebla and is commemorated in Mexico and the United States as the Cinco de Mayo. Many Americans believe that on this day Mexico celebrates its day of independence, so much so that in 2008 President George W. Bush supposedly sent his Mexican counterpart a note of congratulations to that effect. In reality, the Battle of Puebla simply turned out to be a Pyrrhic victory of no military importance. The Mexican euphoria of triumph under the command of Gen. Ignacio Zaragoza Seguín was short-lived. Only temporarily detained, the French moved forward, defeating the forces of Juárez and occupying Mexico City. But in a country in need of a victory amidst so many defeats after the commencement of the War of Independence, this victory has been celebrated way beyond its near irrelevancy. Once Mexico City fell, the country was in the hands of the French, even though France never occupied much of Mexican territory. The invaders didn't have to. The power that controls Mexico City controls the country. Once again, the inability to decentralize power was Mexico's undoing.

Juárez and his government fled north to the city of Chihuahua and then further north to the city of Paso del Norte across from El Paso, Texas, today known as Ciudad Juárez, where he remained until the French left Mexico in 1867. In support of the Mexican cause, and against the wishes of Congress, Abraham Lincoln ordered Gen. Ulysses Grant to provide arms to the remnants of Juárez's forces. Grant had 30,000 muskets mysteriously disappear from a Union armory, left on the border between the two countries.

Under pressure from the conservatives in Mexico and the support of Emperor Napoleon III, Maximilian von Hapsburg, a younger brother of the emperor of Austria, and his wife, Carlota, daughter of Leopold I, king of the Belgians, were sent to Mexico. Arriving in Mexico City they were crowned Emperor Maximilian I and Empress Carlota, but only after Maximilian renounced all claims to any European thrones.

Maximilian was not what the conservatives had hoped for. A liberal in his thinking, he offered amnesty to the exiled Benito Juárez, and the position of Prime Minister, which Juárez disdainfully refused.

During Maximilian's reign he did much to beautify Mexico City, including the restoration of the present-day Chapultepec Palace. Maximilian built the Paseo de la Reforma, Mexico City's most important and beautiful avenue, designed after the Champs Elysées in Paris. Originally, the broad avenue was called the Paseo de la Eperatriz (Avenue of the Empress), after his wife Carlota. It seems that Maximilian's hobby was building large projects such as his Piazza de Duomo in Milan.

In his book *Noticias del Imperio* (News from the empire), written in 1865, Fernando del Paso describes how the foreigners adapted to their new home. In a fictional letter written by the Empress Carlota to a friend, we get a glimpse of what life might have been like under the French:

> But I was telling you about the capital . . . well, there are a few oases for foreigners. We French have a lot of them of course. The Germans can go to a club, Das Deutsche Haus to drink their Alsatian beer while the British spend the weekends at the Mexico Cricket Club [now the Club Reforma] near Tacubaya; a very pretty spot, which is known as the Saint Cloud of Mexico. Ah yes, you should know that this kind of comparison is very fashionable, so we hear that Xochimilco is the Venice of America, San Angel is the Aztec Compiegne, Cuernavaca [fifty miles southwest of the capital] is the Mexican Fontainbleau—it was Maximilian who thought of

that one—and the Castle of Chapultepec is the Schönbrunn of *Anáhuac* and so on.

The French occupation was short-lived, especially once the Civil War in the United States came to an end. In 1867 William H. Seward, U.S. Secretary of State under Presidents Abraham Lincoln and Andrew Johnson, invoked the Monroe Doctrine, warning Mexico that if the French did not leave peacefully there would be consequences. The French, and their conservative Mexican supporters, were well aware of the meaning behind the hidden threat. The Mexican War of 1846–1848 was a clear reminder from the past; they decided the expedient measure was to leave. They also faced the problem of Benito Juárez and his growing army in the north. The outcome was likely not in their favor.

Seward is best remembered for purchasing Alaska from the Russians in that same year, known as "Seward's Folly" and "Seward's Ice Box."* At the risk of being labeled a malinchista, no Mexican historian credits the important role Seward played in getting the French to leave Mexico. The same goes for American historians, who give little credence to Seward's role in freeing Mexico from French rule. If the French departure was inevitable, the lack of bloodshed is clearly due to Seward's intervention on behalf of the U.S. government.

Not all remnants of the French army left. Many were European mercenaries who decided there was a better life to be had in Mexico than at home. Most of these soldiers migrated west and settled in the states of Jalisco and its capital Guadalajara, and Nayarit and its capital Tepic. One of the cultural gifts these relocated soldiers bestowed was creating the Mexican music known as the mariachi. This music, played to celebrate weddings, began in the state of Jalisco then spread to the rest of the country. Mariachi was derived from the French word *mariage*, pronounced *mar-e-aj-e* by the Spanish-speaking locals.

When I was living in Guadalajara, it was not uncommon to encounter people with non-Spanish European last names. I remember driving through the small city of Tepic on the way to the Pacific Ocean and seeing fair-skinned women ambling along the street dressed in typical Mexican peasant dresses.

---

* The purchase of Alaska was also known as President Johnson's "polar bear zoo."

My Mexican friends always reminded me, "Those are the beautiful women we inherited from French sexual proliferation."

Maximilian also decided his adopted country offered a better future. After all, part of the decision to make him emperor was his agreement to renounce his claims to the thrones of Europe.

As Mexico regained its independence under the presidency of Benito Juárez, the Austrian prince, who favored the liberal causes of Mexico, felt that the government should grant him amnesty. Maximilian was tried for treason in 1867, found guilty and, despite the pleas by many European governments, was executed in the city of Querétaro some sixty miles northwest of the capital. His last words were *"Viva México!"* The city of Querétaro is the capital of the state of the same name, where Father Junípero Serra built his five famous missions back in the eighteenth century.

Carlota, who by this time was considered certifiably crazy, spent the rest of her life secluded in Belgium and Italy. She never recovered her mental health, and apparently never knew of her husband's death.

Maximilian and Carlota had accumulated quite a treasure in gold and silver coins and other bullion. Carlota arranged for this booty to be sent to Europe via the Port of Galveston, Texas. A band of renegade ex-Confederate soldiers stole the booty that had been hidden in bags of flour somewhere in Texas. Like the treasure of Montezuma, it has never been found.

Many historians wonder why Juárez did not spare Maximilian's life. A letter Juárez wrote Maximilian refusing his offer to become prime minister gives a clear reason:

> Certainly, sir, the history of our times registers the names of great traitors who have violated their oaths, their word and their promises, they have betrayed their own party, their principles, their ancestors and everything an honorable man holds sacred. Furthermore, in all these cases, the traitor has been guided by a vile ambition of power and a miserable desire to satisfy his own passion and even his own vices.

This letter was a clear harbinger of events that followed, leading up to the Mexican Revolution.

As a result of the French occupation and the earlier American intervention of 1846, Mexico embraced a foreign policy that exists to this day. Known as the Juárez Doctrine, it states, "*Entre individuos, como entre las naciones, el respeto al derecho ajeno es la paz* (Among individuals, as among nations, respect for the rights of others is peace)." Mexico has steadfastly complied with this doctrine to this day. Inevitably, this resulted in a clash with the United States when Mexico, as an ally, refused to support American intervention in Asia and the Middle East.

Abraham Lincoln and Benito Juárez had much in common. Both lived through troubled times and fought a war during their presidencies. Both championed the downtrodden and the mistreated. In the case of Lincoln the cause was the abolition of slavery; in the case of Juárez, it was the plight of the indigenous people who were slaves in all but name.

Upon the death of President Benito Juárez in 1872, the country once more retreated into chaos, bringing on the longest dictatorship in Mexican history. Much like the Spanish colonial rule, the *porfiriato* enjoyed its enlightened moments, but it also had a dark side that set the stage for the Mexican Revolution of 1910.

DICTATORSHIP, REVOLUTION, AND CHAOS (1876–1929)

U NDOUBTEDLY, SOME OF THE MOST DEFINING moments in Mexico's past were the events leading up to the Mexican Revolution during the dictatorship of Porfirio Díaz (1876–1910). The porfiriato was the immediate cause of the Revolution that lasted from 1910 to 1920, and the aftereffects that eventually brought the country back together by 1929. If the Mexican Revolution started as an agrarian uprising in search of bringing change to the oppressed campesino, often living under deplorable conditions, it soon turned into a civil war between many ambitious military leaders. This was a revolution that might have been avoided if the country had paid more attention to the needs of rural Mexico under the thirty-five-year Porfirian dictatorship.

The tragedy of the revolution is undoubtedly centered on what became known as La Reforma Agraria (the Agrarian Reform). Redistribution of land under the ejido communal system turned into a massive failure. By 1940 the revolution had spread to the urban middle and upper-middle class. The intervention in all walks of life—from education, to the economy, to ownership and management of the country's natural resources and utilities—had terrible consequences.

American meddling was also always ever-present. However, Mexico soon realized that foreigners were necessary to help bring Mexico into the twentieth century.

Not only did the Mexican Revolution turn ownership of various sectors of the economy over to the government, but it gave birth to a series of reforms doomed to fail. This period also created a unique system of government that lasted from 1929 to 2000. No other country saw any merits in the Mexican experiment—one that turned a once-rich nation into a third-world quagmire by creating institutions that lent themselves to corruption and mismanagement on a grand scale.

Despite its many failures, the revolution changed the face of Mexico forever. It was truly a turning point in Mexican history. The nation that emerged from the ashes of the old founded a new era represented by many social experiments that had disastrous results. Never to be seriously questioned, the revolution has risen to become "the myth of lay sainthood," as described by Enrique Krause, a prominent Mexican historian.

8

The Mixtec Indian Tsar
(1876–1911)

◆

UNQUESTIONABLY ONE OF THE MOST CONTROVERSIAL figures in Mexican history, Porfirio Díaz defined the Mexico of extreme contrasts. His remains are buried in the Cimetière du Montparnasse in Paris, last resting place of the elite, including a who's who in philosophy, music, letters, and the arts. Among the more notable are Charles Baudelaire, Simone de Beauvoir, Samuel Beckett, Pierre Larousse, Jean Paul Sartre, and Susan Sontag. The list is a long one. The only other military personage buried there is Alfred Dreyfus, of the famous Dreyfus Affair. While the French had no second thoughts about the greatness of Díaz, Mexican historians and the Mexican people are still debating the pros and cons of the Porfirian Era.

The Porfiristas would like to see his remains returned to Mexico and Díaz given his proper place as a figure who, despite his wrongdoings, literally thrust the country into the Industrial Age. This inevitably requires a revisionist approach to the 1910 post-revolution thinking that he was a cruel dictator who should be left to rot in Paris.

What are we to think? Referring to him as the Mixtec Indian tsar gives us a look into the complexities of a man who was born a humble Oaxacan Mixtec Indian mestizo, and who went on to rule Mexico as an iron-fisted dictator for thirty-five years. In the end, there is no question that Díaz was responsible for the Revolution of 1910, which changed Mexico forever. Here was a man who not only forgot his roots, but also answered to nobody but himself. He became the ultimate malinchista, with an insatiable appetite for embracing foreign ideas and foreigners as a solution to his country's problems. In appreciation, countries around the world, especially in Europe, rewarded him with medals of the highest order. When one looks at his official photograph it is a miracle he could stand up straight from all the metal he had to support on his chest.

Those who honored him ignored the fact that Porfirio Díaz disregarded the impoverished *pueblo* from whence he came. He actually went out of his way to make them more miserable. Why? Nobody seems to have the answer. Maybe he wanted to put as much distance as possible between himself and his humble beginnings.

The Porfirian dictatorship followed a simple political philosophy of *pan o palo* (bread or the stick)—take what I have to offer you or face the consequences. This slogan sounded similar to the modern day narcotrafficker's saying *plomo o plata* (lead or silver)—join us or die.

By taking a closer look, readers can come to their own conclusions about a man who had a clear understanding of how to catapult his country into the twentieth century but could also say of his followers, "A dog with a bone neither barks, steals or bites," and of his enemies, "*mátalos en caliente* (kill them now)."

◆

Much like his Oaxacan contemporary, Benito Juárez, Díaz attended a seminary to study for the priesthood. But a military career attracted him, and he soon left to join the army, where he quickly rose through the ranks. His career parallels the rise of Benito Juárez, whose liberal beliefs Díaz espoused, so much so that in 1863 Juárez offered him the position of secretary of defense as army commander-in-chief of the Mexican military forces exiled in the north as a result of the French invasion in 1862.

In 1864 Emperor Maximilian asked Díaz to join his government. Maximilian even tried to get Díaz to head up an army guaranteeing the emperor's stay in power after the French military forces decided to leave Mexico and the exiled Juaristas were back in Mexico City. Throughout this early part of his career, Díaz steadfastly refused to accept any position that was not in total support of Benito Juárez. At times he acted like a protective older brother.

These military offers must have gone to his head, because by 1870 he saw real opportunity in becoming Juárez's successor. When he found it impossible to take over the Mexican government through legitimate elections, he used the backing of the army to appoint himself president in 1876, four years after the death of his Oaxacan mentor. He remained in power until his resignation and subsequent exile in 1911.

If there was a representative government during his thirty-five-year rule, it was in name only. The actual government was divided into two groups, the *científicos*, today known as technocrats, and the *rurales*, squadrons of mounted police who instilled their own version of law and order in the interior of the country with complete authority to impose or circumvent the law as they saw fit. The real intent behind the rurales was to protect the interests of the large landowners, known as hacendados.

Porfirio Díaz understood that the fundamentals of the Mexican economy were anchored in agriculture and mining. When it came to agriculture, the científicos believed that progress could only be made by landowners with the financial means to produce the food supply needed for a growing urban nation. The peasant's only function was to provide the cheap labor necessary for the development of this agricultural base. The rurales became the law enforcement arm who assured that the campesino understood his position in the new scheme of things. Any pretense to continue the land reforms put in place by La Reforma under Juárez, which included protecting the rights of the campesino, ceased.

To this end, in 1883 Díaz passed a law stating that a farmer had no claim over his land unless he could show a formal title that was legally notarized and registered. This eliminated most of the holdings owned by a poorly educated campesino class that at best could barely read and write. Only the large haciendas could meet this requirement, resulting in a reverse agrarian reform in which the hacendados simply added on to their already large holdings by taking the land held by the campesinos. In Díaz's mind, cementing the allegiance of the large landowners allowed him to concentrate on his vision of a progressive industrialized nation similar to the United States and Europe. The only recourse these campesino farmers had was to work for the large haciendas, where they in effect became indentured servants living in misery and despair.

To make sure he could legally dispose of his enemies, Díaz implemented La Ley Fuga (the escape law), which allowed for any of the dictator's enemies to be shot under the pretense that they had tried to escape after being detained.

To put this in perspective, when the owner of a hacienda in the state of Morelos took Emiliano Zapata—one of the future *caudillo** leaders of the

---

* *Caudillo* usually refers to a leader on horseback, or a post-revolutionary warlord.

Mexican Revolution—to Mexico City with him to care for his horses, Zapata was said to have made the following observation: "It was then that I realized that horses were better fed than human beings."

If we want to appreciate the enormity of wealth of these hacendados, many of whom were absentee owners who left the management of their properties in the hands of overseers, we only have to look at the holdings of the Creel-Terrazas family. Once again, it's microhistory that gives us a clear and concise picture of what rural conditions in Mexico must have been like. The concentration of wealth was beyond imagination. Maybe Tsarist Russia could claim some similarities.

Don Luis Terrazas Fuentes (1829–1923) was the patriarch of the Terrazas family, which owned fifty haciendas throughout the state of Chihuahua, totaling in excess of 7 million acres. A member of the Porfirio Díaz inner circle and one of the científicos, Don Luis, when asked at a party of visiting dignitaries if he was from Chihuahua, is said to have answered, "*No soy de Chihuahua . . . Chihuahua es mio* (I'm not from Chihuahua . . . Chihuahua is mine)."

His holdings included 500,000 head of cattle, 225,000 sheep, 25,000 horses, and 5,000 mules. When a group of cattle buyers from Chicago wanted to purchase 50,000 head, legend tells us he answered, "What color?" In just one of his haciendas in the town of Encenillas, he employed over 2,000 campesinos.

Don Enrique Creel (1854–1931), son-in-law to Don Luis, was not nearly as wealthy. He only owned a million-and-a-half-acre hacienda, but he had a far closer relationship to Porfirio Díaz than his father-in-law. He was twice governor of the state of Chihuahua.

Despite the expropriation of much of their land at the subsequent hands of the Mexican Revolution and the Agrarian Reform, José Reyes Baeza Terrazas, offspring of the Terrazas family, became the municipal president (mayor) of the city of Chihuahua from 1998 to 2001. Three years later he was elected governor of the state (2004–2010). On the Creel side, from 2000 to 2005, Santiago Creel Miranda became the secretary of the interior, the most powerful political cabinet position, under President Vicente Fox. He went on to become a presidential hopeful of the conservative party, PAN, and president of the Senate.

Porfirio Díaz believed that if Mexico was to progress into the twentieth century, a modern industrial infrastructure had to be put in place. However, the country had neither the capital nor the technical know-how to bring this about.

Mexico's only alternative was to open the borders to foreign investors and foreign companies to do the job for them. Following the advice of his científicos, Díaz initiated the great era of foreign exploitation.

Porfirio Díaz favored European investment and culture over that of his next-door neighbor. The problem was dealing with his people, who had not forgotten the country that relieved them of half of their territory. Despite Mexico's animosity towards the United States, the financial investment and industrial development opportunities did not stop the American entrepreneurs and adventurers from becoming the leading exploiters of Mexico's mining and oil resources, while building the infrastructure that slowly prepared Mexico to join the community of developing industrialized nations. This feeling can be best expressed by the Mexican saying, "*Que haríamos sin los gringos, pero nunca hay que darles las gracias* (What would we do without the Gringos? But we must never thank them)."

Approximately 60 million acres of privately owned land ended up in the hands of foreigners. By 1894 one out of every five acres of privately owned property in Mexico was under the control of non-Mexicans, mostly U.S. citizens. This alone might have been enough to launch an agrarian revolution. What was Porfirio Díaz thinking? Did he not understand the word malinchismo? Had he forgotten his humble origins?

◆

I have followed the story of a company that made history, not only in Mexico, but also in Great Britain. This company launched the oil boom that turned Mexico into the second largest producer of crude in the world.

In 1898 the científicos invited a British firm, a civil engineering contractor specializing in building railroads and harbors, to come to Mexico and build a railroad connecting the Gulf of Mexico and the Pacific Ocean. They were also contracted to expand the Veracruz harbor, the main Mexican port on the Gulf of Mexico. The firm was then known as the Pearson Conglomerate, or the Pearson Firm. At the time, the company was under the management of Weetman D. Pearson, grandson of the founder. Today the company goes under the name the Pearson Group and is a giant British publishing company that owns the *Financial Times* newspaper, 50 percent of the *Economist* magazine, and Penguin Books as part of their extensive portfolio.

Weetman Pearson came to Mexico, and, while surveying the best route for the proposed railroad, his crew discovered one of the world's great crude oil reserves. Known as El Potrero del Llano, this oilfield created one of the largest oil companies in Mexico. It was called El Águila and in no time made the Pearson family a fortune. In 1921 the declared profits were 85 million pesos in gold, the same equivalent in dollars.

In 1910 the British government rewarded Weetman Pearson with a peerage. He became Lord Cowdray, and in 1917 he became a viscount.

The present-day Cowdrays live in a grand manner, thanks not only to the black gold produced by the El Águila oil consortium, but also from the yearly payment received from the Mexican government in compensation for the nationalization of its interests in 1938. This annual compensation is believed to have extended into the 1980s.

In 1965, I was hired as a fund-raiser by the Financial Committee of the ABC Hospital (American British Cowdray), known in Mexico City as *el hospital inglés*, to raise money from the English-speaking community to build a new ABC Hospital at its present location fronting the American School. My first office was in the old hospital located on a piece of property given to Lord Cowdray as a gift from President Porfirio Díaz. In 1968, when the ABC Hospital moved to its present location, the old hospital was torn down and became the home of the Camino Real, one of the city's landmark hotels. It was befitting that Queen Elizabeth and Prince Philip stayed there on their official visit to Mexico. Their picture is still prominently displayed in the lobby.

The ABC Hospital in Mexico City has served the American, British, and Canadian communities, as well as the Mexican community, for well over half a century. It is one of the landmarks of Anglo beneficence, and the best reminder of the Pearson family presence in Mexico. By mere coincidence, I am a partner in a firm that has been the advertising sales representative of the *Financial Times* in Mexico for over twenty years. When I bring up the story of where the Pearson fortune came from with the *Financial Times* people in New York, they don't have a clue as to what I'm talking about. Like some other famous fortunes that originated from the exploitation of Mexico's mineral and oil resources, it has been hidden from public view.

The largest of the great oil companies was the Pan American Petroleum and Transport Company, owned by Edward L. Doheny. In the motion picture

There Will Be Blood (2007), the character of Daniel Plainview, played by Daniel Day-Lewis, is a loose depiction of Doheny's life. Doheny never made any kind of contribution to the country that made him rich, but chose instead to donate part of his fortune to California universities, especially the University of California, which has buildings named after him.

If El Águila is one of many examples of foreign exploitation of Mexican natural resources, William Randolph Hearst, of the Hearst newspaper chain, was no slouch either. He owned a one-million-acre ranch in northern Mexico called Rancho Barbicora, where he was also involved in mining copper in an area called Cananea, the location of the richest copper deposits in Mexico.

But when it came to copper mines, nothing compared to the holdings of Col. William C. Greene of Wisconsin, who created the Cananea Copper Company known as the CCC. He became famous after a wildcat strike by his 4,500 mine workers in 1906 that eventually required the intervention of troops sent by Porfirio Díaz. Many historians consider this strike as the harbinger of the Mexican Revolution of 1910. The mines were nationalized by the Mexican government in 1971. Two decades later they were privatized and sold to the present owners, Grupo México.

Another interesting fortune made in Mexico that is also hidden from the public eye is the one accumulated by former President George H. W. Bush, the father of George W. This story will be told in a later chapter.

The national sellout of Mexico's natural resources to foreigners in the Porfirian years, the concentration of wealth by the hacendados, and the miserable conditions suffered by the Mexican peasant, coupled with the exploitation of Mexican workers in the mining and oil industry, became the causes for the Mexican Revolution of 1910.

◄►

One of the similarities Porfirio Díaz shared with Emperor Maximilian was a propensity to build projects befitting an empire. To celebrate the centennial anniversary of the commencement of the 1810 War of Independence, Porfirio Díaz commissioned the construction of the Palacio de Bellas Artes (The Palace of Fine Arts), now home of the Mexican Ballet Folklórico. Groundbreaking commenced in 1900, and the building was eventually finished in 1934. This massive European-style opera house was built of Italian marble. One of its many outstanding features is the curtain covering the stage, which came from Tiffany's in New York City. Díaz assigned engineers who completed the Ángel de la Independencia (Angel of Independence) statue in 1910, now the symbol of Mexico City, and the elaborate Italianate Hemicycle Memorial to Benito Juárez in Alameda Park. Across from this memorial, if you are touring the city, don't miss the famous giant Diego Rivera mural *A Dream of a Sunday Afternoon in Alameda Park,** which depicts some of the leading figures of the Porfirian Era. The mural is housed in the Museo Mural Diego Rivera in the Plaza Solidaridad, honoring the victims of the earthquake of 1985.

By 1910 the Mexican countryside was up in arms against the Porfirian dictatorship, and in 1911 Porfirio Díaz was forced to resign. He went into exile in Europe, and spent the rest of his life in Paris. His resignation speech to Congress was extraordinary, showing a clear disconnect between himself and the Mexican people: "I do not know of any fact imputable to me that would have caused this social phenomenon, but permitting, though not admitting, that I may be unwittingly culpable, such a possibility makes me the least able to reason out and decide my own culpability." This was surely an overstatement of a delusional mind. Despite the disconnect to reality, he then concluded, rather prophetically, "In order for me to continue in office it would be necessary to shed Mexican blood, endangering the credit of the country, dissipating its wealth, exhausting its resources and exposing its policy to international complications."

When deposed by Francisco Madero in 1911, the first president of the revolution and the man who was largely responsible for sending Porfirio Díaz into exile, the latter exited with these prophetic words of events to come, "Madero has unleashed a tiger; let's see if he can ride it." Madero couldn't, nor could the country for many decades to come. Despite Díaz's resignation, Mexico did shed blood from 1910 to 1920 and fulfilled the other prophecies he attempted to avoid by his exile to Europe.

Living modestly and in total obscurity in Paris, Don Porfirio Díaz died on July 2, 1915, at the age of eighty-five. Only his immediate family attended his funeral. The *New York Times* expressed it best when reporting his death in their July 3 edition of the same year: "Not less tragic, not one of those whom General Díaz raised up to be his assistants in governing Mexico and who prospered and

---

* The center section of this mural is used as the cover of this book.

grew rich in the shadow of his greatness was with him when he died. None seemed to even have known that he was in Paris."

Whatever the eventual judgment, for that day is yet to come, Porfirio Díaz was far more honest than the Mexican leadership that followed him in the twentieth century. As misguided as he might have been, he put his country first and foremost in most of his actions.

In retrospect, Mexican historians believe that Díaz was a despicable autocratic dictator who neglected the needs of the poor and needy. Even worse, he was a true malinchista. Others are not that convinced. While nobody disagrees on the man's sins, many Mexicans also feel he genuinely tried to bring progress to his country, if at times using draconian methods to reach his goals. Nobody can deny that he modernized the infrastructure of the nation—improving railroads and ports and beautifying Mexico City were high on his list of accomplishments. One can also never forget that during his tenure, Mexico became the second largest producer of oil in the world.

9

The Revolution Turned Civil War
(1910–1920)

◆

TO MOST AMERICANS THE MEXICAN REVOLUTION is personified by Hollywood films depicting men in dirty white pajamas wearing sandals and a bandolier or two across the chest under a wide brimmed floppy sombrero. In these films, it's hard to differentiate between revolutionaries living in squalid villages and bandits roaming the surrounding hills. The opposition, the federal troops, appears as a cruel bunch of killers, pillaging villages, raping women, and executing innocent people at random. Some of these military leaders wear splendid uniforms that give them the look of a backwater Central American dictator. Sam Peckinpah's epic *The Wild Bunch*, starring William Holden and Emilio "El Indio" Fernández as the pompous and overbearing general, is the epitome of these stereotypes. It is irrelevant that in reality those dressed in army uniforms were in most cases fighting in support of the revolution and not against it.

If you asked who the George Washington and Thomas Jefferson of these times was, you would probably be told Pancho Villa and Emiliano Zapata. Most of the people associated with the revolution are largely unknown outside of their own country. Their stories deserve to be told.

The essence of the Mexican Revolution followed the refrain "*mientras más matas, más gobiernas* (The more you kill, the more you govern)." This ten-year period saw an enormous bloodbath due to the pursuit of collective power by a revolving door of leaders, all of whom had a limited vision of the final objective. A rough estimate of more than one million dead is not to be sneezed at. The continuous internal battle of changing alliances made the events of this period so complex.

Historians generally agree that phase one (1910–1920) of the revolution officially began when Francisco Madero González, exiled in Texas after attempting to run against Díaz for president, called for the overthrow of the

Porfirian regime. This phase ended when then-president Venustiano Carranza de la Garza was assassinated while fleeing an armed rebellion in a booty-laden train to the port of Veracruz on his way to Europe. His plan was to spend the rest of his days living in stolen luxury.

Phase two (1920–1929) oversaw the unification of the country and was at times as violent and mired in political incertitude as phase one. This period is known as the Sonoran Dynasty and was dominated by Presidents Álvaro Obregón Salido (1920–1924) and Plutarco Elías Calles (1924–1929).

The final gasp of the revolution, known as the Rebellión Cristero or the Christer Rebellion (1926–1929), was a bloody affair caused by the strident anti-clerical laws contained in the Constitution of 1917 that pitted Catholics against the federal government.

The best way to tell this tale is to highlight the major political actors, most cast from the ranks of the military. They often played tortuous roles on the global stage, at times even lacking a direction in which to lead the country.

These men were self-appointed leaders with ideas that reflected their individuality and personal ambitions. As the eminent Mexican historian Enrique Krause described them in *Biografía del Poder* (*Biography of Power*), "These leaders came galloping on horseback into the national pantheon of Mexican heroes, emerging as the lay saints of these historic times."

The Principal Players

Selecting a point of departure, we might find it worthwhile to recall the words of Porfirio Díaz in his resignation speech in front of Congress prior to his exile to France: "In order for me to continue in office it would be necessary to shed Mexican blood, endangering the credit of the country, dissipating its wealth, exhausting its resources and exposing its policy to international complications." Even though Díaz resigned and went into exile, this is exactly what happened.

Francisco Madero (President 1911–1913)

He was a hacendado from the northern state of Coahuila. Educated in the United States and France, Madero became convinced of the need for reform due to the injustices of the Porfirian dictatorship, especially in the treatment of the campesino. He was the first leader of the Mexican Revolution and its first elected president. In 1910 he ran against Porfirio Díaz for president. For this failed effort,

Díaz had Madero imprisoned and declared himself the winner with 98 percent of the vote. Voter fraud in those days was hardly a sophisticated science.

After Madero was released, he went into exile in the United States, from where he declared open revolt against Díaz, counting on the support of a nation fed up with the aging dictator. The Mexican Revolution officially began on November 20, 1910, when Madero crossed the Texas border into Mexico. That day is now a national holiday known as El Día de la Revolución.

Díaz was forced to resign, bringing an end to the Porfirian Era. With the military aid of two campesino armies, Pancho Villa from the north and Emiliano Zapata from the south, Madero occupied the capital and declared himself interim president; he was subsequently elected to the position in 1911.

President Madero seems to have been mistrustful of his supporters, so he named mostly family members to his cabinet. Added to this nepotism was his inability to live up to the promises he made to his two most ardent supporters, Pancho Villa and Emiliano Zapata. They decided to abandon Mexico City, forcing Madero to place himself under the protection of Gen. José Victoriano Huerta Márquez, a holdover from the Porfirian dictatorship.

There is another version of why Villa and Zapata abandoned the capital. This legend seems to hit closer to the truth because it defines the problems Mexico had to face well into the future.

Both men were sitting in a cantina drinking tequila when the lights went out.

"What happened?" Zapata asked one of his henchmen.

"I have no idea," the man answered, shrugging his shoulders.

"*Mira, hijo de la chingada madre*, listen you son of a bitch, go to the electric company and find out," Pancho Villa chimed in, absolutely furious at the prospect of having to sit by candlelight. Both had been doing this most of their lives and expected better now that they were in the capital.

"*Sí, mi jefe*," the soldier answered, sombrero in hand, as he scurried out of the cantina. Both caudillos shook their heads in disgust.

Hours went by before the soldier, still with his sombrero in hand, returned.

"*Híjole* . . . why aren't the lights back on?" a disgusted Zapata asked.

"I'm sorry, *mi jefe*. It seems we shot the managers of the electric company, and the rest just disappeared."

The moral of the story is that carrying out a revolution is one thing, but running the country's infrastructure after you've rid the nation of its professional and managerial class is another. This was especially true when the administration of a city was placed in the hands of two rebellious campesino armies composed of militia that could barely shoot straight.

Whatever Villa and Zapata's reasons for abandoning the city, this power vacuum opened the door to the overthrow of President Francisco Madero by Victoriano Huerta. The country was soon in the throes of a civil war.

Victoriano Huerta (President 1913–1914)

He was the son of a cavalry soldier and a Huichol Indian. He reached the rank of division general, but was better known for his alcoholism and cocaine use. Even the well-known British writer, Graham Greene, recognized this when he visited Mexico City and wrote his book *The Power and The Glory*. "We drove past the Columbus and Cuauhtemoc statues and the glassy *Café Colón*, like the Crystal Palace, where President Huerta, the man who shot Madero and then fled from Carranza,* used to get drunk, on past the Statue of Independence, all aspiration and gold wings."

In 1913 the conniving and treacherous Huerta put together a plot resulting in the assassination of President Francisco Madero and his vice president, José María Pino Suárez. The plot, known as *la decena trágica* (the tragic ten days), was headed by Gen. Victoriano Huerta, a holdover from the Porfirian era; Henry Lane Wilson, the United States ambassador to Mexico; Felix Díaz, nephew to Porfirio Díaz; and Bernardo Reyes, a general in the army of Porfirio Díaz.

Huerta took over the government. This action immediately ignited an uprising of the Zapatistas in the south, while Venustiano Carranza, a new player in the revolution, started moving against Mexico City from the north, supported by the forces of Pancho Villa, as immortalized by the lyrics of this revolutionary song:

> *En el norte vive Villa*
> *En el sur vive Zapata*
> *Lo que quiero es venganza*
> *Por la muerte de Madero*

---

* Venustiano Carranza deposed Huerta and became president in 1917.

> In the north lives Villa
> In the south lives Zapata
> What I want is revenge
> For the death of Madero

Huerta fled the country in 1914 and died two years later in the United States of cirrhosis of the liver. With his ouster, most of the remnants of the Porfirian years disappeared as well.

When Woodrow Wilson was inaugurated as president of the United States in 1913, he immediately recalled Ambassador Wilson, recognizing that he had directly participated in the assassination of a constitutionally elected president of a foreign country. At the same time, President Wilson understood that Mexico's political instability was turning into an all-out civil war. American commercial and mining investments were now in jeopardy. In an overt attack on Mexico's sovereignty, in 1914 he sent a fleet to occupy the port of Veracruz with the real threat of invading the country if American interests were put at risk. The actual invasion of Mexico might have become a reality had it not been for the start of World War I, and the real possibility of U.S. involvement in that conflict.

Francisco "Pancho" Villa

"Don't let it end like this, tell them I said something."

A campesino from the state of Durango, José Doroteo Arango Arámbula—better known as Pancho Villa—became a bandit after killing the son of the hacendado who raped his sister. A consummate horseman, he managed to turn into a savvy tactician in cavalry warfare. Known as the Centaur of the North, Ronald Aiken perfectly described Villa in his book *Revolution! Mexico 1910–1920* as a "20th century compendium of Attila the Hun, Robin Hood and Jesse James, with a flavoring of red hot chili sauce."

Some historians said he lived and died to rescue his country from foreign exploitation in defense of the ideals of the revolution. Others believe he was just a bandit who saw the uprising as an excuse to plunder the wealthy hacendados and punish those who challenged his motives. The truth probably lies somewhere in between. While at times this bandit-turned-revolutionary was romanticized as the Mexican version of Robin Hood, there was also his lieutenant,

Rodolfo Fierro, whose actions defied such sentimentalization. Fierro was a thug who gladly executed anyone who got in his way, always in the name of the revolution; at times his victim's crime might be only that Fierro didn't like their looks. He was known as *el carnicero* (the butcher).

History recounts that many great leaders were also well known for their favorite horse. Alexander the Great, El Cid, Napoleon, Ulysses S. Grant, and Robert E. Lee, to name but a few. Pancho Villa's horse was named Siete Leguas (Seven Leagues). Many heroic songs, known as *corridos*, have been written about Villa and his horse. If you're in Mexico and a mariachi band offers you a chance to request a song, ask for "Siete Leguas el Caballo." This ballad follows Villa's horse and his famous rider through all the battles they fought together. Make sure a translator accompanies you.

Among Pancho Villa's better-known exploits was the 1916 attack on the armory in Columbus, New Mexico, resulting in President Wilson sending an expeditionary force into northern Mexico under the command of Gen. John "Blackjack" Pershing. Historians point out this was the only time the lower forty-eight states were invaded by a foreign power.

There is also the story that to finance his army, Villa contracted a Hollywood movie company to film his battles. This meant that the time of day to initiate a military engagement depended entirely on the conditions being such that the cameras had enough light to record the action. The word "charge" was replaced with the words "action camera." Villa eventually made four films, casting himself as the star, in 1912, 1913, 1914, and 1916.

In 1920 a defeated Villa was forced into retirement. The flamboyant figure now became as extinct as the dinosaurs. In recognition of his participation in the revolution, the government rewarded him with a hacienda near the town of Parral, located in the southern end of the northern state of Chihuahua. Three years later, during one of his regular visits to town, he was gunned down in his car by a hail of bullets. His executioners wanted to make sure the man many believed indestructible had no chance of survival. Sixteen bullets, four to the head, did the job. Two of the three bodyguards who accompanied Villa were also killed. According to the surviving bodyguard, Villa's last words were, "Don't let it end like this; tell them I said something." One assumes that "something" were words for Mexico to remember for posterity and the history books. The Centaur of the North did have a sense of the dramatic.

To make sure he would not somehow rise from the dead, his executioners severed his head, which to this day has never been found. Moreover, nobody is quite sure where he is buried. To keep the myth alive, his supposed trigger finger is on exhibit in a small El Paso museum of Villa memorabilia. He was unquestionably larger than life.

If Villa's physical presence was gone, his deeds lived on in books and films. Hollywood alone has produced at least seven such films, starring Wallace Beery (*Patria*, 1917; *Viva Villa!*, 1934), Leo Carrillo (*The Valiant Hombre*, 1948), Yul Brynner (*Villa Rides*, 1968), Terry Savalas (*A Town Called Hell*, 1971), and Antonio Banderas (*And Starring Pancho Villa as Himself*, 2003). Despite his shortcomings, most historians agree that he is one of the most important figures during this period. If that is true, the heroes of this revolution left a lot to be desired.

Emiliano Zapata

In all probability, the only revolutionary in the first phase who truly believed that what he was doing was for the betterment of the Mexican peasant, Emiliano Zapata was a man who put his people and his country, as he understood it, above everything else.

Born in the southern state of Morelos, he became the counterpoint to Pancho Villa in the north and a true believer in the principles of the revolution. "*Tierra y Libertad* (Land and Liberty)" became his slogan. One of his problems was his near-illiteracy, and his knowledge of the geography of Mexico was confined to the states surrounding his home state of Morelos, known as Patria Chica (small homeland). Because of his inability to read or write, he was constantly susceptible to what those around him were advising him. Despite his limited knowledge, and when compared to the bloodthirsty and pillaging ways of Pancho Villa, he was almost a saint. One of his most famous lines, "It's better to die standing, than live on your knees," became one of the slogans of the Republicans who opposed Gen. Francisco Franco in the Spanish Civil War.

For most Americans, Emiliano Zapata is best remembered by Marlon Brando's portrayal, with Anthony Quinn as his brother Eufemio Zapata, in the award-winning film *Viva Zapata!* He is unquestionably one of the heroic figures of the revolution and the man to whom the peasant class of Mexico most relate.

Venustiano Carranza (President 1917–1920)

Like Madero, Carranza was from the northern state of Coahuila, and, like many others, he was an hacendado. Elected governor of the state of Coahuila (1911–1913), he became a reformer. After Huerta's coup, which toppled the Madero government, Carranza fled from Mexico City to the north, where he established his own government in exile backed by a budding local army known as the División del Noreste (constitutional army of the northeast). With the support of Pancho Villa's army, known as the División del Norte, and the División del Noroeste under the command of Álvaro Obregón,* they moved against the Huerta regime. Emiliano Zapata and his Zapatistas supported them from the south.

With the overthrow of the Huerta regime in 1914, Carranza became the de facto president in 1915, supported by the official recognition of the United States. He was subsequently elected president in 1917, but not for long.

Unfortunately, Carranza was more interested in constitutional transformation than in agrarian reform, earning him the animosity of two of his major supporters, Villa and Zapata, who soon turned against him and continued the bloody civil war. Once more these two peasant generals were up in arms against the government. The neverending change of partners continued unabated.

By 1915, the tide of revolution had turned against these two caudillos. In the north, a new Carranza ally, Gen. Álvaro Obregón and his División del Noroeste successfully took on Villa, forcing him into retirement, while Carranza's army invaded Zapata's Patria Chica. Zapata realized he was no match against this new federal army under Carranza, so rather than be defeated he made an attempt at reconciliation. A secret meeting was arranged with an officer in Carranza's army by the name of Col. Jesús Guajardo. When Zapata opened the gates to the hacienda where the meeting was to take place, he was, like Villa, assassinated in a fusillade of bullets from Guajardo's troops. Venustiano Carranza was largely responsible for the Mexican Constitution of 1917, though he was not in favor of many of its provisions. This was to be the third and present constitution of Mexico.

Despite having the support of the United States, Carranza was a secret admirer of the German kaiser as is clearly shown in the famous Zimmerman Telegram of 1917, from Arthur Zimmermann, German foreign secretary, to Heinrich von Eckardt, the German ambassador to Mexico. Unfortunately for

---

* Álvaro Obregón became the president of Mexico from 1920 to 1924.

Carranza, the content of the telegram also reached the British ambassador to Mexico, who passed it on to the United States. It was not well received.

> We intend to begin on the 1st of February unrestricted submarine warfare. We shall endeavor in spite of this to keep the United States of America neutral. In the event of this not succeeding, we make Mexico a proposal of alliance on the following basis: make war together, make peace together, generous financial support and an understanding on our part that Mexico is to re-conquer the lost territory in Texas, New Mexico and Arizona. The settlement in detail is left to you. You will inform the President of the above most secretly as soon as the outbreak of war with the United States of America is certain and add the suggestion that he should, on his own initiative, invite Japan to immediate adherence and at the same time mediate between Japan and ourselves. Please call the President's attention to the fact that the ruthless employment of our submarines now offers the prospect of compelling England in a few months to make peace.

The idea that Mexico could take on the United States militarily is as far-fetched as the pussycat that looks into the mirror only to see a lion starring back at him. Mexico was never a lion. This telegram caused such outrage in the United States that it became one of the main reasons for the United States to enter the war against Germany and its allies. What is not clear is why the Germans thought the Carranza government, despite their anti-American position, would be open to such an offer.

By 1920 the eroding support of the United States, Carranza's resistance to many of the articles in the new constitution, and his bleeding the treasury for his own personal enrichment spelled the end of his presidency. Carranza managed to turn just about everyone against him, including the Catholic Church, the conservatives, and the campesinos, who held him responsible for the assassination of Emiliano Zapata. After an attempt on his life, he headed off to exile in Europe with as much of the Mexican treasury as he could load onto the train, destined for a waiting ship in the port of Veracruz. He never made it. His train was ambushed near the city of Puebla, where he was summarily shot on May 21, 1920. The end of his presidency brought to an end to phase one of the revolution. In Carranza's favor, he was a strong supporter of a government run by civilians. He hoped that the future of Mexico in the hands of army generals could be avoided; yet that would not prove to be the case.

Venustiano Carranza is also remembered as a proponent of the national political sport of corruption. The word *carrancear* became synonymous with "self-enrichment by illicit means," a practice that grew so popular throughout many future government regimes. These words were also used to accuse politicians who had fallen out with the administration in power. It simply meant to accept bribes, as well as use the national treasury as one's retirement fund. If we want to try and establish the origin of "institutionalized corruption" as part of the nation's landscape, this has to be as good a time as any.

One can conclude that had the Russian Revolution of 1917 not taken place seven years later, historians might have taken a closer look at its Mexican counterpart. Both were the result of dictatorial rule that kept a large peasant population living in chains and bordering on starvation. The abuses of a ruling class during the Porfirian Era set the stage for a blood-drenched revolution, the fundamental cause of which was to liberate the peasant from his near-slave status and introduce him to a better life. The Russian Revolution had many of the same objectives, if you substitute Porfirian for Tsarism. Both reveled in assassinating allies-turned-enemies. Both left their treasuries bare and their countries in debt. Both thought they were creating a pluralistic society accompanied by a more democratic government. Both believed socialism was the answer to the future success of their countries. Whatever the goals, both revolutions failed and were bound for the scrap heap of history's failed experiments. Whatever else one can say about these bloody affairs, in the end whoever benefited was surely not the peasant in whose name the revolution was fought.

But there are certain conclusions that seem obvious. Thanks to the machinations of four people who plotted the assassination of President Francisco Madero and Vice President Pino Suárez in 1913, the country turned overnight from a genuine revolution to a civil war. Had these assassinations not taken place, the first phase of the revolution might have been an entirely different story, with less bloodshed and fewer convoluted alliances.

The difficult aspects of this revolution-turned-civil-war were the complexity of the events. Mexico's past is like laying out a straight rope where each progressive phase behaves in a linear fashion, the events from 1910 to 1920 were like a rope infested with knots, each one having to be temporarily untied to try and give meaning to a series of uprisings and changing alliances that in the end never lived up to the expectations of those who participated, nor of those who led them. If each knot represented an obstruction on the road to creating a better Mexico, then many of these knots stayed in place.

So what was the point of so much violence and political intrigue? Shakespeare said it best in his famous comedy Much Ado About Nothing. There is no question these bloody events changed the face of Mexico forever, but if the main objective was social justice, then that goal always stayed beyond reach. If there was one social class that was left out in the cold, it had to be the campesino, who not only paid for the revolution in blood, but must have shaken their heads as they looked around and asked—what was in it for me?

The violent side of the revolution of 1910 eventually wound down, and by 1920 Mexico began the slow process of reconstruction, with established order in a new model of government that went into effect in 1929. This new system resulted in a series of reforms that impoverished the nation even further, kept wealth in the hands of foreign interests, and created a unique system of government that only Mexicans came to believe was workable. After all, no other nation in the world ever considered this future Mexican model as remotely functional. At its core, what eventually evolved into a one-party system known as the Partido Revolucionario Institucional (PRI), embraced a form of xenophobic censorship, centralized power in the executive branch, and economic isolation from the rest of the world. Power became centered in an inefficient bureaucracy and its surrogates who benefited by supporting the system. The PRI became the perfect platform for corruption on a grand scale, not only resulting in a constant emptying of the treasury, but also stripping the natural resources of a once-wealthy nation.

The revolution, and its aftermath, also created a series of government-controlled sacred cows that slowly bled the nation's resources. A country traditionally resistant to change, a few of these sacred cows still exist to this day, effectively maintaining a stranglehold on different segments of the Mexican economy. As we shall see, the nonreelection clauses in the constitution substituted one form of dictatorship for another.

To try and understand the complexities of this historic period and its aftermath is a subject that could take up volumes. One thing is indisputable: none of the important figures that emerged from the revolution had the qualities to effectively lead a country into the new century. Another aspect of those who led the revolution was that none of them fit into any kind of mold showing cohesiveness of purpose or clarity of the final objective. Furthermore, they came from such different social backgrounds that it is hard to believe they could even sit in the same room with each other and have a coherent conversation.

Trying to better understand the goals of the revolution, I strongly suggest reading Appendices 1, 2, 3, 4, and 5 to get an idea of some of the articles in the Mexican Constitution of 1917. These articles will begin to make clear the social aims of the revolution (Articles 27 and 123), the xenophobia of foreign intervention and exploitation (Articles 32 and 33), as well as opening the door to a political system of nonreelection (Articles 59 and 83) that for all intents and purposes was an invitation to a unique form of dictatorial rule. However, the revolution was far from over.

10

The Sonoran Dynasty
(1920–1929)

◆

EVEN THOUGH THE REVOLUTION SEEMED to be winding down, it would be up to two men from the northern state of Sonora to bring some normalcy back to the country. They are *la dinastía sonorense* (Sonoran dynasty), and they presided over the emerging Mexico from 1920 to 1929, first as constitution-ally elected presidents, followed by an additional six years in what became known as the Maximato, ending in 1934.

One of these men embodied many of the ideals of the revolution. The other used those same ideals for personal power, only stopping when he was exiled to the United States in 1936. He is best remembered for establishing a political system that lasted until the year 2000 and brought peace to the nation, albeit at enormous expense.

This period might best be described as a time of reconstruction. Unfortunately, much like Humpty Dumpty, "All the king's horses and all the king's men, couldn't put Humpty together again." The nation that emerged from this period of national instability boasted little to be proud of.

Álvaro Obregón (President 1920–1924)

Born in the northern state of Sonora, Álvaro Obregón's early years were spent as a chickpea farmer on a 330-acre farm in his native state. He was born a criollo, but unlike his two famous predecessors, Francisco Madero and Venustiano Carranza, Obregón was more a man of the people. His appeal spanned across the different social strata of the prevailing caste system.

His military career set him apart from his contemporaries. Obregón rose through the ranks until he was promoted to general in command of the División del Noroeste in recognition of his support of Venustiano Carranza's overthrow of Victoriano Huerta. Eventually Obregón's command turned Pancho Villa's División del Norte against him.

Known as the invincible general, Obregón took on Villa and defeated him in a series of battles. Obregón not only displayed great bravery in front of his men but also an ability to use modern artillery and the new weapon of choice, the machine gun, in a tactical manner far in advance of the military strategies of trench warfare employed in World War I that resulted in such unnecessary slaughter. Obregón understood that the machine gun eliminated trench warfare as an option, and he deployed his troops accordingly. Villa did not understand this, and his straightforward cavalry charges over no-man's-land ended in defeat.

General Obregón paid dearly for his bravery with the loss of an arm from an artillery shell at the Battle of Celaya (1914), where he defeated Pancho Villa and terminated the bandit's aspirations of leadership. Despite being an army man, Obregón was also concerned with social change as outlined in the new constitution and even campaigned against the dangers of militarism in Mexican politics. While most politicians publicly espoused these noble ideals, they seem to have been more concerned with their own future than that of the nation. That was not the case with Obregón.

When Obregón realized that President Venustiano Carranza (1917–1920), was more interested in lining his own pockets than in carrying out the promises of the revolution, he resigned from his newly appointed position as war minister and once more became a civilian. As a civilian, he publicly criticized the Carranza regime and campaigned against him with the promise of cleaning up government corruption. He realized that Mexico required a strong centralized government with the confidence and strength to bring together the remnants of the Porfirian Era elites, foreign business interests, ruthless caudillos acting as regional warlords, and local warlords, known as caciques.

These warlords ruled over vast areas of the interior of Mexico and, above all, over the land-hungry peasants who had been the cannon fodder of the revolution. Many of these caciques and caudillos became known as *generales de banqueta* (curbside generals) in reference to their self-appointed rank. Many had no formal military training of any kind, and even less when it came to the requirements to govern.

Despite his leftist and populist political points of view, Obregón also understood the importance of good relations with the United States and the international financial institutions that needed to get aboard if the ideals of the revolution were to survive. Knowing that his country had adopted an anti-American position, he did most of his negotiations through what today we call back door diplomacy. Mexico condemned the United States in public and negotiated with its neighbor in private. This form of diplomacy became the modus operandi of all future relations between both countries.

◆

Among Obregón's accomplishments was using oil to pay off Mexico's foreign debt while bringing some stability to a country that since 1910 had bordered on anarchy and chaos. He was successful in getting the United States to recognize the new post-revolutionary Mexico, but at the expense of having to sign the controversial Tratados de Bucareli that for many labeled him a malinchista. These "gentlemen's agreements" were never ratified by either country but were necessary for good relations between both nations.

Mexico agreed not to apply Article 27 in the Mexican Constitution, especially as it related to the expropriation of private property, such as foreign ownership interests in manufacturing, mining, oil, and agriculture. Americans were also to be indemnified for loss of personal property taken during the revolution. These arrangements made Obregón enemies among those Mexicans who could hardly forget the Mexican War of 1846–1848, the American occupation of Veracruz in 1914, and the Pershing incursion into Northern Mexico in 1916, known as the "punitive expedition."

This cozy but necessary relationship with his northern neighbor once more resulted in Mexican historians not treating Obregón as one of the few true patriots who actually believed in the goals of the revolution. He also made an enemy of the Catholic Church, and a majority of practicing Catholics, due to his stance against organized religion.

In 1924 his swan song was to name a fellow Sonoran, Gen. Plutarco Elías Calles, to succeed him at the end of his four-year term. Calles won the election and at the end of his term of office in 1928,* Obregón again ran for president and won in the election that took place on July 2, 1928. At a victory luncheon on July 17, a Roman Catholic fanatic assassinated him. Supposedly killed with

---

* Originally the term of office was four years. It later became six.

two bullets, a coroner's report that surfaced eighty years later showed Obregón had nineteen bullets fired into his body from various angles. The obvious conclusion was that those at the lunch had colluded in his death. The religious fanatic who was blamed and executed by a firing squad turned out to be a convenient fall guy.

The historian Francisco Martin Moreno wrote about this sensational discovery in a book called *México Acribillado* (Riddled Mexico). Rewriting Mexican history has become a national pastime. The people behind his assassination have never been named. Probably the best clue can be found by looking at who benefited. The answer would have to be Plutarco Elías Calles who, having disposed of his successor, continued as interim president until the following year and for the following six years governed the country from behind the scenes, a period known historically as el Maximato.

Plutarco Elías Calles (President 1924–1929)

Gen. Plutarco Elías Calles became president in 1924 and took office at the beginning of 1925. He is responsible for unifying the country by building a strong central military and doing away with the small-time caudillos and caciques, and their personal armies, who were trying to take over the revolution. He was famous for having said, "*Hay que librar México de los liberadores* (We have to liberate Mexico from the liberators)."

Calles started Mexico on the road to educating the people and distributing land among the *campesinos* in accordance with Article 27 of the constitution. He created the Agriculture Development Bank with branches across the nation, responsible for financing the modernization of the agricultural infrastructure. Unfortunately, little of these funds trickled down to those they were supposed to help. Instead, these agro-banks became centers of corruption for an ever-increasing bureaucratic class that saw the government and its many newly created institutions as piggy banks for a new generation of wealthy public servants.

Again, using the back door concept of diplomacy with the United States, Calles nurtured a budding friendship with Ambassador Dwight D. Morrow, a former banker who became extremely helpful in solving many of Mexico's financial problems, including a foreign debt that was out of control. The *malas lenguas* (evil tongues) or political gossipers, claimed that Calles was a stooge of the American government. Here was one more Mexican leader tainted by the word malinchismo, but compared to his predecessor Calles got off easy. He did not leave office in a wooden box, though he was eventually exiled.

His greatest accomplishment was the creation of a national political machine that officially became known first as the PNR, Partido Nacional Revolucionario (1929–1938). This party evolved into the PRM, Partido Revolucionario Mexicano (1938–1946), followed by the PRI, Partido Revolucionario Institucional, which governed Mexico until the year 2000. Despite the name changes, the party logo has always been known as the tri-color, similar to the Mexican flag. This party eventually ruled Mexico and bled the wealth of the nation dry through mismanagement, political and economic central control, and institutionalized corruption, but did accomplish one major goal: no more coups, no absolute dictators, and a lasting peace internally and with the rest of the world.

Even after leaving office, Calles continued to govern Mexico from behind the scenes in what is called el Maximato (1929–1934).* He was a powerful political figure, and this power turned Calles into a corrupt post-revolutionary politician, a tradition that was integrated into the one-party system he created. The famous saying of the time was, "The president lives in Chapultepec Palace, but the man who runs the country lives across the street," in reference to Calles's home. Despite his corrupt ways, the fact that he brought peace to the country and founded the precursor of the PRI causes Mexican historians to sometimes treat him with a reverence he hardly deserves.

The Christer Rebellion (1926–1929)

Calles, like Benito Juárez before him, was a Freemason who despised the Catholic Church. As president he persecuted the church under that well-known Mexican bureaucratic view of the law: "To my friends the full protection of the law; to my enemies the full enforcement of the law."

He insisted that the Catholic Church abide by the strict application of the anti-clerical laws in the Mexican Constitution by closing monasteries, convents, and religious schools; banning religious demonstrations; and in general cracking down on everything related to the Catholic Church. This launched a new bloodbath known as La Rebellión Cristero (The Christer Rebellion).

---

* Maximato: the word for maximum ruler from behind the scenes during three presidents who between them were only in office six years.

The rebellion was centered in three central states, Jalisco, with its capital Guadalajara; Michoacán; and Guanajuato. These three areas could count on a high concentration of true believers.

The death toll was considerable, with approximately 57,000 federal troops and some 30,000 *cristeros* (Catholics) killed. What is more significant is that there were 4,500 priests in these three states serving their congregations in 1917. By 1934, this figure had been reduced to around 334.

Because of this religious persecution, and at the invitation of the Archdiocese in Los Angeles, thousands of Mexicans in the region where the rebellion was being fought migrated to the west coast of the United States, settling mostly in Los Angeles and San Diego. One can surmise that this may be one of the reasons that well into the 1970s Los Angeles was considered the second largest Mexican city after Mexico City.

By 1934 it became obvious that Calles's behind-the-scenes rule, which still lingered despite his having stepped down from the presidency in 1929, had to be terminated. Lázaro Cárdenas del Río, a liberal governor and revolutionary general from the state of Michoacán, became the next president. The new president accused Calles of crimes against the nation and had him deported to the United States on April 9, 1936. He returned in 1941, and died in 1945.

Among those revolutionary leaders I have highlighted, Porfirio Díaz and Plutarco Elías Calles, both of whom died of old age, and Victoriano Huerta, who died of cirrhosis of the liver while being detained in Texas by the United States, were the only ones to die of natural causes. The rest met their end through assassination. They were introduced to *el saco de madera*, loosely translated to mean the wooden overcoat or burial casket, dying of "lead poisoning."

◆

Having made references to caudillos and curbside generals, I thought I might introduce you to one. During the years from 1964 to 1967, I found myself single and on the prowl in Mexico City. One of my favorite watering holes, prior to its destruction in the earthquake of 1985, was the Maya Bar at the Continental Hilton Hotel.

Many of us young studs gathered at this bar because most of the international commercial airline crews had layovers at the hotel, the main attraction being a bevy of stewardesses. It was also the watering hole of a revolutionary general; his real name shall be kept anonymous in deference to his family heirs. He arrived daily, flanked by his Mexican and American mistresses and, of course, his two mandatory bodyguards. I will call him Don Carlos. In his late seventies, he was ugly in looks and mean in spirit. In time, we would-be studs became his friends, even if only superficially.

His story is worth telling because he was a caudillo in the revolution; a self-appointed curbside general, whose cruel rule over one of Mexico's northern states was notorious. He also carved out for himself a large section of that state, which he turned into his own private fiefdom. He became a gentleman cattle rancher who, much like the hacendados prior to the revolution, was also an absentee landowner.

Unlike other generals of his ilk, he was left alone due to his friendship with Lyndon B. Johnson, before and after he became president, which was established on one of Don Carlos's cattle-buying trips to Texas. Because of this friendship, the Mexican government gave him the title of ambassador-at-large as one of the back-door politicians who had access to LBJ. At least that is what Don Carlos claimed. I suspect he was telling the truth. After all, to have been allowed to hold on to so much land as a post-revolutionary warlord says something about political protection that reached into the highest echelons of government. He was the last of the great *latifundistas*.[*]

I will only add one more anecdote to the general's story so the reader can get a flavor of who these warlords were and how they acted. Upon receiving a telephone call at the Maya Bar, he informed us that there was trouble at his ranch that had to be attended to. When he returned some days later he explained that rustlers had been caught stealing cattle. To dissuade this from happening again, he personally oversaw their execution by hanging without the benefit of a trial. One might get the impression this form of vigilante justice was more appropriate in a western movie and not real life in 1966.

It was quite common for these bandit-generals to take wives from the upper class. Many women accepted this arrangement as a means to protect their families from becoming victims of the revolution. Resigned to their fate, they made the best of it, in many cases educating these peasant leaders to the extent that they became acceptable in the elite circles of the new post-revolutionary society.

---

[*] *Latifundio* is the single ownership of a vast track of agricultural land inefficiently managed due to its size.

11

The Americans—
Extras and Bit Players

◆

DESPITE THE MEXICAN REVOLUTION being largely a Mexican affair, Americans, some of whom went on to become famous in World Wars I and II, did participate.

William Randolph Hearst

The first major uprising that was the harbinger of revolution took place in 1906 in the Cananea copper mines, partially owned by Hearst and other Americans. It began with a violent strike that required the intervention of federal troops sent by Porfirio Díaz. Many Mexican historians consider this the event that launched what in 1910 became the Mexican Revolution.

I have always been curious to know why, when visiting the Hearst Castle at San Simeon located on the coast of California, there is no mention in the one-hour film version of his life that some of his fortune and that of his father's came from Mexico. Mexicans are not the only ones revamping their past.

Henry Lane Wilson
(Ambassador to Mexico, 1901–1914)

Wilson was the ambassador to Mexico during the presidency of Theodore Roosevelt (1901–1908) and William Howard Taft (1909–1912). He was one of the four architects of La Decena Trágica (the Tragic Ten Days), which led to the assassination of President Francisco Madero and Vice President Pino Suárez in 1913. In summary, Wilson was a sordid, intriguing traitor who personally betrayed the constitutional president of Mexico, Francisco Madero, and organized the military coup d'état that raised General Huerta to power.

Wilson never disavowed or showed the least sign of repentance regarding his participation of the overthrow and assassination of President Madero and Vice President Pino Suárez. To the contrary, in his 1927 memoirs he wrote,

"After years of mature consideration, I do not hesitate to say that if I were confronted with the same situation under the same conditions, I should take precisely the same course."

One of the great mysteries of the Mexican Revolution is how this man has been given so little importance by Mexican historians. By no means can he be thought a minor figure, considering the events his participation in the successful assassination plot unleashed.

What seems to have motivated Ambassador Wilson to act without official sanction was the belief that under President Madero the United States' commercial interests and heavy investment in Mexico's mining and oil resources were in jeopardy. This does not seem likely when we consider that Madero was not only educated in the United States, but was also given political asylum there after Porfirio Díaz released him from prison in 1910.

Las malas lenguas, the ever-present political wagging tongues, claimed that President Madero refused to pay Wilson the monthly stipend he was accustomed to receiving during the Porfirian Era. If this is true, it was simply one more indication of this diplomat's perfidious behavior.

Henry Lane Wilson was a disgrace to his country. He spent the rest of his life living in obscurity.

◆

In 1967, my mother came to visit me in Mexico City. She had been living in Montevideo, Uruguay, even though she was born and raised in Boston. The truth is I had not seen or talked to her since 1960. I knew little about my family tree, having been sent off to boarding school at an early age.

During my mother's stay in Mexico City she informed me that my grandfather had served in the U.S.-Mexico embassy under Ambassador Henry Lane Wilson when she was ten years old in 1910, when the Mexican Revolution began. I remember quite clearly the conversation:

"We used to live on the outskirts of the city," she informed me.

"I need more information than that. Who knows where the outskirts of the city were back in 1910?"

"I remember that we lived in row houses reserved for diplomats."

"Anything else?"

"At the end of the street there was a statue of a Spanish Emperor on a horse, but Mexicans referred to it as El Caballito." She was talking about the Caballito statue I referred to in an earlier chapter, which at that time was on the corner of Paseo de la Reforma and Bucarelli in what is today very much downtown. The row houses are still there but have been turned into public housing, divided into multi-family units.

Lt. Frank Jack Fletcher

Rear Adm. Frank Friday Fletcher was the U.S. Navy admiral of the fleet that occupied Veracruz in 1914 as a prelude to invading Mexico if the revolution continued to plunder private and industrial property owned by American interests. The admiral's nephew Lt. Frank Jack Fletcher was also present in the occupation of Veracruz aboard the USS *Florida*. The nephew went on to become a vice admiral and the operational commander of the American fleet that defeated the Japanese in the key battles of the Coral Sea and Midway in World War II, battles that were crucial in turning the tide of war against Japan in America's favor.

Capt. Douglas MacArthur (1914)

One of the five five-star generals in the history of the United States, MacArthur is best remembered for his World War II exploits in the Philippines, his tenure as military governor of postwar Japan, and as the mastermind behind the Inchon landing in the Korean War.

Although he was considered a military opportunist and risk taker, MacArthur coveted being awarded the Medal of Honor. He came quite close to receiving it during the American occupation of Veracruz in 1914. The standing order of the day was that American troops should not venture beyond the city limits. MacArthur thought he knew better. Had it not been for his habit of not following orders from his superior officers, he might have earned this highest of all military honors.

MacArthur took a recon patrol into Mexico, and when they were discovered by federal troops, they had to fight their way out along a railroad track. In recognition of his bravery in leading his men to safety, he was recommended for a Medal of Honor. He was turned down because he took on this mission without the authority of his commanding officer and in defiance of standing orders. Eventually, this trait became his undoing when he was disgraced and fired by President Harry S. Truman during the Korean War.

Brig. Gen. John "Blackjack" Pershing: The Punitive Expedition (1916)

The intervention across Mexico's border was launched under orders from President Woodrow Wilson, who wanted Pancho Villa punished for raiding the arsenal in Columbus, New Mexico. One year later Pershing became the general in command of American ground troops in World War I.

Legend has it that Pershing, who was based at Fort Bliss just outside of El Paso, was an admirer of Pancho Villa and met with him along the El Paso/Ciudad Juárez border. At many of these meetings both the Villistas and Pershing's officers posed for pictures. I first saw some of these photographs at Anderson's Restaurant in Mexico City. This camaraderie came to an end when Pancho Villa decided to cross the border in search of weapons by attacking the armory in Columbus, New Mexico.

Pershing's incursion into Mexico got as far as Parral, in the state of Chihuahua, some four hundred miles from El Paso, Texas. This was the same town where Pancho Villa was assassinated in 1923. Despite the fact that the entire U.S. army was mobilized in preparation to invade Mexico, the United States' involvement in World War I in 1917 became its number one military priority. Future engagements, mostly along the Texas border, turned into a series of guerrilla skirmishes that ended with Villa successfully evading defeat or capture.

2nd Lt. George C. Patton (1916)

Patton was a militarist who always wanted to be in the middle of a fight. When World War I started in 1914, he asked to be reassigned to the French cavalry, but his request was denied. The following year he was sent to Fort Bliss outside El Paso, Texas, where he was assigned to the Eighth Cavalry Regiment under the overall command of Brig. Gen. John "Blackjack" Pershing.

After the attack on the arsenal in Columbus, New Mexico, 2nd Lt. George Patton had finally found the action that launched his career, eventually earning him the nickname "Blood and Guts." By the end of World War II he rose to the rank of a three-star general.

As an aide to General Pershing, he left his mark when, on a ten-man patrol in enemy territory, he engaged and personally killed Gen. Julio Cárdenas and one of his men. The general was a Villista in charge of the bodyguard contingent protecting Pancho Villa. Legend has it Patton brought the two bodies into camp tied down on the roof of a truck. In recognition of this act of bravery he was commissioned a first lieutenant.

Patton killed both these men with the single-action Colt revolver that became his trademark throughout his career. He even carved two notches on his favorite weapon to commemorate the kills. During World War II, he actually took the trouble to show off his notched revolver to King George VI and Queen Mary, while telling them the story of his Mexican adventure.

The Five-Star Generals

In the United States there have been five generals who earned the fifth star, all of them in World War II. They were Generals Douglas MacArthur, Omar Bradley, George Marshall, Dwight Eisenhower, and Henry "Hap" Arnold. We have already seen the involvement of Douglas MacArthur in the Mexican Revolution, but there was also peripheral involvement by Omar Bradley and Dwight Eisenhower.

In 1916, Omar Bradley was stationed along the Mexican border and became directly involved in confronting the constant border crossings by Mexican bandits and Villistas assaulting trains and blowing up tracks as they foraged for weapons and anything else they could get their hands on. Dwight Eisenhower's participation was a little more obscure. In 1916 he was the commandant of a military academy in San Antonio, Texas. However, there is a picture of him standing in the second row of a meeting between General Pershing and Gen. Francisco "Pancho" Villa's men, supposedly somewhere along the border. That picture, if it is still there, can be found hanging in Anderson's Restaurant in Mexico City.

Ambassador Dwight Whitney Morrow

Morrow was a banker and diplomat, whom President Calvin Coolidge named ambassador to Mexico, where he served from 1927 to 1930. He was also elected to the U.S. Senate from New Jersey. He remained in that office for two years before his death in 1931.

Morrow was one of the best ambassadors to Mexico. He became a close friend of President Plutarco Elías Calles, with whom he had breakfast on a weekly basis. Because of these meetings he became known in Washington as the "ham-and-eggs ambassador," while becoming a trusted adviser to the Mexican president, especially on matters dealing with the financial problems facing the country. He was instrumental in helping Mexico successfully negotiate its burgeoning foreign debt.

He owned a weekend retreat in the nearby resort town of Cuernavaca, some sixty miles from the capital, where he commissioned the famous Mexican artist Diego Rivera to paint a mural in the Palace of Cortés off the main square. This mural is one of the main tourist attractions in that city.

Ambassador Morrow invited Charles A. Lindbergh, the first man to fly solo over the Atlantic in his famous plane the *Spirit of Saint Louis*, to his home in Cuernavaca. During his stay, Lindbergh fell in love with and married Anne Morrow, the ambassador's daughter. She and her husband were the center of the Lindbergh baby kidnapping case, which became the legal precedent for many of the kidnapping laws in the United States.

THE ROAD TO DISASTER
(1929–1985)

W ITH MOST OF THE NATION'S INSTITUTIONS in place as a result of the Mexican Revolution and the Constitution of 1917, Mexico could now pursue the destiny it had fought so hard and so long to achieve. If it is true that a country's institutions define its behavior, Mexico was no exception.

"The Road to Disaster" may seem an unfair description of the period from 1929 to the giant earthquake that struck Mexico City in 1985. Nevertheless Mexico's newfound institutions were an open invitation to plunder the wealth of a nation, mismanage its resources, and create a popular belief that, while whole generations profited from this new system of government, nobody had any faith in its legitimacy except as a means to self-enrichment.

The six-year, one-term presidency ruled by a one-party system known as the PRI at times seemed to achieve some progress. Unfortunately, the country's leaders buried their heads in the sand and listened to nothing but their own echoes. The new governing class knew what was best for the country, and that was that. Mexico got the government it deserved, and it was not a pretty picture. This was also the time of President Lázaro Cárdenas del Rio (1934–1940), the humanitarian general who changed the face of Mexico's future by creating social, political, and economic changes that at times appeared to be grandiose accomplishments, but eventually ended as a disservice to the nation he so wanted to help.

The year 1968 was a defining moment that saw social upheaval spread throughout the United States and Europe, and Mexico did not go untainted. The Tlatelolco massacre and its aftermath are surely one of the darkest moments in Mexico's past. Unfortunately, although the Mexican people complained, in the end most stood by as spectators. That year also saw the rise to power of two presidents I have named "The Mexican Miracle" and "The Buffoon." They were extraordinary examples of repression, corruption, and incompetence.

This period ends with the giant earthquake of 1985. This tragedy revealed blatant corruption for all to see. If this earthquake had occurred later in the day, many more thousands could have died in buildings that did not meet the construction standards set by the government. Here was corruption revealed to the naked eye, where no excuses could hold up. Strange as it may seem, the earthquake marked the end of an era and the beginning of a Mexico that would have to implement many necessary changes if the nation was to join the new world led by a more transparent government on the road to a multinational economy.

12

Gone With The Wind— Agrarian Reform (1917–1991)

➤

The road to hell is paved with good intentions.

IN THE INTRODUCTION OF A REPORT TITLED *Mexico's Gift to the World* (1992), Jerzy Rzedowski of the Ecology Institute in Patzcuaro, state of Michoacan, had this to say:

> Due to the unusual variety of climates, rocks, soil and "physiography," Mexico has every kind of vegetation known on Earth. This vegetation ranges from tropical forests, deserts and plains, to high mountain regions, making up the three sides of a triangle, inside which, there are many coniferous and mixed forests, wide leaved, caduceus and perennial trees as well as palm groves, savannas, many kinds of bush vegetation, aquatic vegetation, swamps and coastlines.

From the beginning of the New Spain colonization, Philip II, king of Spain, was so impressed by the reports sent to him from Mexico on the lush vegetation of this giant colony that in 1570 he ordered one of his trusted advisers to catalog this rich compendium of flora and fauna. This begs the question, are we talking about Mexico, or are we describing a paradise out of the machinations of fertile minds out to impress their liege? There had to be an answer to these descriptions of abundance in the past and the realities of the present. Something had definitely changed.

When the world thinks of ecological nightmares and fertile lands turned to waste, we usually turn to Africa where the Sahara Desert encroaches year after year onto lands that once fed people. Why go so far? You have only to take a look at Baja California and the Mexican/U.S. California border discussed earlier. California's agricultural abundance, contrasted with Baja California's near desert wasteland, suggests climate favored one and not the other. Unfortunately the real story, while conveniently fitting this description, hides a truth Mexicans choose to ignore.

◆

My brother, who today is a rancher and soybean farmer in Brazil, came to visit me in Mexico back in the 1960s. He is an agronomist, specializing in pasture improvement. By the time he visited me he had worked for the Department of Agriculture of New Zealand and had been employed by one of the Big Five of Hawaii, improving the cattle pastures on the island of Maui. He had also worked on a 50,000-acre ranch in Montana and a 300,000-acre estancia in Uruguay and was on his way to Brazil to manage an experimental ranch jointly owned by the King Ranch in Texas, the Rockefellers, and the Swift Meat Packing Company out of Chicago.

During his visit, we decided to take a car trip from Mexico City to Acapulco to spend a few days getting reacquainted after so many years. The drive passed through a variety of landscapes. From Mexico City at an altitude of 7,100 feet, to sea level 260 miles away, where the terrain becomes a mountainous skyline covered in a blanket of rich green vegetation interspersed with small lots of farmland being worked by a burro-drawn wooden plow guided by a campesino tilling the soil with his two-thousand-year-old technology. Here was a glaring example of revolutionary progress under the banner of agrarian reform.

While sitting around the pool in our Acapulco hotel, I noticed my brother was in a pensive mood. Suddenly he got up and told me he would be back in a few minutes.

"I'm sorry to tell you this," he said upon his return, "but I'm on a flight to Mexico City and have asked your wife to book me through to Brazil."

"What are you talking about? We've driven all the way to Acapulco, and now you're just going to leave?"

"That's just the problem . . . the drive to Acapulco."

"What do you mean?" I thought the lights in his mind had suffered a brownout.

"It's the Mexican countryside. The erosion and lack of love for the land tells me that the people who live here simply don't care."

"So why is that so important you have to leave?"

"Let me see if you can get the picture," my brother explained. "The presence of human land abuse on our trip down here amazes me. I find it incomprehensible."

He then went on to explain about Hawaii and most of the islands in the Pacific, including New Zealand. "They have a problem. Those islands are volcanic rock with limited topsoil. Yet through land engineering they are green and productive." He didn't stop there. "You're living in a rural shit hole, and apparently don't know it."

He ended his remarks prophetically. "I don't know why so many people talk about Mexico and its great future. A country whose people don't love the land, which doesn't have farmers who understand that someone has to feed the urban areas, is in deep trouble."

He explained that one of the main reasons millions of Mexicans living in rural areas now have to look to the United States for work, is because most of them came from what at one time were productive farmlands.

This brings to mind that much-repeated Mexican saying, "The Creator fashioned a land and gave it enormous abundance. When he realized what he had done, he covered this paradise with Mexicans."

Brutal stuff, but at least Mexicans seem to understand that it was not nature that turned an environmental paradise into one giant laboratory of failure. It was man's folly, and it came under the banner of that stepchild of the Mexican Revolution known as Agrarian Reform.

To understand these reforms it is necessary to delve into two important concepts dealing with the ejido, Mexico's version of a commune, and what Oscar Lewis, who wrote *The Children of Sanchez* and *Five Families*, called "The Culture of Poverty."*

The Mexican Ejido

An ejido, sometimes referred to as *propiedad comunitaria* (communal property), is a commune made up of a series of plots of land expropriated from their pre- and postrevolutionary owners by the government and given to the landless peasants in the form of a lease. The campesino, with only a rudimentary knowledge

---

* "The Culture of Poverty" is an essay written by Oscar Lewis (1966).

of farming, was expected to till the land to feed himself and his family and create a surplus for an ever-increasing urban population.

Theoretically the ejido was supposed to receive technical assistance from teams of government agronomists who would teach the campesino how to become a modern-day farmer. With financing from a central agrarian development bank and its branches throughout the country, farmers could purchase equipment, seeds, livestock, building materials, and most everything else needed for successful farming.

Playing on the near-illiteracy of the campesino, the agrarian development banks became a bureaucrat's road to riches. Rather than helping the campesino, most of the money lined the pockets of government parasites. Furthermore, banks usually require some sort of collateral to issue loans. This immediately eliminated most of the campesino social class.

Why are so many revolutionary governments dedicated to so many economic follies? They believed by reinventing the wheel they could create a better world. Giving away land to campesinos lacking the financial resources or knowledge of modern farming methods might have seemed like the road to rewarding their participation in the revolution.

The Campesino (The Culture of Poverty)

Most developed and emerging nations, like Mexico, have a class system that looks and acts like a ladder. At the bottom you have the lower class, followed by the lower-middle class, middle class, upper-middle class, and finally the upper class.

Once a person understands where they belong on the economic ladder, they will, in most cases, strive to move upward in search of a better life for themselves, their family, and the next generation. However, when people are not aware of the possibility of upward mobility through the economic class ladder, or even know of its existence, they become members of an entirely different social group known in Mexico as campesinos. Sociologist Oscar Lewis, who wrote extensively on this problem in Mexico, best described it as "The Culture of Poverty."

> People with a culture of poverty have very little sense of history. They are a marginal people who know only their own troubles, their own local conditions, their own neighborhood, their own way of life. Usually, they

have neither the knowledge, the vision nor the idealogy to see the similarities between their problems and those of others like themselves elsewhere in the world. In other words, they are not class conscious, although they are very sensitive indeed to status distinctions.

To get a better understanding of what happened in Mexico, we might take a look at some micros in this communal system of agriculture.

In the late 1960s a friend who was a Hollywood director was looking for outdoor locations for a western he was planning to shoot in Mexico. This search took us to an ejido, where we were shown around by a government agronomist.

During our visit we asked him to give us a quick rundown on the inner workings of this ejido. As it turned out he was a frustrated man who had reached the conclusion that working with campesinos was a futile endeavor.

"You see those stone walls. You might notice than in many places they are crumbling," he said pointing. "You see . . . these campesinos are trying to copy their Aztec ancestors. The problem is that the ancients understood that to keep walls from falling you needed to place the pointed end of rocks towards the center so the inward pressure kept them in place." He nodded his head. "These people have forgotten the basics . . . they think they are copying their ancestors without the elementary engineering know how.

"Using round rocks eventually ends up with failing walls." He could not stop there. "Now try to get them to grow anything but corn . . . They just shake their heads, convinced the land cannot sustain anything but that one single staple." He shook his head in resignation. "Agriculture in Mexico is doomed . . . that's the beginning and end of my lecture."

Back in the late 1980s I was invited by the Mexican Bank of Foreign Trade (Bancomext) to attend a meeting in their offices in the city of Veracruz. Ostensibly, this gathering was to see what the bank could do to help the farmers in the state get into the export business. The bank was carrying an uncollectable debt from the sugar cane growers who, despite being subsidized by a government-owned development bank, were incapable of competing in the world markets. At this meeting, there were two American agronomists invited by the bank.

"These people are pathetic," one of them told me. "The state of Veracruz has some of the richest soil in the world, with a climate that lends itself to growing any number of products that could be exported and here they are growing sugar cane, not to mention coffee beans," he sneered, "as if there's not enough surplus of those products in the marketplace. They are convinced the way to be profitable is through an unworkable system of under-financed and technologically outdated communes.

"You only have to look at what Birds Eye, the frozen vegetable packagers, did in the Bajío [the lowlands] area in the central state of Guanajuato. They created a state-of-the-art agricultural industry now run entirely by Mexicans. Just look at their broccoli industry that accounts for 60 percent of what is consumed in the United States. But that's only a small segment of the real potential of the Mexican agricultural industry."

"So what's the answer?"

"Privatize the disastrous ejido program of communal farming, provide modern farming technology and foreign investment, especially into processing and packaging plants for a variety of products that are not sugar and coffee."

"Such as?"

"You can grow just about anything in different parts of the state of Veracruz, but if you want an example . . . any kind of fruit compatible with a semi-tropical environment, which can then be exported as fresh or canned produce. You know . . . things like pineapples and oranges."

He then went on to remind me of the large demand for winter-grown agriculture produce in the United States. Mexico's weather was ideal to fill much more of this demand but for the nation's antiquated farming technology.

When I visited my brother in Brazil to celebrate his seventieth birthday in 2003, he took my wife and me on a tour of his cattle ranch, located on the border of the states of São Paulo and Mato Grosso do Sul. Sitting behind the wheel of his jeep, my wife and I looked out on a green pasture that stretched to the horizon.

"You see that?" he said, pointing. "That's called land engineering. Don't think for a minute that's what it looked like when we got here.

"People complain that we are rich landowners who exploit the land," he laughed. "Who do they think is feeding the world? Every year we get squatters who want our land, and every year we have to pay them to vacate what we struggled to create. Eventually, they are going to win and . . . just as they did after the Mexican Revolution and that country's land distribution program, they will destroy very quickly what took decades to build."

Much like the Mexican agronomist years before, he shook his head. "And then who's going to feed the Brazilian people? Not these squatters whom the state secretly supports to keep them from rising up against the government. Unfortunately, we have no border with a country like the United States and no NAFTA to fall back on."

The problem of campesino squatters on private property is not just a Brazilian phenomenon. Mexico has faced the same issue. A friend of mine who used to live in Cuernavaca, capital of the southern state of Morelos, had a large tract of farmland taken over by squatters. Unlike my brother in Brazil who paid them to leave, my friend waited until the men were at work and the children in school. He then moved in bulldozers and leveled the shantytown. Without the support of the local authorities, he paid dearly for his vigilante methods. Today he and his family live in California. Squatters now inhabit his land.

But the well-educated upper class also contributes to the problem. I was driving a Mercedes Benz owned by a Mexican friend of mine who had just purchased the $70,000 extravaganza. We were on a two-lane country road when he rolled down the window and threw out an empty coffee container.

"Why did you do that?" I complained. This was an educated guy.

"I don't like garbage in my car."

This was just another example of what my brother had complained about forty years earlier when he stated, "The people who live in Mexico have no love for the land."

From my point of view, after years of observation, Mexico has developed an urban-minded culture at the expense of its rural base. If this were just an isolated incident, I might not have mentioned it. After all, the highways of Mexico are littered with so many plastic bags and bottles that a Canadian friend once remarked, "They should replace the eagle as the symbol of Mexico with an empty plastic container. When was the last time anyone saw an eagle in this country?" In fact he was wrong, not about the plastic refuse, but about eagles.

A renowned chemist with his own government sponsored three-story laboratory at the Universidad Autónoma de México (UNAM), the largest university in Mexico, lectures on the problems of water.

"You know," he once told me, "we blame water pollution largely on the dumping of industrial waste . . . but that's a lie." He went on to say, "The biggest polluters are the campesinos out in the countryside. Lacking indoor plumbing and refuse-removal facilities, they pollute our streams, rivers, and lakes with human waste and garbage. They cut down our trees for firewood. They don't know how to rotate crops and they end up exhausting the land, which eventually turns to dust. And when the forests that bring on the rains disappear, they blame the lack of water on a vengeful God . . . they believe praying and lighting candles will make everything right."

What he forgot to mention were the huge annual pilgrimages to visit saints like the Virgin of Guadalupe. Sometimes covering weeks of walking along the highways of Mexico, these believers think that human error causing greater poverty can be resolved with the blessing of the church and its resident saints.

"So why are the campesinos so untouchable in this country?"

"Creating failed institutions is one of the mainstays of what this country is about. You should have learned that by now."

"I have, but I wanted to hear someone else say it."*

---

* For a timeline on Agrarian Reform, Appendix 5 has a complete review of its history from 1910 to the present.

13

Revolutionary Renaissance (1934–1940)

THE NEXT PHASE OF THIS MEXICAN NARRATIVE is the Lázaro Cárdenas era of socialistic change, especially in the areas of the redistribution of land, nationalization, and the creation and implementation of a government system that in time morally and financially bankrupted the nation. Unquestionably, Lázaro Cárdenas is one of the most important figures in modern Mexican history. Little known in the United States, his story is an important one that cannot be ignored. His actions shaped the future of Mexico for decades to come and accelerated Mexico's roller coaster ride to disaster.

The Humanitarian General (1934–1940)

If we take the time to count the number of statues, avenues, schools, and towns dedicated to this Mexican hero, we can shake our heads in absolute amazement at how convoluted Mexican history can be. It is not that the man had bad intentions; it is simply that his intentions turned out badly.

What separated Gen. Lázaro Cárdenas from so many of those leaders who participated in the revolution was his genuine nationalism, his honesty, and his humanitarian intentions towards the poor and the downtrodden. Nobody can ever accuse him of being a malinchista. Maybe, in retrospect, that is one of the reasons Mexican historians hold him in such high regard, forgetting that much of what he accomplished kicked Mexico down the road to disaster. The results of Cárdenas's policies, if not catastrophic, made it quite clear where Mexico was heading, and the nation was gathering speed on the road to disaster.

With the support of Plutarco Elías Calles, Cárdenas was elected governor of the central state of Michoacán, where he was born. His legacy still has an important presence in that state as the socialist populist bent known as *cardenismo*. His successful governorship earned him the presidency of Mexico from 1934 to 1940.

If part of his legacy as governor was his education programs, building schools and roads, and the creation of social services for the disenfranchised, what he is most remembered for is his program of extensive land distribution to the campesinos in the name of agrarian reform. He also embraced socialism as a means to bring economic productivity under the control of the state, a goal supported by trade unions and special interest groups. With the state's economy, the bureaucracy, the unions, and the campesino under his political umbrella, the power structure of the state was in his hands. In Mexican politics, this support is known as the "corporate vote," and became the power base of his future presidency and all the ones that followed until the first real change in Mexico's failed system of government in the year 2000.

Extensive land distribution turned a state with an abundance of green vegetation, forests, and plenty of water and good land to farm into an agriculture tragedy. Today, Michoacán has the distinction of being one of the poorest states in Mexico with one of the highest percentages of migration to Mexico City in search of work. They are in large part responsible for the belts of poverty surrounding the capital and, as repeated so often, the reason for illegally crossing the northern border.

Taking land from the rich and turning it over to the poor only works if you believe in the story of Robin Hood. Governor Cárdenas can be counted among the believers. The legacy of cardenismo thwarted industrial development in Michoacán for decades. Back in the 1980s I remember looking at an industrial park at the edge of the airport in Morelia, the state capital, that was totally overgrown with weeds and high grass—the perfect symbol of a failed socialist economy. The private sector bypassed investing in Michoacán as if it had the plague. Like many of today's populist Latin American leaders, as long as they give the illusion of spreading the wealth among the poor at the expense of the rich, they manage to maintain their popularity—in most cases well after destroying the economies of their respective countries.

Michoacán remains an example of state government failure in that starting around 2006, many municipalities in the state are in the hands of La Familia

Michoacana (LFM). The LFM was associated with the Gulf Cartel* before they became independent and established themselves as an organized crime syndicate in the state of Michoacán. They now influence elections by putting in their own people. In many cases they become the actual law in rural towns offering a better alternative than those provided by the official security forces of the municipalities and the state. When people talk about a "failed state," the state of Michoacán is a good example.

◆

Lázaro Cárdenas was elected president in 1934. His growing popularity, especially among the poor, was in part due to his campaigning with only a chauffeur and aide-de-camp and the promise of cutting his presidential salary by half.

Cárdenas's policies for managing the economy, and his methods of gaining political control when he was a governor, now spilled over into his presidency. Unions, bureaucrats, and parasitic special interest groups became his political base. Salary raises for workers helped consolidate his power. A 400 percent increase in land distribution to the campesinos across the nation brought them on board. With the proven formula that comprised the corporate vote, Cárdenas eventually controlled the election of a majority of officials at federal and state levels. The notion of political opposition hardly pertained to the new Mexico.

To stem accusations that he was becoming a communist in the Stalinist mold, he invited Russian exile Leon Trotsky to Mexico, where he took up residence near the Blue House that was shared by Frida Kahlo and Diego Rivera, both of whom became two of Mexico's internationally acclaimed painters. Trotsky and Frida Kahlo became lovers until Kahlo grew tired of listening to Trotsky's complaints about how much he missed Mother Russia and his estranged wife. She finally ended the relationship. Shortly afterward an assassin ended Leon Trotsky's life by stabbing him with an ice pick.

Cárdenas tried openly to aid the Republican government in the Spanish Civil War but was thwarted by Franklin D. Roosevelt's administration. He then decided to nationalize Mexico's railways. With that success under his belt, the time was right to go after the biggest producer of hard currency in Mexico:

---

* Gulf Cartel: one of the major drug trafficking cartels based in the Northeast of Mexico.

the foreign oil companies. Nationalistic fervor gripped the nation. The intellectual left was having a field day blaming much of the country's ills on foreign exploitation.

On March 28, 1938, Cárdenas nationalized Mexico's petroleum reserves and expropriated all the industry's assets, including refineries, drilling equipment, pipelines, and everything else the government could get their hands on. Once again, the bitter lesson was soon learned that while nationalization was undoubtedly popular with the masses and the left-leaning intelligentsia, no consideration was given to who was going to run the industry, which at the time could boast of being the second largest producer of crude in the world. Many of Mexico's actions as a nation seemed visceral and without much thought to future consequences. What soon became the new government oil monopoly, Petroleos Mexicanos (Pemex), would in time become one of the worst-managed major oil companies in the world, and that is no exaggeration.

There is no doubt that Lázaro Cárdenas was a popular president, socially aware of the injustices suffered by the poorer classes and the campesino. There is also no question that as far as Mexican presidents go, he and Benito Juárez were impeccably honest by Mexican political standards. But the long-term effects of Cárdenas's presidency led his country down that road to disaster. Probably his worst legacy was the consolidation of political interest groups that controlled the country in the future. These groups used their influence in rigging elections, bureaucratic corruption, theft of the treasury, and in some cases stole the natural resources of the country for their own enrichment. They eventually became known as the PRI. The party controlled the political landscape and the economy of the country for the remaining years of the twentieth century.

What is hard to reconcile is that despite his turning Mexico into a one-party franchise ruled by corrupt special interest groups, Cárdenas was largely untainted by the fraudulent practices of the political organizations he created. In this he was echoing the dictator Porfirio Díaz, even though both men were from the opposite ends of the political spectrum.

Upon retirement, Cárdenas lived a fairly modest life dedicated to irrigation projects, the promotion of free education, and medical attention for the poor. He was a proponent of greater democracy and human rights in Latin America.

In 1955 the Soviet Union awarded Lázaro Cárdenas with the Lenin Peace Prize, which is indicative of how doublespeak became a cover for the realities of a one-man executive rule. It is hard to imagine that Cárdenas actually believed he was taking his nation to a better future. But as we have learned from history, "Power corrupts, and absolute power corrupts absolutely."

Thanks to him and Plutarco Elías Calles, Mexico became a benign dictatorship of corrupt rulers who, like the medicine men of the Old West, sold snake oil as the solution to the nation's problems. Jorge Santayanay Borrás, the Spanish philosopher, reminds us that, "Those who cannot remember the past are condemned to repeat it." Cárdenas's son Cuauhtémoc followed in his father's footsteps as governor of the state of Michoacán, endorsing the same policies as his father with the same disastrous results. And like his father, his honesty, or the perception of honesty, kept his political career alive.

14

Oil—The National Patrimony
of the People

◆

IN 1938 PRESIDENT LÁZARO CÁRDENAS nationalized the foreign oil companies held in large part by British and American interests. What originally seemed like a good idea in time turned into a disaster, as the political cry of "Oil is the national patrimony of the nation and its people" became one of the more important slogans of the post-revolution era.

Despite this baseless motto, by 2007 Pemex had become the fifth largest producer of crude in the world—behind Saudi Arabia, Russia, Iran, and the United States—with exports to the United States of over one million barrels daily. However, Mexico is today importing over 40 percent of its gasoline due to a deficiency of refining capacity. Lack of investment in new refineries, poor maintenance, and inadequate planning have left Pemex in shambles. It has also become obvious that the government continues to bleed the oil company of its revenues to pay for a growing deficit in the federal budget. While the price of gasoline at the pump is much higher than it should be for a nation with a third-world per-capita income, most of what the consumer is paying are taxes destined for the government's coffers.

Another unique way to bleed Pemex revenues is having Congress peg the value of a barrel of oil well below the real market price. If, for example, the world market price of oil in a given year is estimated to vary between $70 and $100, Congress might peg it at $45. The difference between the real price of a barrel and that set by Congress goes directly to the federal government. This unique form of pirating eventually turned a sea of oil into a sea of red ink. But that is just the beginning.

In the first place, the top management of Pemex are government-appointed bureaucrats who know little about the oil industry. Not only are they in large part incompetent, but these bureaucrats place their friends and family members on the Pemex payroll. These people are known as *paracaidistas* (parachutists), because they parachute into the payroll office to collect their salaries and then disappear. What the revolving door management also learns during their tenure at Pemex is the art of self-enrichment, not only for themselves, but also for their friends and political supporters.

The exception to these poor managers was Jorge Díaz Serrano, an oil-drilling engineer who became the managing director of Pemex from 1976 to 1981, during the great Mexican oil boom. He was also a partner of George H. W. Bush back in the 1960s. In time, Díaz Serrano paid the price for his American affiliation, which earned him the rancor of the nationalistic political left. His overwhelming success as the head of Pemex, by tripling production and making Mexico the fourth-largest producer at the time, eventually landed him a hefty prison sentence. Success in a bureaucracy, especially one tainted by a foreign connection and the mark of the scarlet *M* for malinchismo, could not go unpunished.

In 1983 the government accused Díaz Serrano of self-enrichment during his tenure as the director of Pemex. This hypocrisy was hardly new, considering that enrichment was his accusers catchword for those falling out with the political establishment. As reported by the *New York Times* in the article "Pemex Case Sentencing" on May 8, 1987,

> Jorge Díaz Serrano, the former head of the Mexican state oil monopoly Pemex, has been sentenced to 10 years in jail on charges of personally enriching himself during his tenure. . . .
>
> Mr. Díaz Serrano headed Pemex during the 1976–81 oil boom years and was once considered a potential candidate for the presidency of Mexico.

Those who claimed nationalistic purity as essential in managing the economic money machine of the revolution viewed Díaz Serrano as a malinchista. Many felt his relationship with the senior Bush was a sellout to the gringos. His success notwithstanding, Díaz Serrano needed to pay for these sins. The famous phrase "enrichment by illicit means" was the perfect excuse. Once again the old political axiom was brought out of the closet, "To my friends the full protection of the law; to my enemies the full enforcement of the law."

In 1953 the senior Bush created a company called Zapata Petroleum in Houston, Texas, partnering with Bill and J. Hugh Liedke, wildcatters best known for leading the hostile takeover of the Pennzoil Company. Within a few years the company made millions from the venture, giving Bush the opportunity to create a subsidiary, Zapata Off-Shore, for the express purpose of building his own platforms to drill for oil in the Gulf of Mexico.

In 1960 Díaz Serrano got in touch with Bush, and between them they created an offshoot of Zapata Off-Shore and named the company Permargo (Perforaciones Marinas del Golfo), which involved supplying drilling equipment, machinery, and pipe for Pemex with its large untapped oil reserves in the Gulf. These deals were wrapped in mystery, since Permargo was never mentioned in Zapata Off-Shore's annual reports. When Zapata Petroleum and its subsidiaries were investigated by the IRS, the books conveniently disappeared. Zapata Petroleum, according to an article in the *Houston Business Journal* of April 23, 2003, "drilled 130 oil wells in the Gulf of Mexico without a single dry hole."

One can only speculate how many fixed bids were won by Zapata Off-Shore and Permargo to supply oil rig equipment for Pemex in the Gulf. But then, speculation is the very fuel of legend and lore. And it makes for a great story.

I recently attended a cocktail party and found myself talking to a Houston matron who had social contacts in the oil industry. "Honey, if you lived in Houston and were in any way involved with the oil patch, most knew old George was well connected with Pemex. I myself had the opportunity of meeting Jorge Díaz Serrano. I can tell you, he was a real Latino charmer. Had us bored housewives quivering in our pantyhose."

Due to the lack of effective management, Pemex fell into the hands of the workers union known as the Sindicato de Trabajadores Petroleros de la República Mexicana (STPRM), led by organizational genius and notorious crook Joaquín Hernández Galicia, alias La Quina. He was so powerful that when President Carlos Salinas de Gortari (1988–1994) decided to get rid of him, the government had to send troops to storm his home before he was finally captured after a fierce gun battle. In 1992 he was sentenced to thirty-five years in prison for possession of illegal weapons and presumptive murder. However, as happens so often when PRI cronies are sent to jail, he received amnesty in 1997. His real crimes of corruption and illicit enrichment were never mentioned. Nobody was going to embarrass the PRI government that he had supported for nearly half a century.

When Lolita de la Vega, a well-known TV Azteca anchorwoman, interviewed La Quina May 5, 2001, on national television, he wrapped himself in his nationalistic cape and spouted so many untruths he would have made Pinocchio blush. Truth be known, he was only repeating the left-leaning political elite's populist dogma.

I was a member of the PRI when it was still in its revolutionary stages, nationalistic and the protector of the nation. We had some pretty good presidents, principally Lázaro Cárdenas, who despite all the criticism never sold one single piece of the nation until President Miguel de la Madrid [1982–1988], put us into the GATT [General Agreement on Tariffs and Trade]. Before that, the PRI was still defending the nation and the ideals of the revolution that cost two million lives [best estimates are around one million]. Unfortunately, now you have the Harvard President [President Salinas de Gortari had a degree from Harvard] and other foreign universities that instead of thinking about Mexico they think for the foreigners.

If you think of a backward country, like our own in technology, you have to realize that the Tratados de Bucareli was where the Americans stopped us from producing everything from screws to engines.* We are simply a nation of assembly plants for all these years, and as I said 20 years ago we are going to end up being *braceros* [Mexicans migrant workers in the U.S.] in our own country. In fact right now we are *braceros* in our own country.

Another problem facing Pemex was its inability, under the constitution, to accept direct foreign investment. This meant that Pemex became Latin America's

---

* This treaty said nothing of the kind. It dealt with reparation of American stolen property during the revolution in exchange for U.S. recognition.

largest borrower in the capital markets. Depending on the state of the Mexican economy, the risk factor on interest rates on loans could become costly. But it did not end there.

Tax evasion is the national sport of Mexico, largely due to Mexicans preferring to pay lawyers and accountants rather than taxes to line the pockets of corrupt officials. To make up for the shortfall from tax evasion, Pemex currently pays over 30 percent of all federal taxes in a country whose tax ratio to GDP is one of the lowest in Latin America. Mexico collects around 16 percent of GDP, compared to 30 percent in the United States. The results for Pemex are no building of new refineries, ownership of a petrochemical industry that is obsolete, and a natural gas potential that at times ends up being burned into the atmosphere for lack of funds to build an adequate gasoduct system for effective distribution.

BusinessWeek magazine said it best in an article titled "Pemex May Be Turning From Gusher To Black Hole" that appeared December 12, 2004:

> Pemex is the Mexican government's cash cow. The state-run company pays out over 60% of its revenue in royalties and taxes, and those funds pay for a third of the federal government's budget. . . .
>
> With the federal government draining its coffers, Pemex doesn't have enough money to invest in serious exploration. . . . It now owes a staggering [U.S.] $42.5 billion.

These are just some of the problems facing the national oil company, which was supposed to become the national patrimony of the people. The legacy of Lázaro Cárdenas's nationalization of most basic industries brought Mexico just one step closer to disaster. The problem has yet to be resolved, despite the awareness of the vast majority of Mexicans that some real change needs to be enacted.

This national disgrace brought on the necessity of reform in the twenty-first century, which was vehemently opposed by elements of the PRI and the leftist PRD party under the leadership of Andrés López Obrador. These orthodox nationalists preferred to see one of the country's largest sources of foreign capital continue the populist illusion of being the patrimony of the Mexican people rather than correct the mistakes of the past.

15

The Nation That Fell Asleep

◆

So far in describing Mexico on the road to economic and financial disaster, I have focused on two aspects of the Mexican Revolution: the Agrarian Reform and the nationalization of many key industries, with oil being the prime example.

One of the reasons I have spent so much time on the Agrarian Reform and the distribution of land to the peasants is because it is an area where we can actually measure the difference between the private and public sectors. While 80 percent of farmland went to the campesino in the creation of the ejido, the remaining 20 percent was still privately owned. To ensure these farms would not become haciendas, the government passed a law that no individual could possess more than 220 acres, hardly enough land for an efficient, modern, agricultural industry. But here is what happened.

If individual property owners could only own 220 acres, additional land could be bought in the name of the wife, sons, uncles, cousins, and close friends, known as *prestanombres* (name lenders). A privately owned farm could grow to the point that an investment in modern methods and equipment was possible for a profitable business. By the 1970s and '80s, that 20 percent private ownership was producing around 80 percent of the food needed to feed Mexico's growing urban population. Eventually, with the advent of NAFTA and the opening of the border to U.S. and Canadian low-cost and high-quality agricultural products, the Mexican communal system was bankrupt. Imported grains, dairy products, beef, and fresh and frozen produce were flooding the Mexican supermarkets. One had only to step into Costco and Walmart to see all those American products with Spanish labels. The campesino, with his antiquated farming methods, was on the road to extinction.

With the agrarian reforms in place, nationalizing the railroads and the oil industry was merely the first in a series of compounded errors that followed.

Other industries also became victims to the infestation of government takeovers. Among these industries were mining, maritime shipping, telephone service and installations, the distribution of electricity and all power stations, and the fishing industry, just to name a few examples. The communications sector, which included newspapers, film studios and radio stations, could be privately owned but were tightly controlled by a censorship board in the Secretaría de Gobernación (Ministry of the Interior). When television became available, the government gave the major concession to the one and only news channel, Televisa, which in return accepted censorship to assure the dissemination of the government's points of view.

Muzzling the fourth estate allowed for unchecked government mismanagement and corruption on a grand scale. As for the distribution of news, Mexicans became adept at reading between the lines in search of the truth.

This dismal state of affairs in agriculture and the nationalization of most basic industries was also accompanied by the creation of a centralized government in Mexico City in which power resided with the executive branch. This executive branch was, in reality, a government run by presidential decree. Elections were controlled by the corporate vote, guaranteeing the continuity of the one party in power since 1929. For all intents and purposes, the country was in the hands of the PRI, which went as far as to make the claim that not only did it control the political institutions of the nation, but announced that it was also the custodian of the economy.

If the economy was in bad shape, then the blame was placed squarely on the private sector. When there was good news to report, with few exceptions, the media outlets fell in step praising those government institutions they secretly held in contempt. One might say, "Hell hath no fury like a government scorned." There were no eagles in the media, just a chorus of well-fed singing canaries in golden cages.

The technocrats and the intellectual elite saw socialism as the perfect model. Those opposed simply saw them as hypocrites and labeled them "champagne communists" in reference to their expensive habits. If that were not enough, there were two more insidious outgrowths of the Mexican Revolution that are still in place to this day. The two are the non-reelection clauses in Articles 59 and 83 of the Constitution of 1917.

Article 59: "Senators and deputies to the Congress of the Union cannot be reelected for the immediately following term." Though not mentioned, municipal presidents, elected for a three-year period, were also not allowed a consecutive second term.

Article 83: "The President shall assume the duties of office on the first of December for a term of six years. A citizen who has held the office of President of the Republic, by popular election or by appointment as ad interim, provisional, or substitute President, can in no case and for no reason again hold that office."

Lest there be no confusion as to who controlled the country, the PRI even used the Mexican flag as its party logo. The PRI claimed that this system of government was ideal for a country that had suffered through an alarming number of coups and internal strife. They reminded the masses that Gen. Antonio López de Santa Anna became president on eleven nonconsecutive occasions, which also meant he had to have been thrown out of office the same number of times. The people had to hark back to the revolutionary years between 1910 and 1929 when Mexican governments were not only a revolving door but were also plagued by political assassinations. Leaving office in the *saco de madera* (the wooden overcoat) had not been that uncommon.

Mexicans take great pride in telling anyone who will listen that this system, which became the cornerstone of PRI power, did keep the country politically stable, barring a few blips, through the years of 1929 to 2000. Nobody asked the obvious question: If the Mexican model of government was such a good idea for third-world countries, why had nobody else seen the light?

Unfortunately, the political calm was only on the surface. The deeper one ventured into this unique system of government, the more one realized the whole political structure smelled most foul. One-term limits for elected officials came at a terrible cost to the nation. They might have listened to Richard S. "Kinky" Friedman, the Texas political commentator, who suggested "there be two term limits; one in office and one in jail."

The six-year presidential term became known as a sexenio (six years). Even though every president could lay claim to being elected, any sane person knew the election was rigged. The president was a six-year dictator, albeit a benign one. As we will see, there were at least two exceptions—two men whose repressive ways made a mockery of any pretense of democratic rule, despite a resistance on the part of Mexican historians to use the word dictator.

Even though the government had a constitutionally elected legislative body, the upper and lower houses were only there to rubber stamp the president's wishes. At least the president was not a dictator for life, his supporters claimed. What is even more curious was how a new president got nominated. Once a nomination took place, his election was a given.

The presidential electoral process started, not with anything resembling a primary where voters got to choose their party's candidate, but with a six-month guessing game of who was to be the anointed one. Mexicans called the future candidate *el tapado*, meaning he who was hidden from public view until he received *el dedazo* (the pointed finger). El dedazo took place when the outgoing president announced the man selected to succeed him. He and his closest advisers made that decision. It is no wonder that open-minded historians considered Mexico one of the longest dictatorships in history, covering seven decades of uninterrupted rule.

Each president's sexenio represents what might be referred to as trickle-down corruption. Most politicians, and nearly all the presidents, are graduates of the Universidad Autónoma de México (UNAM), an institution of 250,000 plus students that is the centerpiece of the nation's universities and the epicenter of socialist doctrine.

It seems that many in the middle class in Mexico City who graduated from the national university at the time the new president was there qualify for a handout in the new sexenio. If we add to the president's classmates, friends, family, distant relatives, political operatives, and all those who felt that they were entitled to a *hueso* (bone thrown their way), we then get an idea why the system of "institutionalized corruption" is so tolerated.

Mexicans accept their system of government because those people in and surrounding the power structure in each sexenio profit like "jackals sidling up to a tiger," as Winston Churchill said of the Italians and their relationship with Hitler. Much of the political handouts come in the way of featherbedding in the state-owned companies. There are the paracaidistas in the oil industry, but it hardly stops there. These parachutists also land on the state-owned company payroll offices to pick up their salaries. Many are just a friend of a friend of a friend of someone way up the bureaucratic food chain. Being on the payroll is hardly an indication that you actually work there. Helping friends on making the right bid for government projects is also quite popular.

Another obvious example of institutionalized corruption is road building—by paying off the government inspectors they then can apply far less cement, concrete, or asphalt than the specifications require. This has an additional advantage. After less than six months these same roads will have to be repaired because they are unable to support the weight per axle they were designed for. Now you can take great pride in all the jobs the government is creating while you repeat the process ad nauseam. Those who believe I'm exaggerating should ask anyone who has traveled the super highway from Mexico City to Acapulco. It was under repair practically from the time the first toll booth went into service.

Then there is El Año de Hidalgo (The Year of Hidalgo). This refers to the fifth year of a Mexican president's six-year term. On this year he goes to the city of Dolores Hidalgo where the War of Independence (1810–1821) began. Amid a patriotic ceremony and the ringing of hundreds of church bells, he rings the bell of freedom on September 16, the day Mexico celebrates its independence from Spain. The other five years of his presidency he rings the bell of freedom at the National Palace in Mexico City.

But the Year of Hidalgo has a more insidious meaning. The Hidalgo is also a Mexican ten-peso gold coin, last minted in 1959. Here the meaning signals that the fifth year of the president's term of office is traditionally the year the executive branch of the government and their supporters clean out the national treasury and steal everything that is not a permanent fixture. Mexicans talk quite openly about El Año de Hidalgo, sometimes with a certain pride that their leaders could be so consistent in stealing the people's money.

When a government employs the one-term non-reelection clause in their constitution, the incentive to serve the people as the means of staying in office is eliminated. Rocking the boat for any kind of change always meets with resistance, which usually turns into making future political enemies. Doing a good job representing your constituents, or doing nothing, is the same in the end if getting reelected is not in play—getting rich is always the best alternative. Despite these realities, Mexican politicians never stop reminding the citizenry that they are there to unconditionally serve the people.

A Mexican politician also has to make sure he can't be accused of being a total political parasite. This requires learning the language of political doublespeak—the technique of making speeches that are so convoluted nobody really understands what is being said, even though the words resonate as important. These speeches hide the fact that there are no promises made, and they are masked in a preponderance of revolutionary rhetoric and zeal. If one aspires to get any-where near the top of the bureaucratic hierarchy, this form of government-speak has to be mastered. How to give the impression of doing something while doing nothing is a professional accomplishment that only a select few are adept at.

You cannot be a Mexican who can read, write, and reason and not be aware of what is going on. To know is to be ashamed, and to be ashamed is to hide behind the mask of shared national guilt. Mexico is a country built on institu-tions that invite corruption on a grand scale. Nobody wants to be left out if they can help it. No wonder Mexico went from being one of the richest countries on earth to where it stands today. The country literally stole itself into near poverty.

Some historians might question why the military at some point did not step in and clean house. The military, at least the upper echelon of the officer corps, was also dipping greedy fingers into the nation's piggy bank.

By understanding how both these constitutional articles work, the reader will get a clearer picture of "the country that fell asleep." There can be no polit-ical innovation, political promises don't need to be kept, and so progress moves at a snail's pace. The private sector retaliates by becoming masters at evading taxes with the national excuse that the alternative is lining the pockets of a totally corrupt bureaucratic caste system. Though the private and public sec-tors are on opposite sides of the fence, both are equally counterproductive.

To get a feel for this national inertia, let's consider the following article that reports real progress and change in Mexico. It appeared in *Time* magazine on September 14, 1953, titled "The Domino Player." The article was referring to President Adolfo Ruiz Cortines who served from 1952 to 1958.* Nothing that appeared in this article came even close to being realized. Whoever wrote this report obviously knew little about how the Mexican political system worked under the PRI. Promise the moon, but never rock the ship of state. In general, the U.S. media was quite naïve when it came to Mexico.

> The republic has a new and different President who has embarked on noth-ing less than a wholesale program for cleaning up Mexico. . . .
>
> In the Mexico of the past, graft and corruption in high and low places was part of the very system of government.

---

* He was known as the "Domino President" because he was an ardent domino player.

With the backing of the rising middle class there has already been a change in the standards of public morality. As such revolutionary ideas as honesty and truth spread through the government, the new President and the new Mexico can look ahead to an even more democratic life. The politically populist magazine *Siempre* proclaimed it: THE ERA of TRUTH.

One might conclude the article was written when the PRI's continuous dictatorship ended and the first open elections in Mexico took place when Vicente Fox, of the PAN got elected president in 1999. Wrong assumption. The article appeared over a half century before.

Even after Mexico held its first open elections going into the year 2000, when for the first time a balance of power was created between the executive and legislative branches of government, the attitude of most Mexicans continued to reflect their mistrust, cynicism, and lack of interest in participating in the new democratic order. Most Mexicans I know talk openly about politics. There is always much to talk about, and dealing with the latest scandal is the centerpiece of these conversations. Mexico never seems to run out of these outrages centered on the latest politician's creative plan of self-enrichment at the country's expense. One must never forget that famous Mexican saying, "Show me a politician who is poor, and I will show you a poor politician."

When I get bored listening to the diatribes, I put up my hand and say, "Can I give you my opinion?"

No one really wants to know what a foreigner has to say. Only Mexicans are qualified to talk about the bizarre politics of the country, but politeness is a Mexican trait, and I will be heard despite the fact they know what's coming.

"Go ahead," they reply.

"Do you know the name of the federal deputy who represents your district in Congress?"

There's a general sigh of resignation. They've heard this before. "So what's new? You always ask the same questions."

"Not to be repetitive, but if you knew their names, you could write him or her a letter expressing your disapproval."

"How many times do we have to tell you . . . don't be stupid . . . nobody knows the federal deputy that represents them in Congress, and if you're going to ask us the name of our senator . . . nobody knows that either."

The moral of this story is that Mexicans have no faith in their government, nor do they believe in the political selection process of the legislative branch of government, despite the primary system in place since the PRI was sent home in the presidential election of 2000. As a result, they have no idea who represents them, nor do they really care, unless it's family, or a friend. Then the bells of opportunity ring loud and clear. In their minds, elected officials are only interested in self-gratification of the monetary kind. Mexicans still don't seem to understand, except maybe intellectually, that people get the government they deserve.

There is another side to seventy-one years of this perverse system of government, which partially ended in 2000. As noted in his book *The Labyrinth of Solitude*, Octavio Paz talks about Mexicans hiding behind masks and concludes, "The impression Mexicans create is like the Orientals, hermetic and indecipherable." So what are they hiding?

Most Mexicans are ashamed of their country's acceptance of revolving-door presidents who, regardless of their accomplishments, are tainted with corruption and self-enrichment. Some sort of mental gymnastics has to take place so that Mexicans can live with themselves in a comfort zone that denies their participation in their county's "road to disaster."

How does one reconcile that Mexico went from a rich country, with the natural resources one needs to create a modern, first-world, industrialized nation, to a third-world country where 16 to 20 million of its people have to seek work in the United States as undocumented workers? Working the labyrinth, according to Octavio Paz, is how this is accomplished. Mexicans don't like to be reminded that they just stood by as spectators and beneficiaries to a long line of self-serving governments pretending to represent the needs of the people. The Mexican people's acceptance of the PRI system of government they supported is conveniently placed in the "I did not participate and therefore I can't be held responsible" category. But participate they did, if the opportunity arose.

Corruption is another issue that must be faced. Mexican parents do not teach their children the ways of institutionalized corruption. Like most parents, they teach their children to be honest and hard-working citizens. So where does parental guidance go wrong? Remember the old saying, "Monkey see, monkey do?" Children follow the lead set by their parents, their peers, and what they experience surrounding them. Dr. Laurence Peter of *The Peter Principle* said it best: "When I was a child I was taught that the people upstairs knew what they were doing." That same erroneous assumption could be applied to family and the country.

Once more, it is important to remind the reader the rationalization that taking bribes is a way of life that assumes, if the government is corrupt, that those who participate are justified in playing the game. This especially holds true for the national sport of tax evasion, which is a form of corruption in itself.

◆

Leaving the impression that nothing has changed is a mistaken notion. Today, despite the grumbling, Mexicans have become more aware of their responsibility as citizens. The government is more representative of the people's choice since the primary system of candidate selection was put in place in 2000. The legislature is no longer a pawn of the executive branch. It is going through the pains of having to carry the burden of passing laws for the betterment of the country, a responsibility the legislative branch of government has never had to assume in the past. A national conscience is growing, despite an active leftist movement that wants to turn the clock back to the bad old, good old days. The much-maligned PRI has a new look, although the dinosaurs of the old PRI refuse to disappear into the ash can of history. The PRI is once more on the road to regaining power at all levels of government.

Denise Dresser, a respected newspaper columnist addressed this subject of PRI resurgence when she wrote in the newspaper *Reforma* on May 17, 2010:

> The PRI is one step away from regaining the presidency only two *sexenios* after throwing them out after 71 years of bad government.
>
> Wouldn't it be nice that a new era of PRI politicians turned out to be a salutary change and not a lamentable return to the past? I wish it were true that the country, as well as the PRI, had sufficiently changed to prevent the resurgence of the worst practices of the past. Any analysis of today's *priismo* contradicts that prognosis based on their view of the future that is being talked about in political circles.

16

1968—Tlatelolco
(The Unnecessary Massacre)

◆

MUCH THAT HAPPENED IN 1968 AFFECTED the world forever. To the astrologically bent, the planets were surely aligned to predict enormous upheavals. If your beliefs were in the tarot cards, then Death, the card of transition, was heralding social revolution. Change was in the air. These omens turned out to be true. This phenomenon affected not only Mexico, but also Europe and the United States.

Despite the Summer of Love in San Francisco and Woodstock on the East Coast, at the end of 1967 the Tet offensive had just taken place in Vietnam, accelerating the growing antiwar movement. Martin Luther King Jr. was assassinated in Memphis, Tennessee, on April 4, 1968, followed shortly by Robert Kennedy's assassination on June 5. These events preceded the Chicago riots. Then the Chicago Seven, under the leadership of Abbie Hoffman, disrupted the 1968 Democratic Presidential Convention in that same city during the last days of August.

In Europe the Warsaw Pact, under Soviet leadership, sent troops into Czechoslovakia to squash the rumblings of liberty and change. In France, the country suffered the first wildcat strike ever involving up to 11 million people. Many saw these events as an opportunity to shake up the establishment. These many changes were not going unnoticed in Mexico.

As the nation took center stage in its preparation for the 1968 Olympic Games in Mexico City, radical students at UNAM saw an opportunity to embarrass the government by putting forth a series of demands for the world to see, under the banner, "*No queremos olimpiadas, queremos revolución* (we don't want the Olympic Games, we want revolution)."

The students demanded the Mexican government free all political prisoners, dismiss the Mexico City chief of police and his deputy, and abolish the security forces known as the *granaderos*,* along with other unrealistic demands. The student activists must have known that no legitimate government was going to forfeit its authority by granting these ultimatums.

To understand why these student demands could be made with impunity, one has to know the meaning of the word "autonomous" when describing a university such as the UNAM. The theory behind the autonomous status of certain select university campuses throughout Latin America allowed for free speech without government censorship and off-campus intervention. This was a form of protecting free speech in many Latin American countries that were under dictatorial rule. While the intent made sense, in the case of Mexico in 1968 a minority of radical students used this freedom to promote their political agenda, an agenda they knew the government would never subscribe to due to the absurdity of their demands. But with the whole world watching the upcoming Olympic Games, the timing was perfect.

President Gustavo Díaz Ordaz Bolaños ordered Secretary of the Interior Luis Echeverría Álvarez to put down what he saw as a growing rebellion with international consequences that would have a negative effect on the Olympic Games. Echeverría sent in the army and occupied the campus in violation of its autonomous status. This heavy-handed response ignited the tragic events that followed. What began as student demands intended to embarrass the government on the eve of the Olympics turned into a public relations fiasco. Unaccustomed to any kind of public outcry against the PRI dictatorship, the government was unprepared to implement an adequate response to the protest.

The uprising soon took on a life of its own. Echeverría overreacted by sending the granaderos and the military law enforcement units to invade the sanctity of an autonomous university, which caused the spark that lit the flames of student disobedience. The students decided to call for a strike, which soon led to closing down the university.

After nine weeks of strikes by the UNAM dissidents, students from around the country began to join them. On October 2, ten days before the inauguration of the Olympic opening ceremony, approximately 15,000 students and their sympathizers marched through Mexico City, congregating at La Plaza de Las Tres Culturas (the Plaza of the Three Cultures), in a neighborhood known as

---

* Anti-riot police

Tlatelolco. It was called the Plaza of the Three Cultures because in its center archeologists had discovered remains of an Aztec temple adjoining a Spanish colonial church next to a modern building used as government offices.

Under orders of the Secretary of the Interior Luis Echeverría, the army and anti-riot police went in to clear out those congregated in the plaza. What became known as the Tlatelolco massacre was in its first stages.

I remember sitting in the Maya Bar at the Hilton Hotel on the corner of the two main avenues in the city that day when gunfire erupted. We piled out to the sidewalk, drinks in hand. At the time we did not know where the gunfire was coming from, but later found out it came from Tlatelolco.

The massacre started at sundown when the granaderos and the military, backed by armored vehicles, started shooting into the crowded plaza. The number of victims is still not known, but as expected, the government reported a low count of approximately thirty, while the antigovernment side reported that the deaths were closer to a thousand. The general consensus put the death toll somewhere between two hundred and three hundred, with many more wounded. Arrests followed, but regardless of the issues and the question of right or wrong, Mexico's international image was tarnished for decades to come. Mexico, and the rest of the world, saw the use of force as unnecessary and legally uncalled for. The Mexican Olympic Games were in shambles.

When Mexicans talk about the Tlatelolco massacre, they never mention their inability to act in support of their nation during this critical time. Nobody talks about a small group of students who were able to destroy Mexico's image abroad at the time when the country was center stage in the world. This group of radicals and their demands turned the 1968 Olympics into probably the least attended Games in modern history. I know. I was working as a volunteer for the Olympic Committee at the time. The stadiums were near empty. For many events, the Mexican Olympic officials opened the gates and let people in for free to give the impression of some semblance of success.

Regardless of the many disasters that fateful October, the Olympic Games themselves were also plagued by the social and political changes taking place in 1968. In the 200-meter track event, two African American male athletes won the gold and bronze medals. When presented with their medals on the Olympic podium, they raised their black-gloved fists in the symbol of Black Power.

◆

Many Mexican historians believe that Tlatelolco was the first glimmer of revolt against the system of a non-democratic government established in 1929. If that was the case, they were sorely shortsighted. Nothing much changed, except that Mexico shot itself in the foot at a time when it was given the opportunity of showing the world it was a progressive country with a stable government, unlike many others in Latin America. After all the wringing of hands and national outrage, Mexicans were incapable of making any short-term changes and seemed apathetic toward doing so. To the contrary, the two presidents who governed the nation from 1970 to 1982 seemed dedicated to pushing Mexico into more acts of repression. The words "road to disaster" never resonated so clearly.

But as happens so often, the leadership of the country was not listening to the people. When President Gustavo Díaz Ordaz was in the process of looking for a successor, he gave the dedazo to the architect of this unfortunate event—Luis Echeverría Álvarez.

Echeverría, the man largely responsible for Tlatelolco, was later charged with genocide but never went to trial. Despite his involvement in this unforgivable demonstration of unchecked government power and his mismanagement of the total affair, he was elected president in 1970. Could anything be more bizarre?

Considering the dishonor he brought on his country, it's hard to believe Echeverría was chosen to succeed a rather benign and generally liked president, and even harder to believe he continues to live in Mexico a free man who has never answered for his crimes. His supporters disagree, claiming he is under house arrest; a canary in a golden cage. He still maintains a faithful following among PRI party dinosaurs.

17

Two Bad Boys—The Mexican Miracle and the Buffoon

◆

Present Luis Echeverría Álvarez and President José López Portillo: these men had much in common. They became presidents of Mexico with a nationalistic agenda that, regardless of the intent, failed miserably. Both were precursors to the kind of populism that some years later would sweep across Latin America, as personified most recently by Hugo Rafael Chávez Frías of Venezuela.

The question that must be asked is why this repressive twosome, considering the damage they did to the nation, never answered for their mistakes? They were not subject to a political trial for high crimes against the nation, nor were they exiled, never to be heard of again. They never even received a minimal slap on the wrist.

Because both pounded away at nationalistic purity and revolutionary zeal without the slightest taint of malinchismo, the pretense that their political actions were above reproach had to be maintained as they marched the country toward financial and economic ruin. This tells us much of how Mexicans think publicly when it comes to the political arena; private opinions are a different story.

The Mexican Miracle, *El Milagro Mexicano*

President Luis Echeverría Álvarez served from 1970 to 1976. From a political perspective, he nationalized the mining and electric industries and ratcheted up the distribution of farmlands to the campesino as part of the Agrarian Reform. He claimed his programs of reform would be remembered as "The Mexican Miracle."

The real miracle was how his administration brought an economically healthy Mexico to near-bankruptcy. To this we can add an increase in unemployment and a decrease in productivity. This Mexican miracle devalued the peso from $12.50 to the dollar to $20.00, and foreign debt, at the beginning of his sex-enio of $6 billion (U.S.), had increased to $20 billion (U.S.) (300 percent) when he left office. Twenty billion dollars may not seem much by today's standards, but not so back in 1976, especially considering the size of the Mexican economy. It was a miraculous accomplishment only to be outdone by his successor.

Echeverría envisioned himself as a champion of the third world and the creator of a true socialist state. To this end, he financed and built a lavish Cuban embassy in Mexico City as a gift from the Mexican people. He embarked on building a "University of the Third World," where students from underdeveloped countries could come and learn the ways of socialism. Today, the university lies in ruins. The grandiose project was a total folly. He also thought it was a good idea to bail out companies that were going broke to give the illusion of low unemployment and an economy on the upswing. After all, wasn't that the responsibility of a socialist state?

To make sure the world understood his socialist credentials, he not only embraced Castro's Cuba but also supported the Chilean socialist regime of Salvador Allende Gossens. When Allende was killed during Gen. Augusto José Ramón Pinochet Ugarte's coup, Echeverría offered political asylum to the remnants of his government, as well as to Chileans who fled the Pinochet dictatorship. Many came to Mexico and now consider Mexico their home.

His next move was to invite the Palestinians to open a Palestine Liberation Front office in Mexico City. When the General Assembly of the United Nations tried passing a vote branding Israel a Zionist nation, Mexico voted in favor of the resolution, believing that somehow Mexico would not pay the price from the large Jewish community in the United States. What Echeverría forgot was that Jews owned a great number of travel agencies and wholesale travel companies. They immediately boycotted travel to Mexico. In response, ex-President Miguel Alemán Valdés, at the time director of the Mexican National Tourism Council, was forced to travel to the United States and beg forgiveness in a series of press conferences.

One of Echeverría's most despicable acts was an attack against the environment. While flying over the interior of the country, he noticed vast areas covered by forests. He was said to have remarked, "Who claimed that Mexico is running out of space for its people to live in? Look at all those useless green forests." He went on to create a special commission to defoliate the forests and make way for the campesino, supposedly capable of converting these areas into productive farmlands.

By this time, leaders in his own party, the private sector, and even the intellectual left were questioning Echeverría's leadership capabilities. His enemies should have known better. They were in for a few surprises.

The city of Monterrey, the industrial center of Mexico, was run by interlocking families of hardworking industrialists centered on the Garza Sada family. The patriarch was Eugenio Garza Sada, a successful businessman and philanthropist. In 1943 he founded the Tecnológico de Monterrey, a privately funded university that now has thirty-three campuses in twenty-five cities and is still expanding. Among his many other accomplishments, he established a regional social security safety net system for workers in his and his family's factories, to the chagrin of the centralist government based in Mexico City. He was not only very powerful, but the city of Monterrey, with its capitalistic bent and American work ethic, stood in stark contrast to the corruption and mismanagement emanating from the capital.

On the morning of September 17, 1973, a guerrilla group calling themselves Liga 23 de Septiembre ambushed the Garza Sada motorcade in a failed kidnapping attempt. In the ensuing shootout, Eugenio Garza Sada was killed. His popularity was such that over 200,000 people attended his funeral.

Information came to light that the federal government knew about the planned kidnapping but did nothing. It was no secret that Echeverría had no love for the politically independent industrialists in the north. Many Mexicans were convinced that the assassination had the president's fingerprints all over it. Wherever the truth lies, the Monterrey industrialists had just learned that there was no such thing as political or economic independence in Mexico.

To make sure the politicians from local, state, and federal levels understood the facts of political life under his autocratic regime, Echeverría created covert enforcement brigades to control his potential enemies. Originally called Los Halcones (the Falcons), they were made up of undesirables, many of them young criminals who received a "get out of jail free card" as an alternative to prison. Their orders were to infiltrate political demonstrations and pick out the leaders so they could be arrested. Their second function was to agitate any peaceful political demonstration and turn it into a violent confrontation against government anti-riot forces known as granaderos. When peaceful demonstrations turned violent, they inevitably lost the support of the public.

When Echeverría became president, the newly appointed federal security chief, Miguel Nazar Haro, was ordered to take Los Halcones one step further and create various contingents of enforcers capable of disciplining political dissidents around the country. They were known as La Brigada Blanca (the White Brigade).

The organization became a secret political law enforcement group for the express purpose of keeping any kind of political malfeasance in check by means of extortion, kidnappings, and violence. Not quite at the level of "death squads," this paramilitary collection of trained thugs became effective in getting the government's message across.

If, for example, a state governor was out of line with the administration, La Brigada Blanca might, with the approval of the Ministry of Interior, kidnap the governor's son and hold him for ransom until the governor changed his political ways. This was just one of the many methods used to eliminate those who harbored any thoughts of opposing Echeverría's dictatorial rule. La Brigada Blanca continued during the next regime, under President José López Portillo.

◆

While living in Guadalajara, capital of the western state of Jalisco, I was invited by a politically well-connected friend to attend an afternoon party at an abandoned hacienda. When we arrived, I noticed two armed guards at the entrance.

"Where have you brought me?" I asked with growing alarm.

My friend laughed. "Just furthering your education."

We entered an open courtyard with around twenty surly types milling around, drinking beer and tequila.

It must have been the look on my face that caused a dwarfish individual to approach me.

"What's wrong *amigo*, you don't like what you see?" I found myself staring at an unshaven man, barely five feet tall. "I think you are looking down on us. I view this as a total lack of respect considering you are here at the invitation of a friend and have been welcomed into my home."

By this time I was in a panic, but my friend started to laugh. This was soon followed by my host joining in. "Scared you, didn't I, gringo. My name is Don Chevo. . . . C'mon, have a tequila." He shook my hand and drew me towards him. "You ever hear of La Brigada Blanca? Well, I'm the commander in this region of the country."

Once the ice was broken, Don Chevo started to boast.

"All these women are my wives," he said and laughed. "*Más o menos*, well, sort of."

He then went on to explain that he was curious to know what would happen if he shot someone lying on the floor in the head. "Would the head bounce, or just stay put?" His eyes narrowed and he suddenly got serious. "You think we're a bunch of *maleantes* (bad hombres)? I can see it in your face." He then gestured to a well-muscled individual, whose head disappeared into his shoulders in the absence of a neck, to come over and join us. He could have been a linebacker in the NFL. "This is one of my sons. I think there are four others around here somewhere."

After the introduction, he ordered his son to tell me about the proudest moment of his life. The answer had obviously been rehearsed.

"When I was being trained at the Marine base in Quantico, Virginia, I competed in a pistol shooting competition." He smiled. "I won."

Don Chevo stared at me, poking his finger in my chest. "You see, my friend, nothing is what it seems to be. Your country is not better than mine. There are no clean hands in this business, especially when it comes to you gringos."

Since this incident happened in Guadalajara, I should mention that President Echeverría's wife was also from that city. María Esther Zuno Arce never allowed anyone to refer to her as the first lady. She insisted on being called *compañera* (comrade), in the classic greeting between leftists, communist revolutionaries, and fellow travelers. She was strong willed and always tried to give the impression that she was a woman of the people, despite the wealth she and her husband accumulated by illicit means during his presidency. The *mala lenguas* (wagging tongues) claimed she never wore mini-skirts so as not to show off her *cojones*.

In 1992, her brother, Rubén Zuno Arce, was convicted by a California court and sentenced to life in prison for being the leader of the Guadalajara drug cartel, and for the torture and murder in 1985 of Enrique Camarena, a DEA officer. One of his associates was Joaquín "El Chapo" Guzmán Loera, today one of the most wanted drug lords involved in the dirty war along the U.S./Mexican border. In 2009 Guzmán gained notoriety when *Forbes* magazine named him the 701st richest man in the world. He was recently upgraded to number 70.

◆

Pretending to be a socialist hardly stopped Echeverría from being one of the most corrupt presidents in Mexican history when it came to self-enrichment. When he left the presidency he owned properties all over Mexico, especially in some of the more expensive neighborhoods in Mexico City, the resort town of Cuernavaca, and most of the upscale beach resorts, among them Cancún and Ixtapa. Yet he always pretended to be a man of the people, in the vein of Salvador Allende and Fidel Castro.

After he retired from office, he continued to be a political force behind the scenes. He became the leader of the PRI's old guard of dinosaurs but rarely appeared in public, preferring to run his business from behind the walls of his fortress home.

In 2005 and 2006, the Mexican government charged him with homicide for the key role he played in the Tlateloco massacre in 1968. Though never cleared of the charges, the Supreme Court kept him from coming to trial based on a thirty-year statute of limitations. The state then changed the charges to genocide, which has no statute of limitations. The presiding judge, despite the law, decided there was a statute of limitations, and Echeverría never came to trial for his alleged crimes. Exposing these past violations of basic human rights was not deemed to be in the nation's best interest.

When he left the presidency in 1976, Echeverría named as his successor his close friend, José López Portillo, a man with little-to-no political experience. I remember at the time the prevailing thinking was the country's future could only get better. López Portillo was more of a technocrat than a politician. In this the nation was proven wrong. If Echeverría was largely a disgrace to the nation, López Portillo was his alter ego.

The Buffoon

José López Portillo was president of Mexico from 1976 to 1982. By the time he came to power the country was already embroiled in the economic and financial mess left by his predecessor. The peso was in free fall and the foreign debt in need of immediate action. The year 1976 was merely the prelude to further disasters. The Mexican manufacturing base was becoming outdated due to the scarcity of entrepreneurs willing to invest, combined with the lack of hard currency to buy imported machinery. The "import substitution plan"* had run its course. High tariffs to keep Mexican manufacturers competitive were no longer stimulating domestic production and the necessary investment that went with it. Added to these woes, the government refused to carry out a tax reform that could stimulate the economy. Instead, the new regime increased its reliance on expensive loans in the international capital markets. Interest rates were going up as the risk of lending money to Mexico increased. Getting one's hands on hard currency, such as U.S. dollars, was becoming expensive.

On the positive side, tripling the production of crude oil under the Pemex leadership of Jorge Díaz Serrano and making Mexico the fourth-largest producer in the world brought on the following boast from López Portillo: "In the world of economics, the world is divided in two . . . those that have oil and those that don't. And we have it!" There was no question that oil was keeping the Mexican economy afloat.

López Portillo followed this statement with more government spending and foreign borrowing against the oil bonanza. The economy overheated and when oil prices fell; Mexican and foreign investors panicked.

During his term of office, López Portillo's ego and nepotism knew no bounds. When Pope John Paul II visited Mexico, López Portillo insisted the Pope pay him a personal visit at Los Pinos, the Mexican White House. The reason, he explained, was so the Pope could give his mother a private mass. This action offended the Mexican faithful and resulted in a public outcry. López Portillo responded, "Why does the public care? I'm willing to pay for it."

Once elected, López Portillo appointed one of his childhood buddies, Arturo "El Negro" Durazo Moreno, chief of the Mexico City Police Department, elevating him to the status of army general, despite Durazo never having been in the military. This was the same man that eleven months earlier had been indicted by a U.S. grand jury on narcotraffic charges. As Mexico City's chief of police, Durazo became rich from extortion and drug trafficking. He once boasted that the heroin confiscated in the film *The French Connection* (1971) amounted to what he sold in one day. He built a huge vacation home, a replica of the Parthenon in Athens, Greece, in the beach resort town of Zihuatanejo, where it sits in ruins, having never been occupied.

---

* Import substitution: Everything imported that could be made in Mexico carried prohibitive high tariffs to protect the globally noncompetitive Mexican manufacturer.

López Portillo then went on to name his son, José Ramón, undersecretary of the treasury, claiming, "My son is the pride of my nepotism."

Other family members who benefited were his sister, Alicia, who became his personal assistant. Another sister, Margarita, was head of the General Directorate of Radio, Television and Motion Pictures, the government entity in charge of censorship. She was thoroughly loathed by most of those associated with motion pictures and the media for her capricious rulings and autocratic manner. Her hobby was writing amateurish screenplays, insisting they be produced for the big screen. Those producers who refused did so at their own risk. Only two of her scripts became films, both of which flopped at the box office.

López Portillo's most blatant appointment was making his mistress, Rosa Luz Alegría Escamilla—ex-wife of one of President Luis Echeverría's sons, minister of tourism. She has the distinction of being the first woman in Mexico to serve in an executive cabinet position. Another of his mistresses was a third-rate Italian actress named Sasha Montenegro. She was known for making films in which she appeared semi-nude and nude. Her career flourished during her lover's presidency. When he stepped down at the end of his sexenio he divorced his flamboyant wife and married Sasha, who bore him two sons. She in turn divorced López Portillo and helped relieve him of as much money as she could get her hands on. In the end, it was simply the transfer of illegally begotten wealth from one set of hands to another.

One can understand why he had at least two mistresses who were constantly in the public eye. His wife, Carmen Romano de López Portillo, was the perfect caricature of an overdressed floozy. Her flamboyant hairdos and excessive makeup made her the absolute antithesis of a first lady. Behind her back she was known as "Red Shoes" in reference to the prostitutes who hung out on the street corners of Mexico City.

I was having lunch at a well-known Acapulco restaurant when she and her entourage made their entrance, insisting she have at a table with an ocean view. None were available, so two tables occupied by visiting American tourists were asked to move.

◆

In 1981 López Portillo guaranteed there would be no monetary devaluation of the peso. "*Defenderé el peso como un perro* (I will defend the peso like a dog)!"

he proclaimed. The dog eventually turned on him, first biting his leg and then his rear end.

By 1982, at the end of his tenure in office, capital flight that began as a trickle became a deluge, followed by the suspension of foreign debt payments in August of that year. López Portillo was forced to devalue the peso by 40 percent. From that moment on, until his death, whenever he appeared in public people barked like dogs in ridicule of his promise. He took refuge in his mansion on top of a hill, which thereafter was known as La Colina del Perro (the Hill of the Dog).

President José López Portillo's last act was on September 1, 1982, during his last state of the union speech to the nation. "*Ya nos saquearon. México no se ha acabado. ¡No nos volverán a saquear!* (We have already been ransacked. Mexico is not finished. They will not ransack us again!)"

With that statement, he then went on to blame the bankers and the private sector for Mexico's financial crisis, claiming, "I'm responsible for manning the rudder, but not for the storm." With that, he proceeded, while his audience listened in amazement and shock, to nationalize the entire Mexican banking system.

If the Mexican people could not get their revenge on this political buffoon, his children from his two wives were far more adept. They relieved him of most of his fortune. To add insult to injury, when López Portillo tried to sell his collection of Fernando Botero paintings, said to be worth a small fortune, he was in for a surprise. Botero himself came to look at the collection, shook his head, and informed the art world that they were all fakes. Even the CIA got its licks in with a secret intelligence assessment produced just over a year after López Portillo's successor, President Miguel de la Madrid, took office. In "The Outlook for Mexico," April 25, 1984, the agency concluded,

> Pressures on former President López Portillo to increase public spending became irresistible after Mexico became a net oil exporter, but the former President's tendency toward grandiose scheming contributed significantly to the disastrous boom and bust cycle that followed. [. . .]
>
> Virtually all social and economic groups have had to accept declining standards of living, scale down their expectations, and compete for benefits and opportunities in a negative sum economic environment. De la Madrid [his successor] has struggled to preserve social equilibrium and to restore public confidence in the political system.

This de la Madrid was able to do with a modicum of success.

When López Portillo died, Phil Gunson of the *Guardian* newspaper wrote on February 20, 2004, "Despite stiff competition for the distinction, José López Portillo, who has died aged 83, was probably the most heartily despised former president in Mexican history."

In the National Security Archives in Washington, D.C., Kate Doyle, an analyst of the López Portillo presidency, wrote the following summary of his presidential years:

> The death of former President José López Portillo on February 17 [2004] unleashed a torrent of public rage and bitter obituaries in the Mexican press. The most prominent opinion makers called him a Machiavelli, a megalomaniac, a gambler, a disaster; mere hours after he passed away, politicians were lining up before the television cameras to offer scathing critiques of his government, his personality. He did not receive a State funeral.
>
> The anger stemmed not only from the actions—or inactions—of López Portillo during his sexenio. Yes, he squandered the wealth of the country's newly discovered oil reserves through mismanagement and corruption. Yes, he engineered the perpetuation of the PRI's "perfect dictatorship," while masquerading as a political reformer. Yes, he led Mexico by the nose into the most spectacular economic failure of the western hemisphere at the time, with fiscal policies that culminated in the country's humiliating bankruptcy and debt crisis of 1982.

What is curious is that nobody seriously trashed him until after his death. Such is Mexican politics. Those that benefited from his sexenio only came out of hiding after he was wearing the wooden overcoat.

If Mexico was forced to suffer through twelve years of these two error-ridden performances, it took a cataclysm to bring the era to an end. It took place in September of 1985.

18

The Final Blow

◆

SEPTEMBER 19, 1985, LOOKED TO BE JUST another sunny day in Mexico City with the probability of rain in the afternoon, common during the summer rainy season. The early-morning dew gave the buildings and tree-lined streets a silvery glistening effect before the giant city awakened to another frantic traffic free-for-all, accompanied by the incessant car honking the city is famous for. And with it, the never-ending gray smog shroud that cast a pallor city dwellers have learned to accept as normal.

But this was early morning, and the giant was still slumbering, hardly the harbinger of an unimaginable tragedy about to strike. Some later believed it was the ancient Aztec gods themselves who were responsible for the coming disaster.

For me this day consisted of overseeing a conference for meeting and convention planners sponsored by a leading U.S. trade publication. Breakfast was at 7:30 a.m. on the top floor of a hotel some distance from the center of the tragedy about to strike. My partner and I were in the hotel lobby, because as Mexican representatives of the trade magazine it was our job to make sure the event went smoothly. That meant escorting the attendees to the elevators on their way to the top floor of the hotel for a breakfast hosted by the minister of tourism.

At exactly 7:19 a.m., the building started to tremble. Unlike most earthquakes, the oscillating movement seemed to last forever. The first thing I noticed was that the water in the pool surrounding a large fountain was rocking like a giant baby's cradle and splashing over the edge in small waves. Next, a fine white powder appeared on the shoulders of my partner's black suit, followed by large flakes of white plaster like unsifted flour that came drifting down from the ceiling.

The lights temporarily went out. I hated to think how those people caught in elevators were feeling. Loud creaking followed, the sound of metal resisting the twisting motion of the seismic event, intermingled with the muted screams of people becoming aware that this was not going to be just another quake.

As quickly as it started, the eerie groaning of the building and the crashing sound of unsecured objects falling to the floor suddenly turned to silence. The emergency lights came on, and in general everything, except the chaotic scene around us, went back to normal. Of course, it was only an illusion.

To understand why our hotel only suffered minor damages, one has to understand the subsoil makeup of the city itself. Most of Mexico City is built on a series of dry lake beds. The soft underbelly in the slowly sinking downtown area is a dried-up lake filled with silt and volcanic clay, which trembles like jelly when earthquakes hit. This forces buildings to sway. The longer they sway, the better chance they have of structural failure and eventual collapse. Large sections of the city, especially on higher ground, are better protected from the oscillating effects of an earthquake. It is the lower areas, built on sediment that were once the five lakes of the original center of the Aztecs, called Tenochtitlan, that were doomed to suffer the most.

The BBC reported, "A massive earthquake has hit Mexico with the epicenter not far from its capital, Mexico City, causing untold casualties and widespread damage. . . . The quake was felt as far north as Houston, Texas, 745 miles (1,200 km) away, and in Guatemala City 621 miles (1,000 km) to the south."

That evening as my partner and I returned to our office, we found an entirely different story in our neighborhood from what we had experienced at the hotel. As we drove along the darkened, near-empty streets, our first challenge was to circumvent the maze of rubble strewn around us. The streets we were driving through looked like downtown Beirut on a bad day. A gray, brooding darkness enveloped the area. When we got to our building, where I lived while in the city, we had to gingerly feel our way up the five floors, immersed in darkness, until we reached our penthouse-office-apartment. The elevator was out of commission. The neighborhood was blacked out.

Using candles and a flashlight, we began our cursory inspection of the damage. The furniture seemed in good shape, but everything hanging on the walls had fallen or was askew. We both suddenly felt dizzy. We later learned the building was leaning ten degrees, but not enough to be uninhabitable. Like sailors on a rolling ship we soon got our sea legs. The city government later froze the rents on buildings that were damaged but not condemned.

The following day, camera in hand, I took a walk through the streets of Colonia Juárez and Roma, two of the hardest hit boroughs in the city. Besides the rubble, there were buildings that had simply collapsed inwards. The floors were there, but the space between them had disappeared. They looked like a stack of metal-and-concrete pancakes. One building I photographed revealed two bodies beneath the rubble. I only noticed the bodies later, when I processed the black and white film. I never saw them when I took the picture. They seemed to be desperately clawing their way to safety. Seconds more and they might have made it. How many bodies were entombed inside, I never knew.

As I walked along, I saw that most of the sidewalks were ruptured, in many cases as if a series of giant fists had punched their way through the concrete from below. Many streets were closed for fear of looting.

There is no way I can describe seeing a tree-lined neighborhood, most of the homes built during the Porfirian era, now broken, the streets destroyed, slabs of concrete and partial brick walls everywhere around me. The destruction did not take place over a period of months, weeks, or days; it happened in less than two minutes.

Dan Rather, an American newscaster aboard a helicopter, described the city as being stepped on, leaving "a giant footprint" that leveled almost everything in sight. Yet, large parts of the city were unscathed. The most dangerous occurrence in the surrounding neighborhoods was falling glass from broken windows.

I later found out that two of my favorite watering holes were gone. The Del Prado Hotel across from Alameda Park was destroyed. The main attraction of this hotel was sitting in the downstairs cocktail lounge and looking at Diego Rivera's famous fresco, "A Dream of a Sunday Afternoon in Alameda Park," which stretched fifty feet across and thirteen feet high. The fresco depicted the major figures in Mexican history during the Porfirian era and the Mexican revolution, centered on the skeleton of a woman dressed in a flamboyant turn of the century gown known as *la calavera catrina*, parodying vanity and also signifying death. Luckily, the fresco survived and can now be seen in its own building across the street from where the downtown Del Prado Hotel once stood.

My favorite get-together lounge was the Maya Bar in the Hilton Hotel on the corner of the two main avenues in Mexico City, Paseo de la Reforma and Insurgentes. The hotel was eventually torn down due to extensive earthquake damage. For me, it was the end of an era.

Sooner or later statistics are gathered and made public, as with most disasters. Only in this way can the authorities assess the extent of the mayhem resulting from the "giant footprint" of destruction the quake left behind.

There has never been an accurate count in terms of deaths. Figures range from 10,000 to 30,000. Whatever the actual count, experts say it was low for such a catastrophic event. Most agree that the timing was essentially the reason. At 7:19 a.m. most people were still in their homes. The office buildings most affected were nearly empty. Many of the neighborhoods outside the downtown area suffered hardly any damage.

The city established the Metropolitan Commission for Emergencies of the Federal District/Mexico City comprising the different government entities involved in rescue operations and damage control. They reported that over 720,000 tons of debris was removed in the first six weeks. There were 2,831 buildings damaged, 880 of which were beyond repair; 516,000 square meters (5,160,000 square feet) of asphalt had to be replaced; and 1,687 schools were in need of repair, affecting over 1.5 million students. Around 200,000 jobs were lost. These statistics did not include damaged water mains and drainage pipes, hospitals, electricity, public transportation, and other city services in need of repair.

The most important statue in Mexico City is El Ángel de la Independencia (The Angel of Independence), built in 1910 to commemorate the centennial of Mexico's War of Independence. Atop this statue stands the figure of a woman known as Winged Victory, weighing seven tons and made of bronze covered in 24K gold. During the great earthquake of 1957, she toppled over into the Paseo de la Reforma.

From that moment on, when the city trembled, people rushed out to see if the statue was still in place. Seeing her, city dwellers were assured the earthquake was not to be feared. In the 1985 earthquake, the worst in Mexico's history, the Ángel—as most Mexicans know her—stayed in place. Supposedly a good omen, it turned out not to be true. A major tragedy was in the making.

Over the course of this book I have time and time again used the words "institutionalized corruption" as one of the more obvious hidden aspects of those masks the Mexican people hide behind. This earthquake, as if the ancient gods had planned it—as so many Mexicans came to believe—lay bare the criminality behind the faulty construction of countless government buildings and schools that were beyond repair.

The construction specifications were designed to withstand seismic activities. When inspecting many of these broken government buildings and public schools, officials discovered that the required steel columns and rebar reinforcements were simply not there. The builders had cheated for personal gain. Building inspectors had been paid to look the other way. Much of the public's money used in building these substandard constructions ended up in the hands of corrupt politicians and their cronies in the construction business. As a result, people died and many countless thousands more could have if the quake had taken place later in the day. Corruption was acceptable, but not when the lives of hardworking citizens and students were put at risk. These exploiters of human life had gone too far.

The news media beat the drums of outrage. Those responsible had to be held accountable, as well as those who had turned a blind eye. Yet, when the outrage ran its course, nobody could name one person or construction company, of all those involved, that faced criminal charges in a court of law. Despite a continuous bombardment of public denials, corruption has always been acceptable behavior. In the end, it was simply business as usual.

I can say, with some degree of historical latitude, that, like the Phoenix, the mythical bird that dies in flames and is reborn from the ashes, Mexico City was ready for a new beginning. It was as if the Aztec gods of yore rained death and destruction on years of accumulated ills, resulting in an intolerable level of national mismanagement and corruption. Mexico needed to change its ways. This blatant example of institutionalized corruption was one tragedy that could not go unnoticed. Maybe Rivera got it right when he painted the skeleton dressed in a white gown as the centerpiece of his famous mural. Rather than signifying the death of the Porfiriato, it now marked the slow death of the 1910 post-revolutionary era and the beginning of a Mexico on the road to change. The process was a slow and costly one.

WINDS OF CHANGE
(1988 TO PRESENT)

B Y THE LATE 1980s AND GOING INTO THE '90s, Mexico's traditional socialism was in a quandary. The Cold War had ended. What Ronald Reagan
called the Evil Empire was on its deathbed. In the crumbling Soviet Union,
perestroika and glasnost were breaking down the walls of isolationism and
censorship in all walks of life. The final blow came in 1989 with the tearing
down of the Berlin Wall, the last vestige of Soviet domination over Eastern
Europe. The victors and the vanquished were not about countries but ideas. In
this conflict between East and West over the minds of human beings, communism lost and capitalism was crowned the victor. By September of 1991, many
of the republics of the Soviet Union demanded and gained their independence.

Globalization, and the free-market concept for industrialized and developing nations, was on the march. This trend soon took on a name—neoliberalism.
If its proponents saw the future in terms of a free-market world economy, its
detractors saw this movement as a formula for widening the divide between the

haves and the have-nots. The latter became the populist movement that spread across Latin America. An ideological war was in the making, and Mexico found itself in the middle of the battle.

Against this background, Mexico had its own glasnost. It became known as *la apertura* (the opening). It was hardly about liberating the country from censorship, as in the Soviet Union, it was about opening Mexico's borders to the winds of globalization. Some supported Mexico's move toward the twenty-first century, but as with most changes, there were also those bitterly opposed.

For Mexico, without going into the gray areas, the ultimate symbol of neo-liberalism became known as NAFTA, the North American Free Trade Agreement, between Mexico, the United States, and Canada. The first spokesman of the populist opposition was subcomandante Marcos, the leader of the Chiapas uprising under the banner of Ejército Zapatista de Liberación Nacional (the Zapatista Army of National Liberation, EZLN). NAFTA went into effect on January 1, 1994; the Zapatista uprising occurred on the same day.

Marcos, in August of 1996, at the Zapatista-sponsored Encuentro Intercontinental por la Humanidad contra el Neo-liberalismo (the Intercontinental Encounter for Humanity against Neo-liberalism), stated, "What neo-liberalism offers is to turn the world into one big mall where they can buy Indians here, women there, children, immigrants, workers or even a whole country like Mexico." Political hyperbole became the mantra of this new movement.

Looking back over Mexican history, it is sometimes hard to know who were the heroes and who were the villains. But then, what could be more Mexican?

19

The Mexican Napoleon
(1988–1994)

◄►

THERE IS A FAMOUS MEXICAN SAYING, "*Ahora te toca bailar con la fea* (It's your turn to dance with the ugly one)." With the advent of a new world order after the fall of the Soviet Union, there were many countries ill prepared to march forward into the arms of the new economic realities of globalization and neoliberalism. Mexico was one of those nations. Many sectors, especially those that controlled the traditional corporate vote,* were aghast at the thought that Mexico might join the neoliberalist ranks. Mexico's brand of socialism, and an economy whose "import substitution program" had restricted foreign invest-ment, was ready to resist any kind of change.

President Miguel de la Madrid (1982–1988) had already taken the first steps to opening the doors of Mexico's traditional economic isolationism. If this transformation was to continue, somebody needed to step forward and dance with the ugly one, for economic and industrial change had an unwelcome partner named resistance and turmoil.

For the intelligentsia, the winds of change had to be neutralized if Mexico was to maintain its revolutionary values. By 1988 a new presidential candidate, the anointed tapado, was about to receive the dedazo, the pointed finger of the PRI and the outgoing president. If Mexico was the nation that fell asleep in the past, this new president was obligated to take on the task of shaking her awake to the new global realities. To put the brakes on the new global market forces, the upcoming 1988 elections needed to defeat the PRI candidate. The only viable alternative was the newly formed Partido Revolucionario Demócrata (PRD), founded by Cuauhtémoc Cárdenas—the son of that Mexican icon Lázaro Cárdenas—which represented the far left and was in opposition to the new global economic realities.

---

* Corporate vote: primarily state-owned companies, labor unions, the bureaucracy, and the campesino.

If we believe in the Napoleon syndrome that suggests people of short stature have giant egos with strong tendencies to always impose their will, then this complex would accurately describe Carlos Salinas de Gortari, the presidential candidate of the PRI. He also had large ears, which gave him a funny bat-like look that made him stand out, much like Adolf Hitler's signature moustache.

Born in 1948, Salinas de Gortari's meteoritic rise inside the federal government gained him the presidency at the age of forty. Unlike many of his predecessors he was well educated, receiving a degree in economics from UNAM at the age of twenty-one, and four years later a master's degree from Harvard's Kennedy School of Public Administration.

Salinas de Gortari never held an elected office, although he was appointed Secretario de Planeación y Presupuesto (Secretary of Planning and Budget), a new government agency created by his predecessor President Miguel de la Madrid. This background did not prepare him to be a politician that could relate to the electorate, but when it came to finances and economics, he was in his element. Nobody questions that he was the definitive technocrat.

Salinas de Gortari initially became unpopular in the presidential election held in July 1988, when he was suspected of losing the popular vote to the PRD and its charismatic candidate, Cuauhtémoc Cárdenas. Mexicans were obviously getting fed up with the PRI and its unending hunger for raiding the treasury, much like pigs slurping in the trough. Only a leftist government with an honest candidate like Cárdenas could reverse the trend.

For the PRI to lose an election was unthinkable, and for Salinas to win by such a small margin, which necessitated considerable computer vote rigging before he could be declared the victor, was unheard of. Presidential candidates from the PRI were usually elected by anywhere from 70 to 90 percent of the vote.

Many people to this day are convinced that Salinas lost the election. The left always considered him to be an illegitimate president who came to power only through electoral fraud. This criticism surfaces to this day. One can only speculate what might have happened had Mexico turned the clock back with another Cárdenas as president. What nobody can refute is that Salinas was never a popular president.

Once sworn in, he embarked on a series of necessary, and in some cases overdue, reforms. While many were popular with some, they were controversial and generally unacceptable to others, especially with those that constantly perpetuated the slogans of revolutionary rhetoric in the media and in academia. On the other extreme there were the powerful national unions.

The Salinas reforms can be broken down into three areas, sometimes referred to as the *salinastroika*, that cover the religious, political, and economic sectors.

Religious Reform

Recognizing that most Mexicans adhered to the Roman Catholic faith and taking into account the importance of the Virgin of Guadalupe as the patron saint of Mexico, Salinas decided to roll back many of the anticlerical laws established by Benito Juárez in the Constitution of 1857 and the subsequent Constitution of 1917. He eventually opened diplomatic relations with the Vatican.

Despite the fact that anticlericalism was a leading principle of the Mexican Revolution, Salinas reversed course by reforming the Clerical Laws. Nuns and priests were once more allowed to appear publicly in their habits and clerical robes. They were allowed to vote. Parochial schools flourished, and many church buildings were privatized. In May 1990, Pope Paul II received an unofficial invitation to visit Mexico. The pope's visit was a complete public relations triumph. Millions of Mexicans cheered and wept with joy as he drove through the streets of Mexico City in his popemobile.

Many of the president's critics felt that opening the door to an official Catholic presence only strengthened the Partido de Acción Nacional (PAN), the conservative party supported by the church and Opus Dei.* In this assessment they proved to be right. The PAN took over the presidency in the year 2000 under President Vicente Fox. The same party went on to win the 2006 presidential elections under the leadership of Felipe Calderón.

In defense of these reforms, Mexico has one of the largest populations of Roman Catholic faithful in the world. However, the PRI and the PRD, which together made up a clear majority in the Senate and the Deputies Assembly, were hardly overjoyed with this development. They saw a clear threat in the resurgence of the Catholic Church and were convinced it was merely the first step in the Church's return to its traditional meddling in support of the conservative elements in the country. The seers were partially right. What Salinas did not take into consideration was that a growing number in the clergy were

---

* Opus Dei: usually refers to lay people doing the work of God. They are also the large financial contributors to the Catholic Church and, if allowed, wield considerable influence in politics.

converting to a new interpretation of Catholicism that became known as the Theology of Liberation. The "new catholicism" would have a profound effect on Mexico and many countries in Latin America.

Political Reform

In October 1990, Congress reformed the electoral system by creating an independent institution known as the Instituto Federal Electoral (IFE), no longer under the control of La Secretaría de Gobernación (Ministry of Interior), the political arm of the executive branch of the federal government. The new organization introduced a voter ID that became *la credencial única*, the official ID of the Mexican people. This national identification card automatically registers citizens into the electoral system free of any political affiliation or pressure. The new IFE went even further by taking over the funding and registration of all national political parties, as well as overseeing elections to make sure they were honest.

The results were immediate. In the presidential elections of 1994, for the first time Mexico invited international observers to be present. The elections were considered the fairest since the establishment of the PRI monopoly on politics. Transparency became a new buzzword and in 2000 opened the door to Mexico's first truly open presidential election.

Salinas also took on the unions, the most powerful being the STPRM, which controlled Pemex and was led by Joaquín Hernández Galicia, better known as La Quina. As previously noted, La Quina was a man who thought himself and his union more powerful than the president himself. Their union's strength was not only in numbers; they were the only ones capable of running Pemex, the petroleum monopoly and sacred cow of the revolution, which made the ridiculous claim of being the patrimony of the nation. If Pemex belonged to the people, the only benefits to the public were high gasoline prices.

La Quina made the decision to face off against Salinas. He claimed that the president was ruining Mexico through his program of privatization, of neoliberalism, and by being elected through voter fraud. He even made his accusations personal by charging the president with murdering the Salinas family's maid when he was a teenager. La Quina should have known better. You don't mess with a Napoleonic ego.

On January 10, 1989, Salinas sent the army to raid the STPRM union stronghold in Ciudad Madero in the northeastern state of Tamaulipas. After a firefight, La Quina and his confidants surrendered. Accused of murder and for having a cache of illegal arms, he was put on trial and sentenced to thirty-five years in prison. As a stalwart member of the PRI, La Quina's sentence was commuted after serving only five years.

Economic Reform (*La Apertura*/The Opening)

President Miguel de la Madrid, Salinas's predecessor, initiated the process of opening the Mexican border by lowering the tariffs of the protectionist policies of the past, which resulted in most privately owned Mexican companies being incapable of competing on the global stage. Most of these medium and small Mexican companies manufactured low-quality, overpriced products. By lowering tariffs, Miguel de la Madrid took the first steps to opening the Mexican economy to foreign competition. He also introduced liberal economic reforms that encouraged foreign investment, and initiated the privatization of government owned companies. As an example, the *paraestatales* (state-owned companies) were reduced from more than a thousand in 1982 to just over four hundred in 1988. What Miguel de la Madrid started, Salinas paid the price for; privatization may have been one of the reasons the PRI squeeked out such a narrow and questionable victory in the 1988 presidential elections. Salinas continued la apertura with terrible consequences to his popularity and to the Mexican middle class.

Unfortunately, Mexican industrialists did not realize what was happening in their own backyard. They did not imagine that globalization could become an unwanted guest sitting on their doorstep. With the coming of Salinas, Mexican factories started closing or were bought by far more efficient international companies that saw Mexico's tariff reductions as creating a more level playing field for foreign investment and the ability to compete with the previously government-protected companies. If the Mexican small- and medium-sized businesses were paying the price of globalization, the results of these changes conversely showed that the macroeconomic indicators for Mexico were never so bright.

For example, as a result of la apertura, inflation that reached 159 percent in 1987 had dropped to 7 percent by 1994. The devaluation of the peso, the lowest in two decades, was kept in check. The Salinas government even renegotiated Mexico's foreign debt.

The Mexican banking industry, which had been taken over by the state in 1982 during the regime of President José López Portillo, was privatized, though not returned to its original owners, opening the doors to takeovers by foreign banks. Leading the pack were the Spaniards, who seemed on a mission to regain their influence in Mexico. Hernán Cortés, disguised as a banker, was again conquering Mexico.

Salinas then took on the most controversial issue of all, that failed institution of the revolution known as the Agrarian Reform. La Desincorporación Ejidal (Disbanding the Ejido) in 1992 privatized the communal farm properties, allowing the campesinos to sell their properties and even take out mortgages.

"In the past," Salinas declared, "land distribution was a path of justice; today it is unproductive and impoverishing."

With the disbanding of the ejido came the elimination of subsidies in inefficient government-run processing and packaging plants, which ended up destroying the production and exports of canned products such as pineapple and other preserved fruits and vegetables. However, the idea that the ejido has disappeared from the Mexican landscape is false. Many of these communes have not gone through the legal process of privatization. This is especially true in the rural south where the campesinos, less educated than their northern brethren, still believe in the Agrarian Reform and the Revolution of 1910.

But the jewel in Salinas's crown had to be the signing of NAFTA, which went into effect January 1, 1994. After years of negotiation, Mexico, Canada, and the United States signed the first major free-trade agreement on this continent.* In anticipation of NAFTA, Salinas's administration was already on a dangerous spending spree to create the necessary infrastructure, most notably in the construction of new four-lane highways connecting Mexico's major cities with the border.

Although President Salinas had the cojones to put in place these reforms, history reminds us they came with a heavy price. Toward the end of his six-year term the economy started to unravel. The first and foremost problem was Salinas's vaulting ambition. He wanted to be remembered for taking Mexico from the third world into the first world without passing through the intermediate stage of an emerging nation. He intended to use the Mexican economic

---

* See Appendix 6.

success story as a career move after leaving office. He was already campaigning for the presidency of the newly formed World Trade Organization (WTO) to be launched at the beginning of 1995, the year after Salinas left office.

To try and accomplish his goals, he went on a spending spree to the point that the dollar reserves servicing Mexico's foreign debt were down to a mere nine billion dollars. This situation was not unusual at the end of a six-year presidential term. Past presidents spent as much as possible in their last elected year, without much thought to the future problems their successors would have to contend with. In Salinas's case, offsetting this dangerous situation was the fact that he counted on the continued influx of foreign capital investment into the expanding Mexican economy.

Much has been said about the eventual economic and financial meltdown of 1994. The disaster that followed, known as *la crisis de noviembre* (the November crisis) in Mexico and the "Tequila Effect" in South America, was exacerbated by global lack of confidence in the Mexican peso and the country's growing political instability. This political crisis was brought on by the EZLN uprising in Chiapas on January, 1, 1994, the day NAFTA went into effect. The timing was no coincidence. In March of that same year, an EZLN uprising preceded the assassination of Luis Donaldo Colosio, Salinas's chosen candidate for the next president. These two events, on top of the government's unchecked spending spree, created a lack of confidence in foreign investment and the financial markets in a country known for its political stability.

So why is Carlos Salinas so reviled by the country he served? The answers are not that difficult to understand if we untie the knots that make the Mexican narrative so convoluted.

I am convinced that Mexico's real hatred for Salinas resulted from what he wrought on the Mexican middle and lower-middle classes who were unable to compete in the global marketplace. Their livelihood came from small- and medium-sized companies that went broke or were bought up by foreign investors as a result of la apertura. If added to this one considers the financial meltdown of 1994 that rested squarely on Salinas's shoulders and the subsequent devaluation of the peso, it is not hard to understand why he is so disliked. The problem went even further. With the loss of confidence in the peso those Mexicans who had invested in La Bolsa Mexicana (the Mexican Stock Exchange) saw their savings wiped out in a matter of weeks.

During the Salinas presidency the growth of the middle class came to a standstill, at best. The biggest hit came in the loss of personal wealth. The worst scenario was that thousands of businesses disappeared leaving the owners, their families, and their extended families, in dire financial straits. Those who put their trust in the Mexican Stock Exchange were scrambling to stay out of the poorhouse. Many of those affected were under the impression that the protectionist economic policies of the Mexican government were entitlements, rather than bestowed government privileges with no guarantees.

Corruption came at the end of the Salinas era, and because he was so successful at this endeavor, his legacy became tainted with scandals of illegal enrichment on a grander scale than any past presidents in the PRI era. Corruption on a grand scale was galling to the Mexican people, especially after Salinas made it clear he had no intention of retiring from public life after completing his term of office, a tradition of all ex-presidents. Steal, but disappear, had always been considered acceptable behavior in a country where institutionalized corruption was a way of life. Yet what really made Salinas one of the most unpopular presidents in the annals of Mexico were the unpopular, but necessary, changes he made in a world on the fast track to globalization. Implementing these reforms was truly dancing with the ugly one.

At the center of the Salinas enrichment was the privatization of many state-owned companies that were placed on the auction block and sold to the highest bidder. The Mexican people are convinced that these bids were rigged and that President Salinas kept large blocks of stock, on top of receiving ample bribes, when these state institutions were sold to his cronies. The two best examples were Telmex, the state telephone monopoly, and Banamex, the largest Mexican government-owned bank.

In the case of the telecommunications giant Telmex, it is hard to believe that an entrepreneur named Carlos Slim* had the financial means or the technical know-how to buy a telephone company that would in 2007 lead to *Forbes* magazine naming him the richest man in the world, ahead of Warren Buffett and Bill Gates. Little is known about Slim's past except that he worked as a cab

---

* As of March 8, 2012, *Forbes* magazine continues to name Slim the richest man in the world at $69 billion. Bill Gates is a distant second with $61 billion.

driver and has an engineering degree from UNAM. An article that appeared in the March 14, 2007, edition of the *Los Angeles Times* under the heading "Once Upon a Time in North America—The Rise of Carlos Slim," claimed he had accumulated $400,000 (U.S.) by the age of twenty-six and from there went on a buying spree of companies. That's all the article says about accumulating enough wealth to be a serious contender for purchasing a telephone monopoly with millions of users. Once Slim knew he was on the inside track, raising the necessary cash with the aid of two foreign telephone giants became easy. Salinas's cut is not known.

The second major privatization was Banamex. One of the new major stockholders was Roberto Hernández Ramírez,* a man who, as claimed by one wag at a gathering of members at the exclusive Bankers Club, "has trouble paying his American Express bill." There were other nefarious deals that vaulted Carlos Salinas from an underpaid government servant to a man whose wealth could be measured in the hundreds of millions of dollars.

For many, Salinas was more reviled than Presidents Luis Echeverría and José López Portillo put together. At the end of his presidency he went into exile in Dublin, Ireland, a country that has no extradition laws with Mexico. His exile also ended any post-presidential aspirations. He eventually returned to Mexico despite antagonism from a public that wanted him brought to trial. He never answered for any of his crimes of enrichment by illicit means. Regardless of Salinas's ability to evade prosecution, his brothers Raúl and Enrique did not fare as well.

Raúl Salinas was sentenced to fifty years in prison, convicted of being *el autor intelectual* (the mastermind) behind the assassination of José Francisco Ruiz Massieu in Mexico City on September 28, 1994. Massieu was the brother-in-law to President Salinas and a member of the PRI party who had been nominated as the future majority leader of the Chamber of Deputies. Raúl Salinas was also convicted of self-enrichment while employed by his brother's administration. Some political pundits consider him to have been his brother's bagman. When arrested, Raúl Salinas had in his possession false passports and documents that led to secret and not-so-secret bank accounts under many different names. In Switzerland, the government impounded $90 million of his ill-gotten wealth,

---

* He partnered with Alfredo Harp Helú, who was later kidnapped, and helped bring on the financial crisis of 1994.

which eventually was returned to the Mexican government. The affair ended with a retrial, where his sentence was reduced by half after the courts deemed there was no clear motive for the assassination of his brother-in-law.

On December 6, 2004, Carlos Salinas's other brother, Enrique Salinas, was found murdered in his car with a plastic bag over his head. There seems to be no clear motive, and the murder has gone unsolved.

To date, Mexico has been unkind to Carlos Salinas de Gortari. Nobody can deny he made mistakes. Nobody can deny his self-enrichment by illegal means. Nobody can deny that the middle and lower-middle class took serious economic hits during his term of office. At the same time, he took a stagnant economy by the horns and instituted measures of reform that were unpopular but necessary in a world on the fast track to globalization.

He was never liked, but no one can say he wasn't effective. In spite of his gluttony for wealth, I believe time will vindicate many of the difficult decisions taken during his presidency. Maybe if he had not chosen to dance with the ugly one and just kicked the can of change down the road, his present place in history might have been different. But he chose to confront the nation's problems, including the creation of NAFTA, which made him a true malinchista in the eyes of those that embraced nationalism as the road to public acceptance.

20

1994—The Perfect Storm

—◆—

In politics there are no coincidences, only conspiracies.

LYNDON B. JOHNSON

Occasionally a historic monster earthquake causes the subsoil to tremble not once but many times in a series of aftershocks that compound the original damage. Such great damage is not caused only by nature on the rampage. In
history, too, unforeseen, man-made aftershocks can follow momentous political
upheavals, catching an unprepared nation off-guard and inevitably forcing change.

Such was the case with Mexico in the year 1994.

Much like a Shakespearean play, the opening scene established the dramatic premise that foreshadowed events to come. In the case of Mexico, the
presidency of Carlos Salinas de Gortari was entering the last year of his sexenio. Salinas was scheduled to leave office on December 1st, 1994; the timing
was perfect for a man with continued vaulting ambitions and the presidency of
the WTO in his grasp. But Shakespeare also wrote that "vaulting ambition" was
the undoing of such leaders.

Act I

With the signing of NAFTA between Mexico and Canada and the United States
on December 8, 1993, increased foreign investment, lower inflation, and a
more stable rate of foreign exchange for the peso, Mexico's future looked
bright indeed. Salinas then launched the final phase of what he believed was
going to be the legacy of his administration. With NAFTA to take effect on
January 1, 1994, Salinas decided to go on the traditional spending spree of the
last year of his administration. He gave little thought to the dangerous deple-
tion of Mexico's foreign reserves. With NAFTA looming, Mexico's northern

neighbors would rush to invest in the attractive manufacturing base Mexico had to offer. Unemployment figures would go down. Mexicans could count on higher wages working for foreign investors. More tax revenue would flow into the federal coffers.

There was nothing to worry about. Or so it seemed. Salinas believed this spending spree in public works and infrastructure would show the world that Mexico was a worthy partner in the community of emerging industrial nations. In anticipation of NAFTA, during the early 1990s Mexico made a huge investment in four-lane highways connecting the major Mexican cities to the border. The logistics of effective and rapid trailer transportation was one of the keys to the future success of this treaty.

Salinas seemed oblivious to the anti-malinchista undercurrent that prevailed in many political and social sectors of the nation. He seemed particularly detached from the undercurrents of political fervor that preferred socialism through nationalism to any kind of intervention of foreign ideas. There was nothing that exemplified this intervention more than NAFTA going into effect on January 1, 1994.

The opening act of this modern Shakespearean tragedy was clearly established. The stage was set for a perfect storm.

Act II

The day NAFTA officially went into effect, far away from the capital, the southern state of Chiapas suddenly began an uprising against the government. This largely indigenous chiapaneco population was not only living below the poverty line, but most of the available land for agricultural development was being exploited by a few privileged criollos.

The first thing to keep in mind is that the dismal social conditions in Chiapas had not worsened under the Salinas presidency. In fact, many believed the government was actually taking steps to improve matters. Regardless of whether conditions were getting better, staying the same, or getting worse, the timing of the Chiapas uprising on the day NAFTA went into effect is far too much of a coincidence to think it was not orchestrated from outside of the state of Chiapas. In retrospect the uprising turned out to have little to do with the plight of the Chiapaneco Indians but much to do with destroying NAFTA. The anti-malinchista forces were on the march.

The Chiapas uprising, and what became known as the EZLN, was led by a masked man calling himself subcomandante Marcos. Unlike the ragged campesino army, Marcos and the masked cadres he brought with him were at least six inches taller than the average foot soldier. He and his cadres were obviously outsiders who arrived to train the cannon fodder of the Chiapaneco army. Marcos and his cadres were dressed in black military regalia, which included combat boots, sophisticated communication phones, and the latest weapons. This was not the case with the indigenous insurgents. They wore the typical Indian dress of baggy white pants, shirt, and sandals and were armed with machetes or ancient single-shot rifles.

When subcomandante Marcos started spouting the revolutionary rhetoric that capitalism, neoliberalism, and globalization were the source of scores of social and economic evils, something was definitely wrong. His uneducated and near-illiterate followers, who for the most part spoke only their indigenous language, could hardly be expected to understand the complexities of these new political theories exploding across the world. Marcos was obviously talking to an audience far beyond the borders of Chiapas. Then there was the question of who was financing this armed insurrection, which has never been answered.

The next slap in the face for Salinas came from the Catholic Church under its new philosophy of social reform. Salinas's administration had been the architect of liberating the Catholic Church from the anticlerical laws in the Constitution of 1917. His government now saw this political initiative backfire. Traditionally, the Church had always supported conservative institutions, such as a strong centralized government and a private sector that included big business and landowners. Who else could meet the financial needs of the Catholic Church? Living in abject poverty, the Chiapas campesino certainly could not.

What became the Theology of Liberation was concentrated in the impoverished countryside of many countries in Latin America. These beliefs matched perfectly with the populist political dogma being foisted on the indigenous population of Chiapas by subcomandante Marcos and his ideologues.

The purpose of the church's Theology of Liberation emphasized the Christian mission to bring justice to the poor and oppressed, particularly through political activism. Its theologians consider sin the root source of poverty, recognizing sin as exploitive capitalism and class warfare by the rich against the poor. The most prominent of these theologians in Chiapas was the bishop of San Cristóbal de las Casas, Samuel Ruiz García. In time he became the lead negotiator between the centralized government in Mexico City and the uprising led by Marcos. Although supposedly impartial, it soon became obvious this new theology favored the demands of the insurgents.

With the support of the left-leaning national and international media that conveniently overlooked the subtleties behind the uprising's final intent, Chiapas soon became a major news story that criticized the federal government's injustices towards the poor and the downtrodden. In no time, the Chiapas story undermined Mexico's stability and international reputation. The result was that foreign investors were starting to be turned off to the Mexican opportunity offered by NAFTA. The reputation of a politically stable country was now being questioned by the same investors the nation was counting on.

To think most Mexicans supported NAFTA is to be in denial. The middle and lower-middle classes saw their economic well-being in jeopardy, confronted by the juggernaut of well-financed foreign competition. The ultra-nationalist intellectual left had always believed that Marxism, or at least socialism, was Mexico's road to the future. They opposed NAFTA and subsequently supported the Chiapas insurgency as a way to destroy, or at least cripple, the treaty. In this, they were partially successful. Everything that remotely could be branded as malinchismo, more so if it related to NAFTA and the age-old nemesis of *imperialismo yankee*, had to be avoided even if it meant the destruction of the nation's economy and its financial institutions. Having got the Chiapas uprising onto the world stage, the left was soon touting Marcos as the new Che Guevara.

How was the country to move forward by turning the clock of progress back to the days the nation fell asleep? Did the leftist ideologues really believe the retreat into economic isolation had a future? The answer to this mystery was as perplexing back then as it is today.

What has always surprised and confused me as a spectator of these events is why nobody has investigated who was behind Chiapas and where the necessary financing was coming from? Armed uprisings cost money. One has only to remember the advice given by Deep Throat to Bob Woodward and Carl Bernstein during President Nixon's Watergate scandal, "Follow the money."

To think that subcomandante Marcos was the sole force behind these events is also absurd. Eventually, Marcos was identified as Rafael Sebastián Guillén

Vicente, a graduate of UNAM, Mexico's national university and the breeding ground of future Mexican politicians and leftist radicals. Despite his crimes of sedition and armed revolt against the Mexican state, he has never been prosecuted by the federal government. If you add to this that the indigenous Chiapas campesino is still living below the poverty line, what can be considered the net benefit of the Chiapas uprising? The truth was a loss of confidence inside and outside of Mexico, and the first step in the economic and financial tragedy that followed.

Act III

Mexico next experienced a chain of events with near-catastrophic results to the Mexican financial markets and the foreign investment so necessary to replenish Mexico's dollar reserves. Here is what happened.

A series of car bombings took place in Mexico City and the interior of the country shortly after the commencement of the Chiapas uprising. The kidnapping of a billionaire banker—Alfredo Harp Helú, a close friend of President Salinas and one of the most important investors in Banamex* and Avantel, the second-largest telecommunications company in Mexico—foreshadowed events to come. Harp was kidnapped in Acapulco on March 14, 1994; his abductors asked for a ransom of $90 million. He was released 106 days later, after his family reputedly paid $30 million. The real effect of the kidnapping was to send the Mexican stock market into a free fall. The Mexican government, army, and security forces seemed to be losing control over the country. This was just the beginning.

In November 1993, President Salinas gave the dedazo to his successor. His name was Luis Donaldo Colosio, and like most presidential candidates within the never-ending PRI dictatorship, he was a close friend and political ally of the outgoing president. Not only had Colosio been Salinas's campaign manager, but during his administration Colosio held various important cabinet positions.

Tragedy struck on March 23, 1994, when at a political rally in Tijuana, across the border from San Diego, Colosio was assassinated by a lone gunman. The assassin, Mario Aburto Martínez, was immediately arrested. To this day, the reason for the assassination is cloaked in mystery.

---

* Banamex was bought by Citicorp in August 2001 for $12.5 billion (U.S.).

On April 28, just over a month later, one of the chief investigators in the Colosio assassination, Tijuana police chief José Frederico Benítez, was also murdered. If there was a connection, nothing was said officially. But, the murder of Colosio created plenty of speculation. In his book *Bordering on Chaos* Andrés Oppenheimer had this to say: "Colosio's death shook the country like no other news in recent history. It buried Mexico's pretension of being immune to the political violence that had long shaken Latin America. What was worse, the government appointed special prosecutor soon disclosed that there had been a concerted action to carry out the murder, fueling speculation that the hit had been commissioned by powerful establishment figures."

At the center of the storm was the Salinas conspiracy theory. According to this theory, Colosio had made speeches criticizing the excessive concentration of power in the executive branch of government and had promised a series of reforms, mainly, to end any vestige of authoritarianism by the ruling PRI party. These statements supposedly so outraged Salinas that he planned to have Colosio removed as a candidate by having him assassinated. These conjectures were never backed by facts.

If the question asked by investigators was, "Who benefits from this crime?" the last person they could point the finger at was Salinas de Gortari. The assassination cost him dearly, but that did not stop the conspiracy theorists from disseminating their insidious propaganda. Why would Salinas compound the insecurity of foreign and national investors who were already feeling the effects of the events in Chiapas? Regardless, investigators were still not dissuaded from centering their investigations on the president.

The next political aftershock was the high-profile assassination of José Francisco Ruiz Massieu, Salinas's former brother-in-law, on September 28, 1994. Raúl Salinas, the president's brother, was tried and convicted for masterminding his murder.

By this time, the Salinas's reputation for bringing Mexico into the family of first-world nations was in shambles. Not only had the flow of foreign capital dried up, but Mexican and foreign investors were converting their pesos to dollars. The Bank of Mexico's dollar reserves were getting dangerously low.

These events were merely the prelude to the final act of this Shakespearean tragedy. The final element of the perfect storm commenced in December

1994, shortly after Ernesto Zedillo Ponce de León, the new president of Mexico, took office.

Act IV

Ernesto Zedillo became president on December 1, 1994. He named Jaime Serra Puche as his new finance minister. Three weeks later, Serra Puche made a fatal mistake. Due to the economic crisis brought on by the disastrous events of 1994, and the fact that the treasury and foreign reserves were running on empty, the only solution was to crank up the presses and print more money. When that happens, currency devaluation has a tendency to follow. But Serra Puche's error was in announcing a devaluation before it actually took place. This became known as "The December Mistake."

The reaction was immediate. Foreign investment and Mexican capital fled the country. Those who could change pesos into dollars and other hard currency did so. The value of the peso officially dropped from 3 to 1 down to 10 to 1 to the dollar. Unofficially, the peso was trading at 30 to 1. Companies with dollar debts, and those importing supplies to run their plants, which had to be purchased in dollars, went into bankruptcy or faced the possibility of going out of business. The Mexican stock market plummeted. Inflation soon followed, increasing over 50 percent in the next few months.

The bad news was going to get worse. The meltdown of the Mexican financial markets and the economy was spreading across Latin America like the ripple effect from an underground earthquake. Like most disasters, it soon had a name—the Tequila Effect. The masterminds behind the Chiapas uprising couldn't have been more pleased. The winds of nationalistic populism versus globalization and neoliberalism were having a field day at the expense of a once-healthy nation.

While Act IV of this Shakespearean tragedy was taking place on President Zedillo's watch, the blame was laid squarely on the Salinas presidency. Zedillo suggested that the best thing for Salinas to do was go into voluntary exile, rather than face a nasty trial on that old catchall charge, self-enrichment by illicit means. This he did in Ireland, where he fell in love, remarried, and embarked on writing a thousand-page memoir, *Mexico, The Policy and Politics of Modernization*, in which he justified the actions of his presidency.

What Mexico needed to do was rid itself of this modern-day Shakespearean tragedy and think more in terms of a western, where at the last minute the cavalry comes to the rescue. There was indeed a white knight to come achargin' over the horizon, bearing the standard of the stars and stripes. To the chagrin of the intellectual left in Mexico City's upscale neighborhoods, watching their country implode without getting their hands anywhere near the fire, an American rescue operation was hardly in their playbook.

The Final Curtain

Leading the charge to save Mexico was none other than President William J. Clinton. He was well aware that a failed state on his southern border was unacceptable. There was too much at stake, especially with NAFTA on the line. A financial and economically healthy Mexico was essential for trade, which was at the core of relations with the United States.

When Congress refused to act, Clinton decided to exercise his right to executive power. *Time* magazine observed in an article titled, "Don't Panic: Here Comes Bailout Bill," which appeared February 13, 1995:

> With the Mexican peso sliding, only $3.5 billion left in Mexican currency reserves and financial markets throughout Latin America on the brink of collapse, the President last week invoked his executive authority to grant Mexico $20 billion in loans and loan guarantees as the centerpiece of a coordinated bailout. Following Washington's lead, the International Monetary Fund (IMF) agreed to provide Mexico with a further $17.8 billion, and the Swiss-based Bank for International Settlements kicked in an additional $10 billion.
>
> In the short term, the U.S.-led rescue saved Mexico from defaulting on $26 billion of the government's Tesobonos/bonds that came due this year—a disaster that would have driven the vast majority of foreign investors out of the country and much of the rest of Latin America. With the threat of default averted, the Administration argues, Mexico can begin to restore itself to health. Says Under Secretary Lawrence Summers, "the success of Mexico's economy now rests on Mexico."

Most skeptics in the financial markets and inside the Washington, D.C., beltway felt Clinton was throwing money down the drain. They would all be proven wrong. The high-risk Clinton bailout paid off. The Mexican financial markets and those throughout Latin America stabilized. NAFTA and foreign investment were once more on a roll. Mexico paid off its debt in less than two years. Unlike the classic Shakespearean tragedy, this story had a happy ending. Most important, there were lessons to be learned. Vaulting ambition by presidents with near-total dictatorial powers had to be avoided. Spending had to be kept under control. The time had come to open the election process. There was a need for a government in which the executive, legislative, and judicial branches maintained a balance of power. Unchecked corruption had to be brought under control if the cynicism that pervaded the Mexican people was to change. *Fútbol* (soccer) was the national sport, not tax evasion. Mexico finally decided, at least for the immediate future, not to repeat the mistakes of the past.

21

A New Beginning

◆

IF MEXICO WAS TO JOIN THE COMMUNITY of nations that could legitimately claim to be truly representative of the people, then Mexico needed to reform the electoral process. The time seemed right for that change.

The President of Transition

Vicente Fox Quesada was brought up on the family ranch near the town of San Francisco del Rincón, a short distance from the city of León, the shoe and western boot capital of Mexico. Throughout his life, the 1,220-acre Rancho San Cristóbal was the place he always called home. It was the one sanctuary he could retreat to, away from the public eye. The ranch raises cattle and ostriches and, in conjunction with one of his brother's farms, grows broccoli for export to Europe, Asia, and the United States.

The young Fox studied business administration at the Jesuit-run Universidad Ibero-Americano in Mexico City. Unlike most aspiring politicians in the past, he broke with tradition by not attending the UNAM. Politics seemed the furthest thing from his mind.

At the age of twenty-two he joined the Coca-Cola Company as a route supervisor, driving a delivery truck. During his travels through many of the villages and towns of Mexico he learned firsthand the poverty his countrymen faced. The promises of the revolution had obviously failed them. Although the Mexican Revolution had been fought in the name of the campesino, decades later, not much had changed. Economically, they still had a bleak future at best. This experience made Fox different from the vast number of Mexican politicians who spent most of their lives in urban centers far removed from the poor rural areas of the country they claimed to sympathize with.

Fox soon caught the attention of top management, followed by a meteoric rise through the ranks. Anticipating a successful future Coca-Cola sent him to Harvard Business School, where he received a diploma in top management skills.

Most people I have met who know Vicente Fox will never give him high marks for being particularly intellectually savvy. However, nobody will deny his dedication to hard work, which in time earned him the position of president of Coca-Cola for Mexico and Latin America. He had the distinction of being the youngest executive to hold this position.

To his admirers' surprise, in the 1980s Fox joined the PAN, on the center-right politically, which got him elected to the Chamber of Deputies in 1988. Running for governor of his home state in 1991, he lost a much-disputed election to the candidate of the PRI. The uproar of electoral fraud was such that the PRI governor resigned and a temporary governor from the PAN party was appointed. In an interim election held in 1995, an overwhelming majority elected Vicente Fox governor of the state of Guanajuato.

True to his roots, Fox became the politician who rarely wore a suit. He always dressed like a Mexican vaquero in western boots, sporting a cowboy belt with a large buckle bearing his name. This trait, and his unusual height, made him a formidable figure wherever he went.

As governor, Fox was fortunate that the party he belonged to, known as *panistas*, and their large Catholic followers had a majority in both the lower and upper chambers in the state Congress. He also had the backing of most of the towns and cities whose municipal presidents also belonged to his party. This allowed Fox a free hand to carry out his agenda without the interference of the opposition. There was no necessity to hone his political skills of negotiation and compromise, which cost him dearly in the future.

Fox soon developed a reputation of rarely being in his office. He preferred spending his time traveling to other countries, studying better ways to approach the problems of the state, which were the same problems faced by the nation. For example, from Bangladesh he adopted a bank model to provide microloans to poor people with no credit history. Having had a successful sales and marketing career with Coca-Cola, he was soon applying his talents to attract foreign investors into relocating their manufacturing plants to the state. As governor, he put in place a special industrial promotion board responsible for attracting investment to the state of Guanajuato. It became a success from its inception.

One of his most significant accomplishments was reforming the state judicial system. Borrowing policies from the United States, judges and top law enforcement officials were now obligated to disclose their personal finances, a practice unheard of in most of Mexico. To set an example, Fox made a full disclosure of his own finances. Civil and criminal cases in the future were assigned by random computer selection to avoid cases being assigned to friendly judges and those known to take bribes.

Corruption at the municipal and state levels in the issuance of licenses and permits was scrutinized to eliminate professional middlemen, known as coyotes, who were adept at circumventing the law by greasing the right hands. Signs were placed in all government offices announcing that no government bureaucrat could accept or ask for a bribe. If such an approach was made, there were sealed boxes where ordinary people could lodge a complaint. The program was a success, helping to regain the people's confidence in the public sector. On top of this, Fox yearly made public the financial balance sheets of the state. The results were out there for everyone to see. People stopped complaining about government indifference to their needs.

In the past, Guanajuato was known as the state with no unemployment because, as the undersecretary of sustainable development once explained to me, "50 percent of the work force is employed here, while the other 50 percent are undocumented workers in the United States." That image started to change. Under Fox, the state became the fifth-largest economy in the country, providing thousands of new jobs in management and skilled labor. This inevitably required more universities and technical schools.

Fox's success soon made him a prominent national political figure. With the growing unpopularity of the PRI and the electoral reforms incorporated in the 1990s, there seemed to be a window of opportunity for breaking the dictatorial hold of the PRI on the presidential office.

The country had come around to the belief that the party in power had finally run its course. The question on the electorate's mind was, were there enough votes to defeat the political machine that had governed Mexico for so many decades? If so, it squarely rested in the hands of that six-foot-three rancher from the state of Guanajauto, Vicente Fox. Not only did he not belong to the PRI; he was a panista affiliated to the PAN, the party of the moderate right. More important, he was a governor with a successful track record. Considering the trend toward populist leftist governments in many countries in Latin America, he seemed somewhat of an anomaly as the standard bearer of change.

The possibility of change took on greater meaning thanks to further reforms implemented by President Ernesto Zedillo in the 2000 presidential elections, when he made it clear he had no intention of naming his heir through the closed system of the past. The tapado and the dedazo were as obsolete as the dinosaur. His successor needed to be named through the system of election primaries, much like the selection process in the United States.

The first real signs of change came in 1997, when the PRI lost majority control of the Chamber of Deputies in Congress. That same year, Fox threw his hat into the ring and took a leave of absence as governor to start a three-year presidential election campaign.

From the outset, his own party was skeptical of his political abilities. Even though he had a proven record as governor of an important state, the fact was that he never had to face any real political opposition in a state where his party reigned supreme. A top executive of a major transnational company was not favorably looked on by a highly nationalistic electorate prone to be anti-malinchista. Undeterred, Fox attained his party's candidacy by uniting his supporters in the PAN and the smaller Green Ecology Party. Moreover, business leaders across the nation were willing to finance his campaign. By 1999, this amalgamation of different groups became known as the Alliance for Change. For the time being malinchismo was placed on the back burner as globalization was having an effect on the mind-set of many of the upcoming generation of well-educated Mexicans with points of view that stretched far beyond Mexico's borders.

Taking a page out of the U.S. presidential elections, Fox challenged the presidential candidates, Francisco Labastida Ochoa (PRI) and Cuauhtémoc Cárdenas (PRD), who was running for the second time, to a public debate. On the day initially agreed on, the other two candidates were no-shows, having decided they wanted the debate postponed. Fox used the airtime allotted for the debate to promote his campaign platform and attack the other two candidates for being scared to face him in an open, televised forum. The experts felt this incident turned many undecided voters in his favor.

During the campaign, a character flaw started to appear at some of Fox's public pronouncements. Like U.S. vice president Joe Biden, Fox had a hard time keeping from making inappropriate remarks. At first these seemed funny, but overall the off-the-cuff comments worked against him. With time he became his own worst enemy. During the campaign, two of his most outlandish statements were 1) calling his PRI opponent *un maricón*, loosely translated as a sissy, and 2) further accusing him of being a transvestite.

Vicente Fox won the election with 43 percent of the vote, followed by Labastida (PRI) with 36 percent and Cárdenas (PRD) with a mere 17 percent. With more than 80,000 observers policing the voting booths to make sure voter fraud was kept to a minimum, the nearest loser made no attempt to contest the outcome.

Fox had changed the political dynamic forever. On July 2, 2000, he not only celebrated his fifty-eighth birthday, but also his election as the first non-PRI president of Mexico since 1929. There was much to celebrate.

It is impossible to talk about the election of 2000 without mentioning the important role played by the last PRI president. President Ernesto Zedillo will not be remembered as a great leader, or as a mover and shaker in the ilk of a Salinas de Gortari. He was truly a mild personality with little charisma. He stood out for his ability to blend into the background. But appearances should not be confused with accomplishments, the greatest of which was allowing the selection of candidates through the use of the primary selection system. At the same time, he did not tolerate the party's interference at the grass roots via the many traditional forms of bribery.

To ensure the campesino vote, the PRI had made it a custom to take building materials, bags of cement, food, and medicines to be freely distributed among thousands of villages and towns. Similar handouts were given to the different groups making up the corporate vote. This largesse was provided from the coffers of the federal government under PRI control. Zedillo refused to participate in this practice. For this he earned the animosity of his party and the thanks of a grateful nation. The PRI was so outraged at Zedillo's behavior there was even talk of throwing him out of the party.

Without President Zedillo's insistence on a clean election, Fox most likely could never have attained the presidency. The stand that Zedillo took and maintained during the entire election process earned him a place among the icons of Mexico's unsung heroes. Without his collaboration, Mexico might not have made its biggest political change since the revolution.

Ernesto Zedillo's career did not end with his presidency. Recognized in academic circles with an MA and PhD from Yale University, he was invited by that institution to become the director of the Center for the Study of Globalization. Harvard invited him to be the commencement speaker in 2003. Again we see the effects of malinchismo—he was honored in the United States and politically reviled by his own party at home.

◆

During the campaign, Fox constantly called on the need for change. One of his promises was to end the excessive control of power in the hands of the executive branch of government. Power had to be shared with the legislature. If elected president, Fox promised that this power sharing would become a reality. Once in office, he kept his promise and resisted any attempt to take over the government as all the presidents had since 1929. As we will see, this became the overwhelming failure of his administration. The PAN lacked a majority in congress. He soon found out the legislature had no intention of giving the newly elected PAN president credit for anything.

Because of his background as a Coca-Cola executive and his success as a governor with no real political opposition, he believed a market-driven economy with the support of the state was the road to success. This was similar to Bill Clinton's administration in the United States and Tony Blair's in the United Kingdom. If it had been a success in those two countries, why not in Mexico? Unfortunately, he was thinking like a pragmatic businessman and not like a Mexican politician.

Though the PAN owned the presidency, the PRI and the PRD had a majority in Congress. As governor, Fox's penchant for adopting ideas from other countries, like microloan banks for the poor, did not sit well with a federal government that traditionally displayed its anti-malinchista credentials.

He also became unpopular with the leftist intelligentsia by his negative attitude toward Fidel Castro's Cuba. A politician might not be supportive in private of the last communist regime in the Americas, but in public, a commitment to the revolutionary ideals of that failed Cuban experiment was essential. One needed to be reminded that both countries were the products of a revolution against a cruel and abusive dictatorial rule. There was no secret that Fox was the intermediary between President George W. Bush and Fidel Castro. Castro had not forgotten that Mexico allowed him to stay as a political refugee when he first challenged the legitimacy of the Batista regime. The cozy relationship between Fox and Bush did not sit well with the orthodox nationalistic anti-yankee left.

Right from the get-go Fox was never popular with the left-leaning press of Mexico and Latin America. If unpopular in the leftist circles of the Latin American intellectuals, he had just the opposite effect with the United States and Europe. Under his presidency Mexico was the shining light of a third-world country. That played well in the first world and the international financial community, but it was a different story at home, where he was soon branded a malinchista and a pawn of the Bush administration. After all, both were elected in the same year. They obviously had a lot in common. If a new generation of Mexicans could accept a malinchista that was hardly the case with the old guard that made up a majority in the legislature.

In Europe and the United States nobody could quite figure out the Mexican mentality. A longtime resident of Mexico made this observation: "Remember, Mexico is a car whose driver signals left but turns right."

Fox forgot to give the left hand signal in public and the opposite in private. Honesty and transparency in Mexican politics is considered naive and gets you nothing but scorn, despite public proclamations to the contrary.

Not only did Congress not see eye to eye with Fox on just about everything, but they were also stymied by the inertia acquired from simply rubber-stamping the whims of the chief executive's decisions in the past. Congress reacted to the idea that they now had to initiate legislation to pass into law like a one-legged man being asked to run a marathon. Congress was being asked to do something they had never done before or were even capable of doing—govern. Liberated from the dictatorial fist of the past, where consensus was out of the question in a one-party system that had never needed to reach a compromise on anything, there were now three parties to contend with, and none had a majority.

Fox was successful in projecting a favorable image of Mexico abroad, but at home his lack of political skills and unwillingness to enforce his will from the power of the presidential bully pulpit made him totally incapable of any meaningful accomplishments.

To make things worse, in 2001 Fox married Marta Sahagún, a divorcée who became the Lady Macbeth of his administration. She was overly ambitious, with eyes toward becoming the next presidential candidate of the PAN and the first woman president. He appointed her the communications secretary of his presidency, which on top of her personal ambitions tarnished what little positive image Fox had left.

The Mexican people had set their hopes on the man who had liberated the country from the PRI dictatorship but was now the butt of jokes. As Fox was a divorced man with four adopted children, snide remarks surfaced that maybe he was not only politically impotent, but possibly sexually impotent as well.

◀

Fox was a close friend of George W. Bush until Mexico refused to support a U.N. Security Council vote legitimizing the U.S. invasion of Iraq. Bush could not understand why his friend and ally voted against the United States resolution, keeping in mind the U.S.-sponsored president of the Security Council at the time was the Mexican ambassador to the U.N. Somebody should have reminded Bush that Mexico's foreign policy doctrine since the time of Benito Juárez was, and still is, "Among individuals, as among nations, respect for the rights of others is peace." Throughout Mexico's history, there has always been a national cry of outrage when this doctrine has not been respected. The invasion of Iraq was no exception.

Relations between the United States and Mexico became frosty. This time Fox expressed himself in writing. Fox retaliated against Bush in his English-language autobiography, titled *Revolution of Hope: The Life, Faith and Dreams of a Mexican President*, by labeling Bush a "windshield cowboy" because he refused to ride one of Fox's horses when invited to his ranch. He also called Bush the "cockiest guy I ever met" and was surprised that such a man had made it to the White House.

The Joe Biden in Fox now surfaced. Among his many gaffes, in May 2005, during a presentation to a group of Texas business executives, he explained, "There is no doubt that Mexicans filled with dignity, willingness, and ability to work are doing jobs that not even blacks want to do back there in the United States." Fox apparently had little knowledge of American political correctness dealing with matters of race. He soon had Reverends Jesse Jackson and Al Sharpton demanding an official apology.

In recognition of his written and public statement errors, in November 2006, just before Fox turned over his presidency to his successor, the TV network Telemundo released a tape in which Fox admitted, "Now I can speak freely. Now I can say any stupidity. It doesn't matter anymore. Anyway, I'm leaving." On December 1, 2006, Fox's successor, Felipe Calderón, became the next president of Mexico.

◄►

In retrospect, Vicente Fox was the man who broke the PRI's seven-decade dictatorship; for this alone, the nation should be grateful. Unfortunately, the Mexican people came to expect reforms Fox was never capable of delivering. While nobody openly said it, the Mexican people expected him to act like the majority of autocratic presidents who governed in the name of the PRI. That's the way to get things done, they reasoned. The people forgot he campaigned on the promise of delegating much of the presidential powers to the legislative branch. The people and the media blamed him for not being able to bring together the many different political factions, who still saw Mexico as a quasi-socialist state. While some of the criticism is well founded, it is also obvious that the legislative branch of government was unprepared to govern, especially where compromise was the only road to many needed reforms. Regardless, the inability to pass the necessary reforms, notably the much-needed fiscal and tax reforms and reforms in the energy sector, was laid squarely on his shoulders.

I was recently at a weekend getaway with seven of my Mexican friends. During the cocktail hour the conversation turned to the Fox presidential years. A poll was taken to see who of those present had voted for Fox for president. All raised their hands. A second poll was taken to see who looked favorably on his years in office. Nobody raised his hand. Among those present were two retired generals, an architect, a civil engineer, a retired corporate accountant, a business machine salesman, and a retired sales director of a major U.S. corporation in Mexico.

Today, Fox is remembered simply as the president of political transition. If that is his only legacy, then he deserves to sit among the heroes of his country.

The new millennium also brought on some serious changes in the political landscape of Mexico and Latin America. The ever-increasing divide between the haves and the have-nots was becoming more protracted and dangerous for the stability of the region. Socialism was once more coming back into vogue. The real danger, however, was a new breed of populist leaders, who like the mythical Greek Hydra were rearing their many heads. The danger was the lack of a Heracles to step forth and smite the monster.

22

Populism and the Mexican Messiah

◆

As Mexico struggled for continued economic and political stability, a major socioeconomic force was sweeping across Latin America, threatening those nations that fell under the spell of its utopian promises. Mexico was in the crosshairs of a political trend that could end many of its accomplishments since la apertura—the privatization of badly run, state-owned companies, accompanied by the globalization of the economy and the open and fair presidential elections in the year 2000.

The left was convinced that the era of neoliberalism and capitalism had run its course. The politics of the future had to benefit a majority of the people, not just a select few. The socialists believed the net effect of neoliberalism was to widen the gap between rich and poor. A new era, known as political populism, was on the march. This movement divided countries into the people and the elites. Among the latter were those who inherited their wealth, as well as those who became wealthy through hard work. Daniele Albertazzi, in his book *Twenty-First Century Populism*, described the elites "as depriving, or attempting to deprive, the sovereign people of their rights, values, prosperity, identity, and voice." In other words—rich versus poor.

If socialism seemed like a good alternative to some on the left, others felt populism had a far broader reach in satisfying the common good. Words such as productivity and efficiency were associated with a private sector that was primarily interested in monetary gain and was therefore exploitive by nature. It was up to the people to make the right choices. Since the people were incapable of such trust, it was the strong, all-powerful, centralized government that was needed to make the right decisions for them. A messianic leader was the ideal, someone who could bring justice and prosperity for the downtrodden. In reality, populism has a dismal record.

There has always been the illusion that turning back the clock might actually benefit the masses. Nobody was listening to Jorge Santayana's dictum, "Those who cannot remember the past are condemned to repeat it."

At the center of the populist movement was that same old unworkable mantra—the redistribution of wealth. Take away from the rich and give to the poor. The redistribution of wealth also included the redistribution of agricultural lands to the campesino. Some of these new leaders went as far as to promote the idea that the state not only owned the subsoil, but also the land itself and almost everything on it.

As the government became the sole owner of the national territory, it could then parcel out property above and below the surface for the good of the people—in other words by government decree. The intellectuals behind this movement reasoned that wealth produced by the "nanny state" could then be used for education, healthcare, jobs, and bettering the infrastructure of the nation. The idea of Utopia was music to the ears of academia and the poor. The state had in its grasp the ability to change centuries of poverty that had plagued Mexico and the rest of Latin America. To be a populist, you also had to be anti-American to the core.

Before turning to the Mexican Messiah, I have chosen four such men in Latin America who espouse this new trend. All four were duly elected, claiming to have discovered the road to a better future for their people. Their promises have been tried in the past and, if temporarily successful, over time brought on more misery than they alleviated.

Juan Evo Morales Ayma, popularly known as Evo, has been the president of Bolivia since 2006. He has the distinction of being the country's first fully indigenous head of state in the 470 years since the Spanish Conquest. During his campaign for the presidency he made it abundantly clear that if not elected his followers would revolt against the government. One way or another, his populist reforms were going into effect in the new constitution he was proposing. The democratic process could work only if elections turned out favorably. If not, then his followers would take to the streets. The Mexican Messiah used practically the same language.

Adored by the indigenous population, Evo is despised in the south where most of the country's wealth is to be found. The south threatened to secede.

The government took steps to make sure that does not happen. In part, Bolivia's apparent success is largely due to the largesse of oil-rich Venezuela, led by Evo's good friend, Hugo Chávez.

In Ecuador, Rafael Vicente Correa Delgado founded the alliance Patria Altiva y Soberana (the Sovereign and Proud Fatherland Alliance). This new party espouses as its slogan the double-speak of "political sovereignty and regional integration." These high-minded words disguise the real intent, land reform by the failed method of redistribution. Correa promises this will bring economic relief for Ecuador's poor. Correa, an observant Roman Catholic, describes himself as a humanist, a Christian of the Left, and a proponent of socialism befitting the new populist trend of the twenty-first century—in brief, the Theology of Liberation.

In 2006 he was elected president by a narrow margin. In 2009 he was reelected by an overwhelming majority. Again, Ecuador survives in part due to the benevolence of Venezuela.

In July of 2009, secret papers were discovered that showed Correa was being partially funded by the Fuerzas Armadas Revolucionarias de Colombia (FARC), the revolutionary populist guerrilla army occupying one-third of Colombia and the major producer of cocaine in the world. At first these papers were considered elaborate fakes to discredit the Ecuadorian government. However, they proved to be authentic. The effect on the Correa administration was nil. More recently, the government of Ecuador has given Julian Assange, of Wikileaks fame, political asylum. Most political observers believe this is Correa's way of attacking the United States.

In November 2006 Daniel Ortega Saavedra became president of Nicaragua with 38 percent of the popular vote. This is the same Ortega who led Nicaragua into total bankruptcy as the leader of the Sandinista movement. Back then he was elected president and served from 1985 to 1990, at which point he was voted out of office. During his first term, he took a page out of the Mexican Revolution's playbook—land reform and the redistribution of wealth. Never mind that both had failed in Mexico; that hardly deterred him. These reforms didn't work in Nicaragua either. The Nicaraguan people reelected him in 2006. The country is on the road to becoming a failed state if someone like Hugo Chávez doesn't come to the rescue.

The most conspicuous of these four populists is a Venezuelan military-officer-turned-politician named Hugo Chávez. He founded the left-wing Fifth

Republic Movement after orchestrating a failed 1992 coup d'état against former president Carlos Andrés Pérez. Chávez was elected president in 1998 under the campaign promise of aiding Venezuela's poor. The road to helping the poor was again the redistribution of wealth through that well-established populist policy—nationalization. He named his movement the Bolivarian Revolution, which he claimed would soon be known as the Bolivarian Revolution of the Americas.

He has been smart enough not to expropriate the foreign companies licensed to extract, refine, and transport Venezuela's oil. Even Chávez must have realized the Mexican model represented by Pemex was and is a failure. He was reelected in 2000 and in 2006. In the meantime, petro dollars not only keep the Venezuelan people living slightly above the poverty line, but there is enough left over to help bolster the dismal economies of Ecuador and Bolivia. Chávez has also made new friends like Russia and the revolutionary government of Iran.

Turning to Mexico, one would suppose rational thinking and a certain amount of basic intelligence would steer Mexico away from repeating the disastrous results of the Mexican Revolution and its aftermath. One should not be so naive. Populism also gripped Mexico under the deft leadership of the man his followers came to know as the Mexican Messiah, *el pejelagarto*,* or simply El Peje.

Andrés Manuel López Obrador, who became known by his initials AMLO, was born in 1953 in the state of Tabasco, also home of the pejelagarto. Like most future politicians, he attended the UNAM in Mexico City, majoring in political and social sciences. He received his degree in 1987 at the age of thirty-four. Records show he enrolled at the age of twenty. Fourteen years to get a degree in political science is hardly indicative of someone interested in getting an education, but then an education is not a requirement for a future leftist firebrand ideologue. His career soon revealed he was more of an opportunist than anything else.

After graduating from university, AMLO joined the PRI and returned to Tabasco, where he was elected the state leader of the party. By 1988 he realized there was not much future in the PRI under the leadership of gubernatorial

---

* The *pejelagarto* is a fish with a pronounced snout to an alligator. It has long and sharp teeth, which is how the it gets its Spanish name, a contraction of the words *peje* (fish) and *lagarto* (lizard).

candidate Roberto Madrazo Pintado. His solution was what Laurence J. Peter in his book *The Peter Principle* called a lateral arabesque. When you reach a certain level in a hierarchy and you can't go any higher, go laterally. This is exactly what the ambitious AMLO did. He abandoned his party affiliation to the PRI and joined the newly formed PRD, the leftist party led by the venerable Cuauhtémoc Cárdenas.

The PRD is largely made up of disgruntled PRI members who, for one reason or another, saw no future inside their own party. The party was an opportunity to jump ship and board a new one. If the PAN was moderate to right, the PRI moderate to left, there existed an opportunity on both extremes. Anyone who follows Latin American politics knows that the extreme right is reserved exclusively for military dictators. Those *priistas* who had suffered defeat or were blocked from further advancement suddenly saw the opportunity of a resurgent political career on the left. Others were born again populists, especially if it meant getting elected by offering the panacea of equality and prosperity for all.

Political analysts agree that most countries need a leftist party with a clear agenda. This was not the case with the PRD. Composed of a majority of malcontents, it is to this day still fighting internally to see who is going to lead the party in the future. It has yet to adopt a clear political agenda. In the meantime, the best it can do is garner votes from the millions who are fed up with the PRI and the PAN.

In 1994, AMLO decided to run for governor of the state of Tabasco against his nemesis, Roberto Madrazo of the PRI. In a fraudulent election, AMLO narrowly lost. Disillusioned, he moved to Mexico City.

If AMLO had lost the election in Tabasco, he was definitely credited for bringing an end to the political future of governor Roberto Madrazo as a presidential hopeful. In the presidential election of 2006, Roberto Madrazo, as the candidate of the PRI, received a drubbing with only 21.57 percent of the vote, unheard of for a PRI candidate in a national election. In the meantime, AMLO became the new president of the PRD.

In 2000 AMLO was elected as the governor (mayor) of Mexico City with 38 percent of the popular vote. In the past, this position has been the death knell for many a political career. The city is considered impossible to govern because of so many special interest groups with their hands out looking to be greased, a large population living in the belts of poverty, insufficient infrastructure—from rapid transit to streets and thoroughfares—well-entrenched corrupt law enforcement agencies, and an equally corrupt legal system recently exposed in a prize-winning documentary "Presumed Guilty," made in 2010. In general, it is a city living on the verge of chaos. Despite the enormity of the problems facing him, AMLO beat the odds against sure failure as experienced by so many that had gone before him.

Nobody in their right mind believes Mexico City is much better off now than before AMLO came to save the city he named "The City of Hope." So what did AMLO do to become so popular? He was savvy enough to know that if a city the size of Mexico City was largely ungovernable, there were areas of opportunity to take advantage of. AMLO also understood that in the world of politics, perception is, in many cases, more important than reality.

Every working day morning at 6 a.m. while most of the city slept, AMLO was on the air reporting his work schedule for the day and his accomplishments to date. Though most people were not listening, they were still impressed that here was a man literally arriving at the office while most of Mexico City was barely awakening to another traffic-laden, smog-filled day. He even drove a modestly priced car to work with the minimum police escort.

As governor of Mexico City, he instigated various social programs, including a monthly check for those residents over sixty-five years of age. He also included unwed mothers and other economically challenged groups in his welfare program. These handouts were immensely popular not only with those receiving the money, but also with their family members who could now count on some relief from taking care of their relatives.

In 2001, he founded the first new university in thirty years, the Universidad Autónoma de la Ciudad de México (Autonomous University of Mexico City, UACM). The curriculum emphasizes philosophy, education, and the humanities. He could now take credit for opening higher education to thousands who had been denied this opportunity in the past.

The Zócalo, the main plaza in Mexico City, home of the National Palace and the National Cathedral, and surrounded by historic Spanish colonial era buildings, had become neglected and rundown. Street vendors, overcrowded housing, and tourist locales no tourist wanted to visit now occupied the historic heart of the nation. Similar to many cities in the United States, an urban renewal program for the downtown area might be doable if the financing was available. A white knight in shining armor, bursting at the seams with money, came to the rescue.

Carlos Slim is the owner of the telecommunications giant Telmex, Mexico's telephone company, and América Móvil, the largest cellular telephone provider in Latin America. The financial success of both these enterprises eventually made Slim the richest man in the world. Approached by AMLO, Slim now saw an opportunity to do something, both for his country and his personal image. This was a great opportunity to deflect the criticism of those who had derided Slim for having such enormous wealth in a country where 30 to 40 percent of the population lived beneath the poverty line. Either his record for charitable contributions was lacking, or his public relations people were doing a bad job.

The urban renewal of the Centro Histórico (Historic Center) became a reality. Slim put up the money, and AMLO shared the credit.

There was not much one could do with the city's corrupt law enforcement agencies. Firing the lot was no solution; that would only create a new criminal class. A corrupt policeman with a badge was preferable to a criminal without a badge. AMLO soon found the answer.

After leaving office as mayor of New York City, Rudy Giuliani founded Giuliani Partners, a security consulting business with national and international clients. The government of Mexico City hired the firm to reorganize the law enforcement agencies of the city. The Giuliani group tried to implement zero tolerance for those violating the law, the cornerstone of Giuliani's success as mayor of New York City. The whole episode was a wonderful public relations coup, but nothing really changed except that crime only worsened. This was especially true in what became known as "express kidnappings."* Most of these kidnappings went unreported. Most victims also believed the police were behind this criminal activity. Mistrust of law enforcement was never so high.

To improve the flow of traffic on the two main arteries in the city, AMLO added sections of double-decker roadways to existing beltways. Extremely expensive and only partially successful, these *segundo piso* structures now stand as monuments to AMLO's term in office. He also put in the metrobus rapid transit system that, for many, created more traffic congestion than it freed. On

* Kidnappings lasting twenty-four to forty-eight hours. Ransom is usually paid by emptying the victim's bank accounts at ATMs and maxing out their credit cards.

the downside, somebody had to figure out how to pay for the city's increased debt.

Backed by an 80 percent approval rating, the perception of AMLO's success as governor of the city vaulted him onto the national scene. In view of the upcoming 2006 presidential election, he was selected as the official candidate of the PRD. The party finally had a winner.

Presidential Election of 2006

From the get go, Andrés López Obrador was the man to beat. His old enemy, Roberto Madrazo, was the candidate of the PRI. A lackluster political operative, Felipe Calderón, represented the PAN. Neither of them had the personal charisma of the man some called "The Messiah."

Going into April, three months before the election, AMLO enjoyed a comfortable lead in the polls. All of a sudden, the picture started to change.

Much like the Republicans in the 2008 presidential election in the United States, the PRD has a reputation of shooting itself in the foot. This election was no exception. Whether it was the ex-PRI members AMLO put on his staff, or subcomandante Marcos of Chiapas fame claiming that he lacked the proper leftist credentials, AMLO's lead started to evaporate. He was also beginning to display his arrogance toward his party, their leaders, and the electoral process. Most populist leaders believe they are chosen to solve the social problems of their respective nations, whether the public agrees with them or not. The Messiah was no exception. He could always be relied on to have the answer, even when it was unattainable.

AMLO refused to show up at the first presidential debate, which he considered could only jeopardize his immense lead. On top of this, Cuauhtémoc Cárdenas, founder and moral leader of the PRD party, begged off participating in any political rallies in support of the candidate. Many other leaders on the left decided to stay at home. By June the election was a toss up

On July 2, the citizens of Mexico went to the polls. As the day wore on, exit polls started to show Felipe Calderón had a slight lead. On July 6, with the final count in, Calderón was officially declared the winner by 243,934 votes, representing a margin of .58 percent over AMLO. The PRD immediately claimed that the PAN had cheated. Approximately 12,000 ballot boxes in 155 districts were recounted manually, resulting in differences favoring Calderón.

Incapable of accepting his loss, AMLO's answer was to declare himself "the legitimate president of Mexico." Until officially recognized, his followers vowed to embark on a program of peaceful civil disobedience. These demonstrations tied up traffic, closed off highway access to and from the city, and accounted for millions of hours of lost productivity.

Was this AMLO's response to the same people who had given him an 80 percent approval rating? At one point, he was quoted as saying, "The big changes in Mexico have never been produced through conventional politics, but in the streets," the classic populist answer after losing an election.

Many who had considered him the solution to Mexico's problems were now embarrassed and turned against him. The intellectual left and the media who supported the change AMLO represented, now had second thoughts. As my leftist Mexican friends ran for cover, it reminded me of Nixon's second-term election. When the Watergate break-in took place, followed by Nixon's eventual resignation, it was hard to find anyone who had voted for him.

Taking to the streets, blocking traffic, and locking down the city became the order of the day. AMLO's hardcore followers went on to block access to Congress on the day President Fox was to give his last State of the Union report. Fox was politically embarrassed and forced to present his speech in writing.

On November 20, the day Mexico celebrates the Mexican Revolution, AMLO held his own celebration with his followers proclaiming him the legitimate president of Mexico. Polls showed that only 19 percent of the Mexican population approved of this action, while 56 percent disapproved. Undeterred, AMLO proceeded to name a shadow cabinet to govern Mexico in absentia.

He then closed off the main avenue, Paseo de la Reforma, and turned it into a city within a city, made up of squatters living in plastic tents. He had become a mere caricature of the man who had led the government of The City of Hope. Any resemblance to a left-of-center politician was gone. He was now a populist with an agenda that appealed mostly to the political opportunists and the nation's disenfranchised. The enemies were the traitorous Mexican oligarchs and foreign interests. It was hardly important that those he accused were the backbone of the nation's productivity base.

By 2009 he was once more on the stump, carrying his message to villages and towns in the country, proclaiming the illegitimacy of the government and his legitimate right to the presidency. Slowly but surely he was losing not only his popularity, but even the support of the leftist press who had been faithful to him. Still, some of the intelligentsia continued the myth that here was the reincarnation of Salvador Allende combined with Che Guevara.

To show off his populist credentials, here is a partial translation of a letter published in one of Mexico's leading newspapers prior to President Obama's state visit in April 2009. To the "great unwashed," it was music to their ears.

The Legitimate Government of Mexico
April 15, 2009
Citizen Barack Hussein Obama
President of the United States of America

Citizen President Obama:

You arrive in our country during unfortunate times when our people live exhausted from poverty, unemployment and insecurity. These bad times, President Obama, have been caused by a group that took over the country to impose the politics of pillage at the expense of the suffering of the masses and in detriment to the public good.

You should not ignore the imperial oligarchy that has imposed neo-liberalism on our country. Our problems originate with the illegitimacy of President Carlos Salinas (1988–1994) who turned over state-owned companies, banks and other assets of the nation to speculators, influence peddlers and corrupt politicians. They now have political power that exceeds that stipulated by the constitution. They also own the important media outlets, which promoted the electoral fraud of 2006.

It is obvious that this mafia cares nothing about the country's destiny. During more than two decades, Mexico has had the least growth of any country in the world. Since 1983, the government agencies in charge of economic growth have been dismantled, as have the generators of employment, agricultural support, and the deliberate destruction of the energy sector of our economy as a means to justify the privatization of electric power and the petroleum industry.

Our young people have no future. There are no employment or education opportunities. There is no social mobility, the only road available is to migrate or a life of crime.

Yours truly

Andrés López Obrador
The Legitimate President of Mexico

This letter represents a perfect outline of the populist movement's philosophy. The division between the people and the elites could not have been more clearly stated. When lies are piled onto more lies, if you believe in a mere 10 percent, has the "big lie" triumphed over the truth? Lies are the feeding grounds of the innocent and uneducated. AMLO is a master at appealing to both.

George W. Grayson, a respected historian of Latin American politics, sums up AMLO in his book *Mexican Messiah*. He argues that while López Obrador is a populist, he is also unlike many of the other populist leaders in Latin America. He describes AMLO as a "Secular messiah who lives humbly, honors prophets, gathers apostles, declares himself indestructible, relishes the role of playing the victim, and preaches a doctrine of salvation by returning to the values of the 1917 Constitution—fairness for workers, indigenous peoples rights, fervent nationalism and anti-imperialism." He forgot to mention the Agrarian Reform.

We have heard this so many times before, and in the end all that these promises accomplish is more misery for the poor. Mexico has had to struggle hard against the winds of populism and leftist ideologies. The country has progressed as a result, and even managed to survive fairly untainted by the financial and economic meltdown in the United States that started in 2007 and has continued into the present.

Andrés López Obrador is one of those messianic figures that suddenly appear on the national scene of countries facing internal social and economic problems. Flaunting enormous egos and the ability to mesmerize the masses with impossible promises, they sometimes manage to take over a country, with disastrous results in the long run. Lenin, Hitler, Mao Tse Tung, and Mussolini are examples of these kinds of leaders. In the United States these are the candidates who make endless speeches on their vision for a better future—a future in name only.

AMLO's popularity in Mexico attained a high in the 2006 presidential election and has been on a downhill course ever since, as with the leftist intelligentsia and the left-leaning press who had put their faith in his promises. One of the more prominent analysts was Denise Dresser in a speech she made on April 1, 2009, as she expressed her disillusion with not only the left, but with politicians in general. "In today's Mexico pessimism coats the land. The country is obsessed with failure and the feeling of being victimized by everything that might have been but never was, that which has been lost, forgotten and mistreated headlined by catastrophes, corruption and leaders that are too small for the country they live in."

Could she also have been talking about the United States?

But the populists around the world can still have hope for AMLO. He has softened his strident image and lowered the tone of revolutionary ideals. In the 2012 election he lost to the PRI's candidate, Enrique Peña Nieto, by a mere 6 percentage points. Not as good as 2006, but still a force to be reckoned with.

THE TROIKA OF
AMERICAN FOREIGN POLICY
AND THE
CULTURE REVOLUTION

M EXICO IS HERE TO STAY, AND IT'S TIME THE United States starts to believe that fact. Here are two observations to keep in mind as stated at the International Forum of Intelligence and Security Specialists held in Mexico City, December 2008:

1. "Mexico deals historically with crushing U.S. ignorance of Mexico's vital contributions to the U.S. economy."
2. "The U.S. in turn deals historically with a Mexican political system that has a paranoid fixation on the perceived injustice of U.S. arrogance and imperialism."

As a reminder, according to the International Monetary Fund (IMF) 2008 report, which tracks 179 nations, Mexico has the eleventh largest GDP PPP (purchasing power parity) in the world and the third largest on the American continents, behind the United States and Brazil. It has a larger economy than Canada. When we talk about Mexico, we are not talking about a third-world country.

The United States imports over 10 percent of its foreign oil from Mexico and accounts for 47 percent of direct foreign investment in Mexico. While 50 percent of Mexico's imports come from the United States, 82 percent of Mexico's exports go back across the border.

Benign neglect has been the policy of the United States towards a neighbor with which it shares an open border. That's a strange reality considering the shared problems in trade, immigration, and illegal drug trafficking.

In a speech made by Carlos Pascual, U.S. ambassador to Mexico, at Stanford University on October 20, 2010, titled "Mexico at a Crossroads," he summed up the administration's policy: "The Obama Administration has committed itself through the Merida Initiative and other security and economic initiatives to support Mexico in its efforts to build institutions, establish a strong rule of law, and to combat organized crime as a necessary step to increasing economic well-being." It is worthwhile to analyze some of these assurances and where we are today.

It is impossible to talk about the relationships between these neighbors without referencing the two negative forces that are constantly the centers of obstruction. On the northern side of the border, we know it as political correctness, the U.S Congress, and lying by omission; while on the southern side, it is the sacred cows of the 1910 Mexican Revolution, that unique Mexican trait known as malinchismo, and the Mexican version of lying by omission. On the positive side, there is the narrowing culture divide between both countries, largely due to the influence of NAFTA.

Whatever their differences, the two countries must learn to live side by side.

23

Lying By Omission
(A Half-truth is a Total Lie)

◀▶

COUNTRIES LIE BY OMISSION, AND THIS IS TRUE when the U.S. and Mexico enter into discussions concerning NAFTA, narcotraffic, and immigration. U.S. ambassador to Mexico Jeffrey Davidow (1998–2001) used the words NAFTA, narcotraffic, and immigration to describe the "troika of American foreign policy" towards its neighbor, NAFTA being the key issue. Davidow held the highest diplomatic rank as a foreign service officer (FSO) in the U.S. State Department. In 2003 he took over the presidency of the prestigious Institute of the Americas at the University of California at San Diego. In the twelve years after Ambassador Davidow explained American foreign policy towards Mexico at the Pinnacle Group luncheon in Mexico City, nothing much has changed.

Since World War II, the foreign policy of the United States is concentrated on an east-west axis. To the east lies Europe and the Middle East, while to the west is Asia. The north-south axis, with Canada to the north and the rest of Latin America to the south, goes largely neglected. Considering this phenomenon it behooves us to look at an example of lying by omission as it pertains to the United States' strategic interests.

The United States will have you believe the Middle East is strategically important because of oil. This is clearly manifested in how the United States kowtows to the corrupt and less than friendly government of Saudi Arabia. Most Americans believe the Saudis, and other sheikdoms in that region, are the most important suppliers to the United Sates of this precious and essential resource and as presumed allies should be given special attention. This is hardly the case.

According to the Energy Information Administration (EIA) in its "Official Energy Statistics from the U.S. Government,"* the United States imports

---

* Energy Information Administration (EIA), "Imports of Foreign Crude to the United States," July 12, 2012.

approximately 10.75 million barrels of crude oil a day. Looking at the top fifteen countries that exported crude to the United States in July 2012, the American continent supplies more than 5 million barrels a day, while the Persian Gulf provides around 2 million. Aside from Saudi Arabia, the other two large producers of crude oil in the Middle East are Iran and Libya. Neither one supplies the United States with oil. The United States' four major foreign suppliers of crude oil in order of importance are Canada, Saudi Arabia, Venezuela, and Mexico. Three are on the American continents, and only one is in the Middle East. Canada alone supplies the United States with more crude oil than the entire Middle East. The only other players in the Middle East are Iraq, Kuwait, and to a much lesser extent the United Arab Emirates. These statistics do not include gasoline and other finished petroleum products imported from Latin America to the United States, while the Middle East only exports crude. These statistics beg the question of why the United States keeps kowtowing to those corrupt princes and sheikhs while all but ignoring Canada, Mexico, and Venezuela. Why indeed? Didn't President Obama bow in front of the king of Saudi Arabia? I didn't see him giving Hugo Chávez the abrazo, the classic Latin American bear hug given by friend and foe alike.

In this shadowy world of half-truths, there are certain reliable facts that can be garnered if we study not only the present but also the past. If we are apprised of the events that brought us to where we are today, we have a clearer picture of what direction the future might take. Doing nothing, under the appearance of doing something, is the worst of all solutions, yet the United States clearly prefers this tactic, especially when the subjects of NAFTA, narcotraffic, and illegal immigration come into play. We know that an aspirin is no cure for a brain tumor. Despite the importance of Mexico to the United States, benign neglect is the order of the day, most evident since the end of World War II when the United States took it upon itself to rebuild Germany, Western Europe, and Japan under the Marshall Plan.

To discuss these three subjects without a passing reference to what is known in the United States as political correctness (PC)* would be remiss on my part. PC is a black mark on American free speech, made up of populist ideas and convoluted words that mask real truths of which Americans would like not to

---

* PC: words and behavior that will not offend a group of people.

be reminded of. Unfortunately, political correctness also affects the relationship between the two countries. That is not to say that Mexico lacks its own version, which comes under the banner of the Revolution of 1910, with anti-malinchismo and excessive nationalistic fervor leading the parade.

The PC ideas the United States spreads that what is good for America is good for the rest of the world, as well as the notion that the United States is the country to whose values others should aspire, are arrogant concepts that might have resonated with meaning during the post–World War II years, but no longer. This attitude is especially repugnant in the case of Mexico, a country that has lived through periods of military intervention and economic exploitation by its northern neighbor.

Because of its unchecked greed, mismanagement at various levels of society, and breakdown in the values it so much admires, the United States has brought on a global recession the likes of which was unimaginable just a few years ago. If we consider the inability of Congress to act effectively, and the endless ethical scandals surrounding lawmakers, what must the rest of the world think of the greatest power on earth?

The United States apologizes to no one and those who are responsible are not held accountable, whether they are individual homeowners or financial corporate institutions and government.

In dealing with Mexico, the United States bandies about words like "illegal immigration," "illegal aliens," "the war on drugs," and "secure our borders." It even has the audacity to talk about human rights when referring to the dirty drug war being fought along its southern border, a war that is putting Mexico's national sovereignty at risk. One might expect a more subdued attitude considering human rights abuses at Abu Ghraib and those PC words "collateral damage," used when referring to the killing of innocent civilians by rockets launched from drones flying overhead and artillery shells gone astray, not to mention the more sinister "enhanced interrogation techniques," a euphemism for torture or "extreme measures," used when referring to assassination under certain nebulous criteria. The word that always catches my attention is "rendition," used when moving suspected terrorists to clandestine prisons located in countries that turn the other cheek to the practice of enhanced interrogation and in some cases extreme measures. The United States recently introduced "lily pads" to its collection of euphemisms. These are undisclosed military bases at strategic sites around the world used for the launching of covert operations.

The universal PC catchwords being bandied about in the U.S. government are, "Bring those jobs back that went overseas" and "Buy Made in the U.S.A." These utopian ideas make everyone feel good. Assuming they took place, the country would immediately recover from the malaise of unemployment. Mexico and NAFTA are two of the main targets of this thinking. The idea of jobs and manufacturing plants moving abroad irks Americans who are being put out of work, or who think they are about to lose their job to overseas plants manned by underpaid and exploited workers.

When the United States looks at Mexico, nobody seems to want to understand why these jobs went south in the first place. The words "not being globally competitive" due to excessive regulations and corporate taxes that are not in line with the rest of the world do not seem to resonate. In the areas of productivity and "total quality manufacturing," essential segments of a successful nation's economic well-being, the United States is falling behind, especially compared to a growing number of emerging nations around the world.

When it comes to the rise of undocumented workers and Mexican immigrants, Americans believe it is because Mexico's ineffectual and corrupt government cannot provide work for its own people. Americans even suggest that Mexico does not do its part to stop the flow of undocumented Mexicans crossing the border. It has never occurred to anyone that these Mexicans are not breaking any laws in their own country. It is only when they cross over into the United States that the violation of sovereignty constitutes breaking the law. What is also curious is why the Unites States sees every Mexican that crosses the border as an immigrant. Most are simply looking for work. Yet the issue of undocumented immigrants and workers is far more complex if we look into the past and the role NAFTA has played in this phenomenon.

Maybe the most disturbing issue is drug trafficking. Americans have come to believe that it is the growers and suppliers who are responsible for the rise of vicious Latin American and Mexican cartels that have now infiltrated their country, creating crime waves and unchecked violence. Even more absurd, most Americans feel that the United States is not responsible for the violence on its southern border. That's a curious perception, considering the money is coming from American drug users. Everyone knows that wars cost money.

The Fox News commentator Greta Van Susteren best expressed these popular attitudes towards Mexico during her show *On the Record* on April 30, 2010: "You would think the Mexican government would at least give the United States a thank-you for the financial help we have given them in this war that they don't seem to be able to control."

The United States never seems to shoulder its part of the blame game. Americans seem to forget that both countries share the same border. They share in the responsibility of solving their problems and their differences, which incidentally, do not include building a fence in an attempt to sever the two nations.

On the Mexican side of the border, it is high time the government stopped protecting those outdated ideals of the Mexican Revolution like the campesino, Agrarian Reform, and Pemex (the state-owned oil company). Mexico is plagued by excessive nationalistic nonsense, institutionalized corruption, and many other issues that are routinely swept under the table. Then there is the old nemesis malinchismo that the older generations have yet to try and find a way to live with.

In 2000, after seventy-one years of one-party rule, Mexico held an open election that ended the dictatorial rule of the executive branch. Since that historic election, internal bickering, and the lack of any one party being able to come up with a majority in Congress has stymied the legislative process. The legislature had become so accustomed to rubber-stamping the will of the executive branch that they seem to be in a quandary about how to do the nation's business.

◆

Benign neglect on the part of the United States towards its neighbor might be difficult to understand but is not exaggerated when we consider then president-elect Obama's attitude in late 2008 when he met with Mexican president Felipe Calderón. The most important shared issues between the two countries were put on the back burner, with the exception of Obama's mantra that NAFTA be renegotiated to bring jobs back to the United States. If NAFTA is to be renegotiated, it should be to expand the treaty, not cut it back, as so many in the U.S. Congress want to do. Expanding the treaty is now taking place by the North American Super Corridor Organization (NASCO),* a privately funded group

---

* NASCO: a network of highway and rail corridors connecting Mexico's major seaports with inland custom ports in the United States and Canada.

made up largely of members of the U.S. Chamber of Commerce and other business entities.

Despite a general consensus that trade agreements benefit the United States, nothing seems to happen. In fact Congress voted down a trade agreement with Colombia, a country that is essential to the interests of the United States in Latin America. Two other potential trade agreements with Panama and South Korea were placed on the back burner. This trend of staying away from trade agreements took a dramatic turn when the Republicans regained a majority in the House of Representatives in 2010.

Rather than just give these important issues a cursory look, it behooves us to have a better understanding of American foreign policy towards its southern neighbor. The two countries share in many mutual problems related to NAFTA, immigration, and narcotraffic. The United States' inability to find a common solution with Mexico to these bilateral problems is not the answer.

24

NAFTA

As a result of NAFTA, by the end of 2008 U.S. Customs reported tens of thousands of trailers crossing the U.S-Mexican border daily, at times as many as fifty thousand containers. The sheer numbers give us an idea how important this treaty is to both countries.

If we don't understand the effects of globalization, which made this free trade agreement essential to the United States, Canada, and Mexico, then we become the victims of our own ignorance. Although NAFTA has not been perfect, the benefits far outweigh the downside for all three countries.

Entering the 1980s, the Mexican manufacturing base was facing a serious problem. The high tariffs placed on imported goods to subsidize and promote nationally owned manufacturing companies, known as the import substitution program, no longer worked. There was pressure from the World Bank, the IMF, and the Inter-American Development Bank (IADB), which insisted that Mexico open the protectionist economy to global competition.

Upon opening the border by lowering tariffs, known as la apertura, Mexico soon found out it could not compete in a global economy. Concurrently, the United States was also feeling the competitive pressures of globalization.

During World War II, the Roosevelt administration placed a freeze on wages. After the war and the end of the wage freeze, labor unions began bargaining for a constant increase in take-home pay and other benefits such as medical coverage and pension plans. Concessions to unions at a time when global competition was nonexistent due to the destruction suffered by most industrialized nations during the war did not impair the growth and health of the U.S. economy. When globalization became a fact of life in the 1980s, unions continued to justify their existence by continually raising wages and bettering benefits, seemingly unaware of the long-term consequences.

When Ross Perot ran as an independent for U.S. president in 1992, he coined that famous phrase dealing with the proposed NAFTA treaty, "NAFTA will cause a giant sucking sound as jobs go south." The problem did not originate with Mexico. The problem was the necessity of creating a more level playing field with emerging industrial nations like Japan, Taiwan, South Korea, India, and eventually China. Mexico, being right next door, was a partial solution in the creation of that level playing field.

The American worker was also losing the high productivity and quality control that had been compensated with high wages. The world discovered that Japanese, Korean, and Mexican workers were not only more motivated but also more productive, as studies on "total quality control"* took place between competing nations. "Made in the U.S.A." no longer set global quality standards. "Made in Japan" and the more competitive prices of Japanese products were more attractive to the global and American consumer.

Despite the new realities, American politicians just hid behind the rhetoric of "American ingenuity and innovation" and forgot to look under the hood to see if the U.S. manufacturing engine was still running. Asking the national unions to bring wages to a more competitive level with other industrialized nations was not an option. Taking on a union could also spell political suicide for the Democrats who relied, and still rely, heavily on their support to get elected. The only other internal option was bringing the American standard of living, based on high levels of consumer goods consumption, in line with other industrialized nations. That strategy was definitely out of the question. The economy of a nation based on consumer spending could spiral downward into a serious recession. The only solution was going offshore, aided by a resurgent manufacturing concept that had been around since the 1950s. It was called production sharing, as in bilateral manufacturing agreements between two countries. Production sharing with Mexico was the obvious answer; both countries had something to gain in pursuit of their national interests.

To face the globalization menace of the 1980s, the first step Mexico and the United States took was to revitalize the *maquiladoras* that had originated in

---

* Total quality control usually refers to number of rejects/million in the production of a product or component.

1965. The maquiladoras were in-bond assembly plants that appeared along the *zona libre* (free zone), which covers a distance of approximately 20 kilometers inside the Mexican border. Both countries now found a mutual benefit in solving the U.S. manufacturing problem, while at the same time creating much-needed jobs in Mexico beyond the control of the U.S. unions and their bloated wages and worker benefit programs.

From the beginning, but especially in the 1980s, what became known as twin plant–production sharing was a success. It was called twin plant because to stay competitive, one plant on the U.S. side produced the capital-intensive end of manufacturing and then shipped these components in-bond to their twin, known as a maquiladora, on the Mexican side of the border. The maquiladora, in turn, provided the labor-intensive side of assembly, and then shipped the finished product back into the United States duty free. On the Mexican side there was the much-needed "transfer of technology" from the United States.

Overnight, American companies moved whole sections of their manufacturing to Mexico. Industrial parks cropped up all along the border to accommodate hundreds of plants that wanted to participate in the maquiladora production-sharing program. If this created thousands of jobs, it also created serious problems in infrastructure. Housing, schools, medical facilities, urban development, and the municipal services that went with them could not keep up. Shantytowns sprang up near the industrial parks. These were hardly an attraction for workers with families who had migrated from the interior of the country.

The worst social catastrophe that took place was the violence against women workers. Many, if not a majority, of the workers in the maquiladora plants were women. The men became resentful, accustomed to being the breadwinners in a macho society. Eventually these resentments turned to violence. This was mostly evident in Ciudad Juárez across from El Paso, Texas.

In 1993, the Organization of American States Inter-American Commission on Human Rights stated:

> The victims of these crimes have preponderantly been young women, between 12 and 22 years of age. Many were students, and most were *maquiladora* workers. A number were relative newcomers to Ciudad Juárez who had migrated from other areas of Mexico. The victims were reported missing by their families, with their bodies found days or months

later abandoned in vacant lots, outlying areas or in the desert. In most of these cases there were signs of sexual violence, abuse, torture or in some cases mutilation.

A bird's-eye view of the problem appeared in the *San Antonio Current* on May 5, 2009: "A collection of legal and human rights organizations are suing the Mexican government before an international court for failing to adequately investigate the torture and killings of women in Ciudad Juárez. It is thought that more than 500 women have been killed in Juárez since 1993."

Both countries needed to find an alternative solution to these border problems.

Mexico and the United States soon realized that if these assembly plants were a success, why not expand inland to the major Mexican manufacturing centers to take advantage of a large labor force that could be trained as skilled workers, without the burden of having to create the infrastructure that was lacking along the border and causing so many social problems. Mexico could also take advantage of the transfer of technology as the roadmap for Mexican industry to become more globally competitive in the future. Building a four-lane highway system, connecting the interior of Mexico with the major border crossings into the United States, solved the old problem of transportation logistics caused by trailers having to travel on overcrowded two-lane highways badly in need of repair. In the past, on-time deliveries, a requirement for quick inventory turnovers, were difficult to guarantee the further a company went into Mexico.

Fifteen thousand kilometers (nine thousand miles) of these new highways were built during the presidency of Carlos Salinas de Gortari. The financial burden of this immense infrastructure investment depleted the Mexican treasury and was one of the causes of the financial meltdown of 1993–1994.

NAFTA met U.S. demands for a larger manufacturing base in Mexico, despite fierce opposition on both sides of the border. With NAFTA in place, the United States was looking at the loss of yet more jobs to Mexico, while the xenophobic nationalists of Mexico were once more having visions of exploitations from the giant of the north.

Canada also came aboard. Trade with the three countries could only expand with the elimination of unfavorable tariff restrictions.

The problem with NAFTA was that there were hardly any regulations to protect the Mexican agriculture industry. There were none for the campesinos' antiquated farming methods. The small ejido communal farms, created by the Mexican Revolution under the banner of Agrarian Reform, could never compete with the highly developed industrial agriculture infrastructure of the United States and Canada. This resulted in a large segment of the population having to look for work elsewhere. Many migrated to major Mexican cities, extending the urban belts of poverty, while millions crossed the border illegally into the United States.

If NAFTA opened the doors for U.S. manufacturers to relocate to Mexico, it also provided the Mexican people with inexpensive American made consumer goods. Large outlets like Walmart, Costco, Sam's Club, Office Depot, Home Depot, and others became commonplace in most Mexican cities. This transition to imported products was even more evident in food products produced by an efficient, state-of-the-art agricultural industry in the United States and Canada. Soon, Mexico was importing much of its grain and dairy products from the United States, as well as much of its beef. Even Mexico's basic staple, corn for tortillas, was partly imported from the United States. By 2008 the price of imported white corn production to make flour was rising due to demand for ethanol production using yellow corn. The end result was that Mexico's under-privileged suffered from an increase in the price of tortillas, the basic food staple of the lower classes.

Mexico's agricultural industry was further complicated by the fact that, according to the NAFTA timetables, on January 1, 2008, the last of the protectionist tariffs on agricultural products were removed, creating an even greater competitive problem to the already dismal agricultural infrastructure of Mexico. Meanwhile, the urban industrial base flourished. In 2007 the American Chamber of Commerce reported that 40 percent of the Mexican labor force was employed in U.S. companies and their multinational subsidiaries. If we add the Canadian, European, and Asian companies using Mexico as a springboard into the U.S. market, one can only guess what percent of the labor force has been left in the hands of Mexican companies. It comes as no surprise that Walmart has become the single largest employer in Mexico. Since foreign investment requires a large infusion of foreign capital, all but one of the major Mexican retail banks soon became foreign owned.

For years, the truth of how much damage organized labor had wrought on the American manufacturing base was kept from the American public, especially in those known as union shop states.* The United States still maintained the image of the hard-toiling American worker, second to none in productivity, barely able to make ends meet. If there were problems, blame them on management's poor planning, bloated salaries, and sweet executive packages. The fact that entire factories were moving offshore was blamed on everything but the effects of globalization on the world economy. Concurrently, NAFTA became a whipping boy for those opposed to free trade, in other words, the forces of globalization.

Anti-NAFTA consensus was easy to create. Lying by omission soon became the order of the day. U.S. companies in Mexico paid meager wages that exploited the Mexican worker. Nobody took into account the fact that the cost of living was considerably lower than in the United States. The only people who did not feel exploited were the Mexican workers employed by the foreign-owned manufacturing and assembly plants. They were delighted to have jobs that provided better working conditions, wages, and benefits than the nationals.

The Mexicans were further accused of creating environmental hazards by refusing to enforce the requirements agreed to in NAFTA that were similar to those in the United States under the watchful eye of the Environmental Protection Agency (EPA). Mexico was accused of poor safety standards inside of plants and substandard trucks that moved merchandise to the border, both of which added to corporate greed and anything else the anti-NAFTA proponents could come up with. No one denies some truth in many of these statements, but the reality was that the American manufacturer was not keeping up with the competition coming from other industrialized and developing nations.

The United States was then faced with the auto-industry meltdown in November 2008. For the first time, the American people got to see the true nature of how the national unions, complicit with management, had affected the American economy. Even after the U.S. auto industry bellied up, the United Auto Workers' (UAW) greatest concession was not to take a cost of living increase in 2009. Barely a whisper of criticism could be heard.

The Japanese have a huge market of cars that sell in Mexico and are imported from their U.S. plants, including most of the Toyota line and the best-selling Honda Civic, assembled in Ohio. There is only one Toyota plant in Mexico, which assembles the Tacoma, while the Honda plant in Guadalajara

---

* Union shop states: In which persons are required to join a particular union as a condition of employment.

only assembles the Honda Accord. These automakers were based in right-to-work states.* Toyota's only unionized plant, based in California, a union shop state, closed its doors in 1999. The plant produced the Corolla, which then moved to Canada, and the Tacoma, which then moved to plants in San Antonio and Tijuana, Mexico.

◆

So where should NAFTA be heading? The answer is to further integrate the economies of the United States, Canada, and Mexico into a more solid North American alliance. The North American Super Corridor Coalition Organization (NASCO) will, if it becomes a reality, unite the Mexican and over-burdened United States seaports and create a network of inland ports, sometimes known as dry ports, that, from a trade standpoint, will eliminate the border between Mexico and the United States and, to a lesser extent, Canada. Integrating the rest of Latin America into a trading block similar to the European Economic Union is a must. The United States and the rest of the American continent should come together into what has already become known as the Free Trade Agreement of the Americas (FTAA). Unfortunately, this may be a lost opportunity, as many Latin American countries have looked elsewhere in search of favorable trade agreements while the United States worries about issues that have nothing to do with the economic well-being of the country, such as same-sex marriage and the never-ending argument over abortion.

Another issue is the metric system, which nearly the whole world is on, with the exception of the United States.† The refusal to "go metric" is just another example of what the rest of the world perceives as the United States' arrogant behavior.

Looking ahead, it is in the interest of both nations to open more border crossings to facilitate commerce. Three key ports of entry are being expanded at San Ysidro, across from Tijuana; Nogales-Mariposa, south of Tucson; and the World Trade Bridge in Laredo, south of San Antonio. A new port of entry was opened on December 15, 2009, at Anzalduas near Reynosa, across from McAllen, Texas, followed by the Land Port of Entry San Luís II on the Arizona

---

* Right-to-work states: secures the right of employees to decide for themselves whether or not to join a union or financially support a union.

† The only other countries not on the metric system are Myanmar (Burma) and Liberia.

border in October 2010 and the Donna–Río Bravo International Bridge in east Texas in December 2010.

Despite these positive trends, the United States keeps looking eastward to Europe and the Middle East and westward to Asia while continuing to pay less attention to the north-south axis of Canada and Latin America. The southern hemisphere is tired of U.S. neglect and indifference as expressed by the LatAm nations when the United States attends Organization of American States (OAS) meetings that deal with trade. Presidents George W. Bush and Barack Obama have both been exposed to frigid receptions when they ventured forth to these meetings.

As the Monroe Doctrine so pointed out, the United States' sphere of influence is the American continent. It was true then, and it is true today. President Felipe Calderón of Mexico said it best in a speech he gave at the Annual American Chamber of Commerce meeting on March 11, 2009: "It is only through greater integration between Mexico and the United States that it is possible to improve the well-being of the two nations."

25

The War on Drugs

◆

THE WAR ON DRUGS INSIDE OF THE UNITED STATES has a nice, politically correct ring to it. President Richard Nixon coined these words in 1972, an obvious copy of the War on Poverty created by his predecessor President Lyndon Johnson. If there is such a war going on in the United States it has to be one of the best-kept government secrets.

Jorge Castañeda, former foreign minister of Mexico under President Vicente Fox, offered the obvious answer to the drug problem in his book *Limits to Friendship*. "The only known solution to the drug issue is a draconian, widespread repression of users or legalization. Americans are not willing to accept either."

Benjamin Arellano Félix, the deposed capo of the Tijuana Cartel, gave a clearer picture of the problem when interviewed by the *Washington Post* on October 31, 2002, at his residence in the Almaloya de Juárez high-security prison, where the most dangerous criminals in Mexico are housed. He said, "The United States has already lost the war on drugs. Violent trafficking gangs will thrive as long as Americans keep buying marijuana, heroin and cocaine."

Is anybody listening?

The odds are on Arellano's side. We have only to look at the Volstead Act that ratified Prohibition in the United States from 1919 to 1933 to see the truth of his statement. Prohibition was the breeding ground for organized crime and what eventually became popularly known as the Sicilian Mafia.

Prohibition had many of the same negative effects on society as the traffic of illegal drugs has had on Mexico. Countless innocent people suffered from the criminal elements' disrespect for the law, a breakdown in law enforcement, a corrupt judicial system, increase in crime, as well as the decline in morality that became the Roaring Twenties.

In 1933 the United States repealed the Volstead Act and alcoholic beverages once more became legal. The refusal to compare Prohibition with illegal drug traffic is an example of lying by omission. This attitude may have something to do with the fact that drug trafficking is a far more lucrative business, or simply the inability to face reality.

The United States is a drug culture, not only in the use of illegal drugs, but also in the use of prescription pharmaceuticals. The drug culture came out of the closet in the late 1960s. Woodstock, the San Francisco "summer of love," and the unpopular Vietnam War were just some of the events that led to the disenchantment of a new generation seeking refuge in a drug-induced parallel universe. Known as the baby boomers, they changed the United States' social values landscape forever.

At the same time, a new world was coming into vogue. The use of drugs, especially among "recreational drug users," was becoming acceptable. These people had a hard time understanding why alcohol and cigarettes were legal while the use of marijuana could land one in jail. Most Americans are unaware that many of today's illegal drugs were legal, at least through 1914, as stated in the Harrison Narcotics Tax Act of 1914.*

The U.S. government believed nations that cultivated cannabis, coca leaf, and opium poppy and trafficked in the finished products (marijuana, cocaine, and heroin) were the root cause of the drug problem. Mexico and Colombia became the major scapegoats on the American continent. To give the impression that the United States was concerned about the traffic of drugs, in 1986 Congress enacted a bill known as the Drug Certification Process, which the United States used to rate the antinarcotics efforts of other countries, especially those in Latin America.

The leading illegal drug consumer in the world decided to grade, much like a school report card, the efforts of other countries in the make-believe war on drugs, exempting itself from any such scrutiny. Those countries that did not meet the U.S. standards of compliance were to be punished. Favored nation status could be cancelled and with it aid and preferential trade agreements.

The producers were shaking their heads in the knowledge that the United States was once more trying to take the moral high ground, blaming its problems on everyone else. The public did not question why the Coast Guard and

---

* Harrison Narcotics Tax Act: federal law that regulated and taxed the production, importation, and distribution of opiates.

the Immigration and Naturalization Services (INS) backed by the Border Patrol, U.S. Customs, and law enforcement in general were so ineffective in stemming the flow of drugs into the United States.

When the Colombian Cali and Medellin Cartels realized that there was far less risk introducing cocaine into the United States along the Mexican border, rather than by sea from places like Jamaica, Haiti, the Dominican Republic, and other islands in the Caribbean, alliances between the Mexicans and the Colombians soon followed. The Colombian cartels provided the merchandise, and the Mexicans provided the transportation across the border. By this act alone, the Mexicans soon replaced the Colombian cartels as the major players in the trafficking of drugs.

Drug trafficking between Mexico and the United States reminds one of the Russian factory worker who used a wheelbarrow to cart odds and ends like paper towels, soap, and other inexpensive articles out of the plant. The guards at the gate always stopped him to confiscate his stolen goods. After this went on for a while, it occurred to one of the guards to ask the obvious question. "Why do you steal when you know we will always catch you?" The guards finally understood that the worker was stealing wheelbarrows.

To put this in perspective, during the 1990s and into the twenty-first century, the media continuously reported those drug intercepts by custom officials along the border checking false bottoms in cars and small trucks, tires filled with marijuana, false oil pans, etc. These stories became a good cover to try and convince the public that the war on drugs was actually working. Meanwhile, thousands of trailers that daily crossed the border from Mexico were largely unchecked. Lying by omission is necessary to keep the drug culture alive. The illusion of doing something instead of nothing kept public opinion under control.

"Narcotraffic is an integral part of the Mexican economy and the government will not only control the traffickers, but will be an active participant," wrote Jorge Fernández Menéndez is his book *El Otro Poder*, a history of Mexican drug trafficking. That observation has been put to the test if we read the news of the violence along the U.S.-Mexican border.

When newly elected President Felipe Calderón came into office in 2006, it was now his turn to "dance with the ugly one." The ugly one turned out to be the out-of-control drug cartels, more powerful than ever, that were literally taking over the different law enforcement agencies and the judicial system along the border and in certain states, like Sinaloa in the interior. An unprepared military and a corrupt police and judicial establishment were given the responsibility to reverse the ominous trend. Mexico was soon involved in a violent internal war it had no chance of winning in the short term. It also faced an additional problem in that human rights organizations in Mexico and the United States were demanding the Mexican army abide by strict rules of military conduct. The *narcos* followed no rules whatsoever, including the elimination of those that opposed them, and often their families as well.

Aware of the possibility of a failed state on its southern border, in October 2007 President Bush asked Congress for a $1.4 billion appropriation to aid Mexico in what is now called the Merida Initiative. The main purpose of the financial support was to fight the cartels that were threatening to turn the northern border of Mexico into a narcostate similar to what the FARC had done in Colombia. Approximately one-third of that nation is still under their control.

As part of this initiative, Mexico was to receive modern military hardware in the way of two or three military helicopters, sophisticated surveillance equipment, and military-grade weapons to match those of the drug cartels. The Mexican government, on the other hand, had to make sure law enforcement was paid and trained better. With additional training they might be convinced to resist being bribed by the narcotraffickers whose coffers brimmed with narcodollars.

The Merida Initiative caused an uproar in the United States. Why was the United States supporting Mexico's corrupt law enforcement agencies and the military rather than bolstering the local and federal law enforcement on the border fighting to intercept drug traffic from Mexico into the United States and insuring the war not spread to American soil? Why indeed? Before retiring in January 2009, U.S. ambassador to Mexico Anthony "Tony" Garza in a speech made in Texas in November 2008 that appeared in the *Dallas Morning News*, said:

> As U.S. ambassador to Mexico, I've tried to be honest with both Americans and Mexicans alike, and the truth is, Mexico would not be the center of cartel activity or be experiencing this level of violence, were the United States not the largest consumer of illicit drugs and the main supplier of weapons to the cartels.
>
> The U.S. and Mexico must fight these criminal organizations together, or we will fail together.

An obstinate Congress, with a large Democratic majority, was not listening. Any suggestion made by an unpopular President Bush had to be scrutinized through the myopic vision of elected officials more interested in playing politics than paying serious attention to what was happening on the border, which threatened to spread into the interior of Mexico and northward into the United States.

The initial refusal of Congress to give this money to its southern neighbor, where the army is largely dedicated to handling natural disasters and not the elimination of well-armed drug cartels, is one of the most sordid examples of misapplied U.S. foreign policy. The bickering and the lack of responsibility assumed by a supposed friendly neighbor clearly showed how self-righteous the United States could be. Apparently Congress did not understand the words, "A clear and present danger."

What President Bush realized, and the American Congress did not, was this offer to Mexico had nothing to do with stopping illegal drug traffic. Bush understood that realpolitik meant that the control of narcotraffic had to be in the hands of the Mexican government. The alternative was unthinkable. A U.S.-Mexico border in the hands of the drug cartels was, and is, out of the question. If this notion was new to the United States, Mexico never doubted its government had to be in control of this business.

The next ploy used by the U.S. Senate to withhold funds was to insist that any money given to Mexico had to include human rights guarantees by the Mexican law enforcement agencies and the army. The senators seemed blind to the fact that, as the *Dallas Morning News* reported on June 7, 2008, "Since President Felipe Calderón took office in January 2007, there have been over 4,000 drug trafficking related deaths in Mexico." Going into 2009, that figure had doubled and was increasing at an alarming rate. By April 2010 the figure was over 18,000. Even worse, the war was now moving into the interior of Mexico. By August 2010 the killings were up to 28,000 with no end in sight. By mid-2011 deaths rose to 40,000 and were still climbing over 45,000 in January of 2012. That figure has now increased to over 50,000.

The Mexican newspapers were daily reporting the names and ranks of law enforcement agents, prosecutors, judges, and news reporters executed, their bodies left for the public to see. Many times they were tortured before being shot or decapitated, as a warning to those who either refused to go along with the system or had been receiving bribes, but did not live up to what the narcos expected of them. There was no more dramatic picture than that of a headless body hanging from a bridge in Ciudad Juárez, across from the city of El Paso, Texas. Decapitated heads tossed into a crowded nightclub in the state of Michoacán was another attention getter.

But the U.S. Senate continued to talk about human rights and corruption in Mexico's law enforcement agencies. The Senate seemed more concerned with protecting the human rights of the narcotraffickers and their families than the Mexican law enforcement officers who were systematically being tortured and assassinated. Once more, the politically correct trend of blaming the victim and protecting the rights of the perpetrators was spreading like an unwanted oil spill in the Gulf of Mexico. Human rights proponents were having a field day.

Eventually, the House of Representatives passed a watered down Merida Initiative bill by the narrowest of margins on June 30, 2008—eight months after the original Bush proposal. Mexico became the recipient of $400 million (instead of the original $1.4 billion) of military equipment and financial aid, which included a fixed amount to be applied in bettering Mexico's human rights record.

Few in the United States government, with the exception of the DEA and elements of the intelligence services, seemed to grasp how the business of narcotraffic works. Anybody who has studied narcotraffic in Mexico knows that you cannot have the enormous wealth created by this business solely in the hands of the traffickers. Underpaid government bureaucrats have to be included in the distribution of this wealth. These riches also have to be shared in return for law enforcement and the army to turn a blind eye, and even support the narcotraffickers when necessary. Those who are not willing to cooperate in the system have no future and may even be facing death as the ultimate punishment. In Mexico, they call it plomo o plata (lead or silver). You either go along, or face the consequences. This enormous wealth also had to be "laundered" into the Mexican economy to become legal tender.

The other problem facing the Mexicans is the insistence by the United States that the country do its share in intercepting drug shipments and burning fields of marijuana and opium poppies, known as brown heroin and "Mexican mud" among U.S. law enforcement agencies. The narcos understand that drug confiscation and crop eradication is a fact of life. They put elaborate schemes in place so that losses are shared among growers and traffickers. Mexico can then show it is doing its part in illegal drug enforcement. It is only when the traffickers refuse to fall in line that the government law enforcement agencies step up their confiscation efforts without making any deals with the drug cartels.

The government has to be careful in this game. Reprisals, torture, and grisly executions immediately increase when this cozy relationship breaks down. Following in the steps of the Arab terrorists, the narcos seem fascinated with the notion that severing heads and putting them on display in public places is good for their public relations image.

This breakdown of understanding between the cartels and the Mexican government is exactly what is happening today. In the short term there seems to be no remedy in sight.

Under the administration led by President Barack Obama, no alarms went off, despite dire reports from respectable think tanks like Stratfor, which provides strategic intelligence on global business, economic, security, and geopolitical affairs. In addition, a report from the U.S. Joint Forces Command (USJFC) dealt with the seriousness of the Mexican border situation.

The new administration was more concerned with the Israeli-Palestinian conflict in the Middle East. Obama named George Mitchell as a roving ambassador to the region of Israel and Palestine. He also named Richard Holbrooke as a roving ambassador to Afghanistan and Pakistan, while neglecting his strategic southern flank. As of summer 2009, Mexico was still without an ambassador on duty. That did not bode well for Mexico.

For reasons that are not entirely clear, in late March 2009 the situation took a turnaround. With hardly any kind of official announcement, Secretary of State Hillary Clinton was on her way to Mexico, followed by a statement from the White House that the president would be making an official visit to Mexico in April. The urgency of the situation along the Mexican border had finally resonated as a wake-up call that there was indeed "a clear and present danger."

In June 2009 the Obama administration finally designated as its ambassador to Mexico Carlos Pascual, a Cuban-American who is a senior fellow in foreign policy at the Brookings Institute, a former ambassador to the Ukraine, and senior director on the NSC advisory staff. Pascual took office in August.

At his senate confirmation hearing in August 2009, when it came to the problems of narcotraffic, Ambassador Pascual reminded the senators that this war was a shared responsibility between both countries. He reminded those present that without the insatiable appetite of Americans purchasing and consuming drugs, the Mexican cartels would not have the financial resources to buy military-grade weapons to carry out a war among themselves and against the Mexican government.

He also reminded the senators that Mexico had already invested $4 billion of its own financial resources, while the United States had released a mere $120 million of the $400 million approved by the U.S. Congress under the Merida Initiative. This reduced amount did not mirror what President Obama promised when he visited Mexico City in April 2009.

During that visit President Obama took a mea culpa attitude when it came to the problem of the traffic of illegal drugs and the consequences facing Mexico. He guaranteed Mexico that the United States would take an active part in the war between drug cartels, the Mexican military, and law enforcement. Once more the world was about to get a taste of what the administration says it will do and what the legislature allows him to do. Like many of Obama's speeches, this one left few footprints.

On June 24, 2009, in anticipation of President Obama's August visit to the Summit of the Americas in Guadalajara, the U.S. Congress gave Mexico forty-five days to provide a detailed report on Mexico's military and law enforcement agencies' violations of human rights as a prerequisite for receiving the allotted funds of the Merida Initiative. Congress was more concerned that the Mexican military and law enforcement agencies behave in a manner that guaranteed the human rights of the drug traffickers and their gangs of hoodlums despite the fact it was not Congress's war to wage.

On July 13, the bodies of twelve Mexican law enforcement officers were found tortured and executed in the city of Morelia, capital of the central Mexican state of Michoacán. Simultaneously, the Human Rights Watch (HRW) in the United States was demanding that Secretary of State Clinton retain at least some of the money approved by Congress under the Merida Initiative, insisting that "the abuses carried out by the Mexican army continue to be tried by military tribunals and not by the civilian authorities." Yet American soldiers who violate the human rights of their enemies are tried by a military tribunal and not by a civilian court.

On August 10, President Obama made a second visit to Mexico, this time in conjunction with Stephen Harper, the prime minister of Canada. Prior to his visit, Mexico presented their report on human rights. As chairman of the Judiciary Committee, Senator Patrick Leahy received the report and refused to present it to his committee, thus effectively holding up the Merida Initiative funds for Mexico. Despite the promise President Obama made to Mexico to support the drug war along the border, he went to Mexico empty-handed. Once more a member of his own party was interfering in the president's foreign policy objectives.

The solution was obvious. If the United States was going to help Mexico in this war, steps had to be taken to keep that aid under the radar and away from the prying eyes of Congress. Ambassador Carlos Pascual was up to the task.

Going into December 2009, a joint U.S.-Mexico command was set up in Mexico City combining Mexican law enforcement agencies, the Mexican army, the DEA, and other elements of the U.S. intelligence services. The objective was simple: the Americans tell the Mexicans where the bad guys are, and they go in and take them out, or else the United States would have to rethink its financial support. That task was not as easy as it seemed, since most of the bad guys were protected by local law enforcement and in some cases the military.

The first big test came on December 16, when Mexico assigned navy marines to storm the penthouse of an apartment building in Cuernavaca, a resort town southwest of Mexico City. In that penthouse the "boss of bosses" of a branch of the Sinaloa cartel was living under the protection of local law enforcement and elements of the army.

Drug lord Arturo Beltrán Leyva and six of his bodyguards were killed in the subsequent shootout, as was a navy marine. Again, the human rights organizations were outraged that these narcos had not been given a chance to surrender; after all, most of them had families. The Mexicans were aware that capturing Beltrán Leyva was one thing, trying to hold him in a Mexican detention center was a risky proposition at best.

The Mexican marine who gave his life in the Beltran takedown was given a hero's funeral. That same night an assassination squad raided his family's home and executed his mother, aunt, and siblings, sending a chilling message that attacks against drug traffickers had terrible consequences. The HRW did not express its outrage, but maybe offered condolences.

◆

It is time the United States and Mexico accept certain realities. An illegal drug–free United States could cause a national disaster, not only for the junkies, but also for recreational users and pill poppers whose life has become impossible without the use of uppers and downers and all sorts of remedies for stress disorders in the workplace. Americans seem to be at odds with the kind of society they have always touted as the best in the world.

In Mexico, the cutting off of narcodollars will also have disastrous consequences in that much of this money is laundered and then recycled into the economy. As an example, savvy people know that Guadalajara, the most modern of Mexican cities with a population growth that went from half a million in the early 1960s to six million at present, was partially built with narcodollars.

A narcoculture has become a reality that Mexicans don't like to admit. There are narcotours in the city of Culiacán, the drug capital of Mexico, much like the Hollywood tours that visit the homes of the stars. This new culture includes ranchero musical groups, who sing the praises of the narcos. Some of these songs reach the top of the music charts.

Much like the Sicilian crime families of the past, the narcos are also deeply religious in the knowledge that statistically they will exit this world at a fairly young age. The narcos are lavish contributors to the church at weddings, baptisms, and funerals, and in many cases have built chapels as an extension of their homes. Many in the Catholic clergy attend these narco chapels and perform mass for family and friends. They have also created their own patron saint to protect them in their illegal endeavors.*

As one cynic pointed out, "Most of those buried in the city of Culiacán cemeteries die a violent death. Few die from natural causes or old age. When death is from terminal illness, lead poisoning is the most frequent disease."

Knowing the truth about narcotraffic is one thing; knowing what to do about it is another. First and foremost—stop lying about it! The idea of an ongoing war on drugs in the United States is just politically correct jargon to make the public believe that solutions to the drug traffic problem are being worked on. No such war exists, at least not on American soil. Accept the fact that if the traffic of drugs continues, and there is no indication that it won't, the control has

---

* Jesús Malverde: a murdered bandit proclaimed a saint because he gave most of his ill-gotten gains to the poor.

to be in the hands of the Mexican government or you risk the possibility of a failed state, at least on the U.S. southern border.

A decision has to be made whether or not to legalize illegal drugs in the future, and to what extent. As far back as 1972, Milton Friedman made the case in *Newsweek* magazine in the article "Prohibition and Drugs" that "Legalizing drugs would simultaneously reduce the amount of crime and raise the quality of law enforcement. Can you conceive of any other measure that would accomplish so much to promote law and order?"*

There is a growing feeling that the way to beat the cartels is to cut off the money supply, as has been successfully done with organized international terrorism. The experts calculate that the cartels receive around $40 billion a year from the sale of drugs in the U.S. market. Of that total amount $20 billion is from the sale of marijuana. Legalize marijuana and you reduce the cartels' ability to wage their dirty war by 50 percent.

If you can't stop people from using drugs, then teach them how to be safe users in the same way that you teach teenagers to have safe sex. Another partial solution is to accept that the use and abuse of illegal drugs is not a crime but a health problem, similar to cigarettes and alcohol.

Probably the best intermediate solution is an advertising campaign on the effects of illegal drug use, steering away from the health issues and concentrating on where the money ends up being spent in Mexico. Something along the lines of "Your Drug Money at Work," followed by a picture of a headless Mexican soldier hanging from a bridge in Ciudad Juárez. That should have an effect on the conscience of millions of recreational drug users and the ever-present proponents of human rights—draconian but effective.

The time has come to recognize that marijuana, opium poppy, and the coca leaf should be treated as legal commodities rather than part of the underground economies of those countries that cultivate them. All three have multi-uses, mostly in the area of medicine.

In 2009, the Bolivian government enacted a new constitution. President Evo Morales then took the unusual step of legalizing the cultivation of the coca leaf plant. He claimed, correctly, that this plant has more uses than simply the production of cocaine. The same can be said for the opium poppy and marijuana.

---

* Milton Friedman: renowned American economist, statistician, and author who taught at the University of Chicago. He passed away in 2006.

On May 12, 2010, the U.S federal government took the first step in coming up with the first sane policy since Richard Nixon first coined the phrase the "war on drugs" back in 1973, when Gil Kerlikowske, President Obama's drug czar announced "a shift in national drug policy that would treat illegal drug use as a public health issue and plunge more resources into prevention and treatment." On this issue there is general agreement on both sides of the border. The federal government was finally taking the issue of drug traffic seriously. But these suggestions unfortunately remind me of that old saying, "If you talk the talk, then walk the walk."

Another issue is the illegal flow of military grade weapons from some eight thousand retail gun shops in those states bordering Mexico. Both the Bureau of Alcohol, Tobacco, Firearms and Explosives (ATF) and Immigration and Customs Enforcement (ICE) are moving in that direction, with initiatives with code names like "Armas Cruzadas" and "Project Gunrunner."

Unfortunately, an offshoot of "Project Gunrunner" is the ill-fated program of "Fast and Furious," also known as the "gunwalking program"* still under investigation by the House Oversight Committee under the leadership of Chairman Darrell Issa.

Another initiative in the works is following the money and the money laundering so important to the survival of the Mexican cartels, which have long been neglected. A joint team of U.S. and Mexican financial intelligence professionals has recently come up with a ten-point program to confront this all-important issue.

If at times progress seems slow, there are definitely some positive signs that both countries are actually working much closer with each other than in the past. Much of this progress is despite the sorry performance of the legislative branches of government on either side of the border.

---

* Gunwalking program: allowing Mexican cartels to buy guns illegally in the United States in an attempt to follow these marked weapons across the border.

26

Immigration

◆

THE TERM "ILLEGAL IMMIGRATION," which has become part of American English jargon, is a contradiction—an oxymoron, if you want to be more technical. Someone crossing the border illegally should not automatically be considered an immigrant.

Americans don't seem to know how to separate the migrant worker from the immigrant and constantly complain that Mexicans refuse to learn English, use social services such as hospitals and schools, and don't pay taxes, forgetting that these workers only came to the United States to work out of economic necessity. A simplified guest worker program would go a long way to curing some of these ills.

They also complain that the undocumented Latino workers include a strong criminal element inside and outside of state and federal prisons. The news media makes a point of sensationalizing major crimes against American citizens perpetrated by Hispanics illegally in the country. Most of these crimes are related to the sale, distribution, and control of illegal drugs. As long as illegal drug use and abuse in the United States is not brought under control or legalized, criminal gangs will only get worse, whether they be Mexican, Jamaican, Colombian, Dominican, Russian, etc.

An additional comment voiced by the United States is that Mexican workers are welcomed if and when they apply for and receive a "temporary work visa," as if this procedure is as easy as getting a driver's license.

Like the notion of an ongoing war on drugs, temporary work permits are nearly impossible to get unless an alien has a sponsor, usually a corporation, with the funds to pay for immigration lawyers who specialize in navigating the maze of bureaucratic red tape. The small businesses that employ the majority of Mexican workers laugh at this kind of bureaucratic nightmare for the mere hiring of low-paying jobs, and in many cases temporary ones at that. Jobs in the agriculture and construction sectors are mostly seasonal.

Legal employment comes under a "Temporary Work Visa (H)," which states that it is: "Required by an alien who is to perform a prearranged professional or highly skilled job for a temporary period, or to fill a temporary position for which there is a shortage of U.S. workers, or receive training from an employer. The employment or training must be approved in advance by the United States Citizenship and Immigration Services (USCIS) in the United States on the basis of an application filed by the prospective employer." In the case of seasonal workers in the agricultural sector work permits come under the "Agricultural Worker Non-Immigration Visa Classification (H2A)."

The millions of Mexicans working illegally in the United States come under the "shortage of workers" definition. Considering the red tape and legalese language, the Mexicans who fall under this category do not have the documents, time, or resources to go through the process, nor do the people who hire them. The phrase "catch-22" comes to mind. Tom Rosser, an immigration lawyer in the firm Mayo Mallette PLLC gave some insight to the problem. In 2010 he was good enough to send me information on the subject, which as a layman I found impossible to understand. He summed it up with this comment: "I want to help you understand the complications of the existing program and why it is so unpopular and unworkable."

A work visa is not to be confused with the "green card," which is totally different. The green card is issued to immigrants that eventually can apply for citizenship.

The question is: How did the United States get into this ridiculous situation of having millions of undocumented living in the country? Another question is where did these Mexicans come from when you consider that well into the 1970s Los Angeles was the second-largest Mexican metropolitan area after Mexico City? We need to look to the past for the answers.

After the United States annexed California in the Guadalupe/Hidalgo Treaty, ending the Mexican War in 1848, there were approximately 14,000 Spanish/Mexican, non-indigenous people, known as criollos, living in the territory. As a result of the 1929 Rebellión Cristero* pitting Catholics against a sectarian Mexican government, approximately 5 percent of the Mexican population in the central states where the rebellion took place were given sanctuary by the archdiocese of Los Angeles. Most of them settled in the San Diego and Los Angeles areas.

When the United States entered World War II and Rosie the Riveter went to work in the factories, who was going to do the heavy lifting and the stoop labor on the farms? Enter the "Bracero Program," a simplified version of today's guest worker program.

In August 1942 this program brought in 50,000 Mexican farm workers and another 75,000 to work on the railroads, all with easy-to-get temporary guest worker permits issued by the American government. More important, they were paying taxes and not using many available social services since their families stayed back in Mexico. By the time the program ended in 1964, there were 4.5 million Mexicans and Central Americans who had legally worked in the United States. Why so many?

The partial answer is that young men who went off to World War II did not want to go back to the low-paying jobs they performed prior to the war, as was poignantly illustrated in the 1946 Oscar-winning film *The Best Years Of Our Lives*, in which a decorated army air force captain, played by Dana Andrews, returns to his hometown to the same job he had before the war—a soda jerk working in a drug store. Likewise the black communities and other minorities, having gone to war for their country, were resisting the low-paying jobs with no upward social mobility assigned to them in the past. This was also true after the Korean and Vietnam Wars. Men who had done military service and fought in wars and risked their lives in the service of their country expected to return to a better life. The problem was partially solved by millions of Mexicans living below the poverty line just waiting for the opportunity to do any kind of work to improve their lives.

Why did the Bracero Program end? The national unions in the United States claimed the Mexicans were taking jobs away from the American worker—at least that's how officials from the U.S. embassy in Mexico City explained it to me when I asked the question back in 1998. Others claimed these braceros

---

* Rebellión Cristero: See chapter 10, "The Sonoran Dynasty (1920–1929)."

worked in unsanitary and inhumane migrant work camps. In retrospect, it would have been much more in the interest of the United States to improve the conditions in these work camps than to cancel the program. The demand for these migrant workers had not suddenly disappeared. I tend to believe the union explanation, taking into account that 1964 was a presidential election year.

The reader can judge who is telling the truth. But what may even be more important is, how many Americans are aware that the Bracero Program even existed? If the unions were successful in rescinding the Bracero Program in 1964, will they be equally successful in making sure that Congress does not enact the necessary comprehensive immigration legislation that has to include an accessible guest worker program based on demand?

◄►

When I turned sixty-five, I went to the U.S. embassy in Mexico City to sign up for my social security benefits. I was directed to the Office of Financial Services, where I fully expected to have the place to myself. How many American citizens living in Mexico had just turned sixty-five and were applying for social security benefits?

The place was packed, not with Americans, but with Mexicans, many of them campesinos accompanied by a family member who could read and write. Who were these people, and what were they doing in the Office of Financial Services? It never occurred to me that these were the braceros who had legally worked in the United States, paying into the social security system for a minimum of forty quarters, and were now claiming their earned benefits.

On August 28, 2009, José Hernández, a NASA astronaut with a BS in electrical engineering and an MS in electrical and computer engineering, was launched into space. He was born in a migrant workers camp near Stockton, California. His parents were Mexican migrant workers who were part of the Bracero Program. There is a reason for this anecdote about the astronaut. Many of these migrant Mexican workers, who eventually stayed in their adopted country, had the same aspirations for their children as those immigrants who arrived from other parts of the world.

In the past, the Bracero Program was a solution to those sectors of the U.S. economy requiring seasonal workers and those jobs most Americans stayed away from. The point is—it worked.

Here are some other points to keep in mind. In 2007, the "remittances" sent back to Mexico by undocumented workers in the United States amounted to approximately $28 billion dollars. There has been a considerable drop in 2008 and 2009 due to tightening up of the border and cutbacks in construction. Another factor is that the Mexican economy is booming, especially in the building and manufacturing sectors.

Remittances are calculated on money orders cashed at Mexican banks that register these transactions. The Mexican government estimates an equal, untraceable amount, most of which arrives through the underground economy—sometimes referred to as the "pirate economy"—in the form of smuggling and the traffic of drugs. Most of these activities can hardly be the work of illegal immigrants; it is far more likely to be from undocumented workers and traffickers.

As for terrorists crossing the border from Mexico, it is far more difficult to enter Mexico if you are a terrorist or an undocumented immigrant than to enter Canada. Mexican immigration and custom authorities have no problem profiling ethnic and racial groups. As a U.S. ally, Mexico is working hand in hand with its American counterparts.

One example was when U.S. immigration authorities complained that Brazilians were illegally crossing the Mexican border into the United States. Mexico then put restrictions on Brazilians coming into Mexico by insisting they have visas that mirrored the strict rules established by the United States.

On a return trip from visiting my brother in Brazil I asked the Mexican immigration officer what effects the new visa policy was having on arrivals from Brazil.

"Brazilians entering Mexico is down about 60 percent," he answered.

In May 2010, Mexican President Felipe Calderón made an official state visit to the United States, where he complained about the new immigration law in Arizona, claiming the law's intention was to target undocumented Mexican workers and immigrants in that state. This caused an uproar because a foreign dignitary was sticking his nose into the national affairs of the host country. This objection was rather curious considering U.S. presidents, when visiting other countries, are many times quite vocal about activities they disagree with in the host nation.

The real problem for President Calderón surfaced when the media got hold of Mexico's immigration laws dealing with illegals coming into Mexico, especially those crossing their southern border from Central America. The Mexican laws on immigration turned out to be far more aggressive than Arizona's new law. What got lost in the melee of accusations was that these people who were crossing illegally into Mexico were only doing so on their way to the U.S. border. They were hardly looking for work in Mexico, with its huge underemployed population. Rather than simply criticize the Mexican government for the standard "human rights abuses," the Americans might appreciate that Central and South Americans are being kept in check before reaching the U.S. border. Detain a Mexican illegal and you just send him back across the border, catch an illegal from Central or South America and you have a problem. You either put them in a detention camp or have the expensive proposition of having to send them home by air.

The moral of these two stories is that Americans always hear how uncooperative Mexico is when used as a platform for entering the United States illegally. In fact, the Mexican government works quite closely with American Homeland Security. That's what a good neighbor does when sharing a two-thousand-mile border with the most powerful country in the world.

On the other hand, crossing the Canadian border into the United States is a cakewalk compared to crossing the rugged landscapes along the arid southern border. In Canada there is at least one town on the border with Main Street as the dividing line between the two countries.* The terrorist aspect of securing the Mexican border also contributes to those lies by omission because it assumes that the porous Canadian border is somehow secure from those fanatics who want to harm the United States.

When it comes to immigration reform, the last attempt at a comprehensive bill was presented to the Senate at the urging of then-President George W. Bush with the backing of Senator Harry Reid, majority leader of the Senate. The Comprehensive Immigration Reform Act of 2007, or the Secure Borders, Economic Opportunity, and Immigration Reform Act of 2007, came before the 110th United States Congress. It would have provided legal status and a path to citizenship for the approximately 12 to 20 million undocumented Mexicans currently residing in the United States. The bill was portrayed as a compromise between providing a path to citizenship and increased border enforcement. It never came to a vote. The bill was based largely on three previous failed immigration reform bills.

---

* The towns of Derby Line, Vermont, and Stanstead, Quebec, function as one community.

These were:

A bill proposed in May 2005 by Senators Ted Kennedy (D) and John McCain (R), sometimes referred to as the McCain-Kennedy or McKennedy Bill

A bill proposed in July 2005 by Senators John Cornyn (R) and John Kyle (R), sometimes referred to as the Cornyn-Kyl Bill

The Comprehensive Immigration Reform Act of 2006, sponsored by Senator Arlen Specter (I), which passed in the Senate in May 2006 but never passed in the House

Like in the past, nobody wants to seriously take on immigration reform, especially if it happens to be an election year.

One might think the bill with the best chances to pass into law is the Development, Relief and Education for Alien Minors Act of 2010 (DREAM), which would open the path to citizenship for those undocumented Mexicans who came into the country under the age of sixteen. The requirements were military service and/or a college education. Think again. Congress has been toying with the idea since 2001 with no end in sight, despite the bill's being passed by the House of Representatives on December 8, 2010. Nobody believes approval from the Senate will happen, despite the tradition of military service during wartime being a short road to citizenship, as long as you're not Mexican.

To try and better understand how the government approaches the issue of immigration, one has only to turn to a speech made by Speaker of the House Nancy Pelosi (D) to an audience of Hispanic leaders in San Francisco on March 18, 2009. In this speech, she pointed out the necessity of immigration reform and even went as far as to call the present immigration laws "Un-American." What she forgot to tell her audience was that as Speaker of the House for the last two and a half years, she and her fellow Democrats had not made the slightest effort in that direction. She did not find it necessary to explain her meaningless words in front of an audience who should have known she was playing the old political game of lying by omission.

President Obama had also promised there would be an immigration reform bill in place by the end of 2009. Senator Charles "Chuck" Schumer (D), chairman of the Senate Judiciary Immigration Subcommittee responsible for getting immigration reform on the docket, had this to say: "The public is tired of the rhetoric and wants a real solution. The 'amnesty, amnesty, amnesty' was white hot two years ago. People still don't want amnesty, but they want a solution." Senator Schumer is undoubtedly the master of hot air and lying by omission. What he forgot to tell the American public in his speech was that neither he nor the U.S. Congress was going to do anything about his passionate words.

President Obama promised to have a bill in front of the Senate by Labor Day 2009 and into law by January 1, 2010. Labor Day and the year 2010 have come and gone, and there is still no immigration bill on the docket. The press somehow forgets to remind the American people of these false promises when it comes to immigration reform. It is patently clear Congress wants nothing to do with this controversial legislation. What better example is there of a half-truth being a total lie?

But Mexico also plays an important part in the blame game. The terrible mistakes of the Agrarian Reform have had a lasting effect; it not only destroyed the agricultural base of Mexico but created enormous unemployment of unskilled workers who had to look elsewhere for work. These people saw the opportunity of crossing the border illegally into the United States where the opportunities for temporary and non-union jobs abound.

A solution for Mexico is to crank up the economy and create jobs for the millions of unemployed campesinos. That is wishful thinking. Cutting back on the birth rate is doable. Mexico's "Planned Parenthood" programs have no doubt been successful. Unfortunately, most of the positive effects have been felt in the middle and working classes. The campesinos don't seem to have gotten the message, especially the men who consider children as a potential unpaid work-force farming their small plots of land.

One of the legitimate concerns of the United States is how to successfully monitor those who live in the country, whether legally or illegally. As difficult as that may seem, other countries have found some fairly good solutions. Mexico is one of them.

A workable solution for the United States to control its population is to have a national identity card with a holographic ID including a thumbprint and photo for citizens and foreigners alike. In countries like Mexico, these cards have to be shown to open a bank account, get into a hospital (excluding emergency patients), register for a school, buy an airline ticket, etc. They are more difficult to counterfeit than a passport.

The American Civil Liberties Union (ACLU) counters by saying it is a violation of privacy, guaranteed in the constitution, to institute such a card. Better a social security card that can be easily counterfeited. Better yet a driver's license that just about everyone short of the blind can get. Yet a national identity card would go a long way to identify citizens and foreigners, as well as documented immigrants and workers, from the undocumented. In most countries, the standard identification for foreigners has always been a valid passport. Once in the United States, a foreign visitor will rarely have to show a passport, or any other kind of identification issued by the host country. The lack of proper identification begs the question of just how serious America takes the concept of homeland security and undocumented immigrants and workers.

The hypocrisy is that to control money laundering, which is the financial arm of terrorist organizations, the United States has insisted that the Mexican government not allow Americans to open a bank account without having to present a current passport. Mexico also insists on an official ID, issued by the Mexican government's immigration offices, or at least a tourist card required by a visitor to the country outside of a border free zone. In addition a person has to have a legitimate address. This can be done through a rental agreement, or a recent utility bill. This triple identification is also needed for a foreigner to be issued a driver's license. No such strict requirements exist within the terrorist-conscious United States. Had this been the case the 9/11 terrorists would have had a harder time acquiring multiple driver licenses.

If the United States were to create a national identification card for nationals and foreigners alike, theoretically the need for a border fence would cease to exist. Easily accessible temporary work permits would definitely help the undocumented worker problem. Instead of always talking about an immigration reform bill that nobody has the stomach for, pass a bill with the suggested title "Temporary Guest Worker Visa Reform Act" that would count on broad support if Congress had the courage to ignore the national unions and other political extremist groups. Just think of the much-needed taxes these people would be paying into the coffers of the United States.

The Fence

It is impossible to talk about immigration along the border without reference to "the Fence." Whatever the pros and cons, here is a reality that Americans seem to ignore, even when it comes up in talk shows by commentators who claim to have given serious thought on the subject.

The Berlin Wall is a case in point. Was the purpose to keep people in, keep people out, or both? The answer is, obviously, both.

The border fence operates on the same principle as the Berlin Wall but for different reasons. Millions of undocumented workers who cross the border in search of seasonal work, mostly in the construction and agriculture industries, are now faced with a dilemma when it comes time to return to Mexico. Getting back into the home country is easy, but what about the return trip to the United States across a fenced-in and protected border the following year? The Fence, as statistics show, makes this a much harder endeavor. The answer? Stay in the United States, and don't risk not being able to get back in.

What the United States has inadvertently done is turn an undocumented worker into an undocumented immigrant. But the problem doesn't end there. What does this undocumented worker live off during the off-season? If he can't find work, maybe joining a gang is the answer. A temporary life of crime preying largely on the Hispanic community can keep him in tortillas and tequila.

Unfortunately there are no criminal statistics to back this up, maybe due to not asking the right questions. A clue might be that, while border-crossings of illegals go down, the population of illegals during the off-season stays about the same.

But there are other areas of the border that strangely enough are unprotected and easy to cross. The 9/11 cry of "protect our borders" sounds like a myth.

◆

In the United States, different law enforcement agencies have different responsibilities that keep them from encroaching on each other. Thus national parks have Park Rangers, and law enforcement agencies like the Border Patrol are allowed but not overly present. For example, the Big Bend National Park administers 245 miles along the Rio Grande. In places this section of the river is so narrow you can walk across.

To dissuade people from crossing back and forth there is an official warning that has absolutely no way of being enforced. It may scare Americans, but does anyone believe the Mexicans crossing illegally are shaking in their tennis shoes?

"There are no legal border crossings in the park—since 2002," states the brochure you receive upon entering. "Crossing over to Mexico at the Boquillas, Santa Elena bridges, or elsewhere on the Rio Grande is illegal and will be prosecuted with up to $5,000.00 fines, and/or one year in prison."

The park administration doesn't seem to get it. What American wants to cross illegally into Mexico? The traffic is coming the other way. There are similar warnings that if you happen to be rafting or canoeing on the Rio Grande and are approached by a Mexican wading out into the river to sell you a curio— don't risk being fined or going to prison for bringing contraband into the United States. Bureaucratic stupidity sometimes has no bounds.

Going further east there is a large reservoir bordering both countries called the Amistad National Recreation Area. Boaters on this giant water reservoir are made aware of what side of the border they are navigating, as there are approximately thirty miles of mid-channel buoys with this dire warning: "National Park Service rangers do not have jurisdiction in Mexico; boaters crossing into Mexican waters should rely on those authorities for assistance."

Looking at the many inlets and coves on this reservoir must have Mexicans using any kind of watercraft salivating at the ease in which one can cross the border into the United States. Even further east one encounters the Falcon Reservoir, a fifty-mile-long lake straddling the U.S.-Mexican border that gained media notoriety when American citizen David Hartly was killed by Mexican pirates while jet skiing on the Mexican side of the lake. The United States is not going to build a fence in these protected national parks and recreational areas.

Most Americans are hardly aware of these anomalies. It's best to make the uninformed believe that "the Fence," the inhospitable desert, and ICE are taking care of business.

But here is the reality. The Rio Grande runs along 1,200 miles of the Mexico-U.S. border. On what side of the river would you put the Fence? Not on the U.S. side, which would concede the river to Mexico. On the Mexican side you would be invading the sovereignty of another country. Yet to hear politicians blathering away about the necessity of a Fence would make one wish they would consider taking a course on North American geography.

Whatever the answers to this immigration mess, first and foremost the United States needs an updated comprehensive immigration reform bill. This has to include a simplified guest worker program application format that eliminates much of the bureaucratic red tape and is based on quotas established by the demands of those small businesses that need these people. Would this be hard to administer? Maybe (we're back to the Bracero Program model), but it's a far better solution than no solution at all.

The real problem is getting people to return to Mexico when their time is up. The truth is most undocumented workers do not feel comfortable in the United States, primarily because they are there for economic reasons and not because they especially want to immigrate. They feel more at home back in Mexico with their families during the off-season.

America has to rid itself of that politically correct notion that millions, if given the choice, would want to live in America. That may have been the case in *West Side Story* and the song "I Want to Live in America," but not today. Mexicans are not governed by a repressive regime, nor are they persecuted for their religious and political beliefs, nor are they at war, except with drug-related organized crime.

The longer the administration and Congress wait, the worse the problem will become, affecting both countries with potential dire consequences. The Fence is not the answer, nor is talking about immigration reform with the pretense of doing something but in reality doing nothing.

27

Immigration South

◆

MEXICO IS NOT A COUNTRY BUILT ON IMMIGRANTS. After the revolution of 1910 Mexico did everything possible to close the door to foreigners and keep as many jobs as possible for its own people as it could, as Article 32 of the Mexican Constitution of 1917 made clear. It states: "Mexicans shall have priority over foreigners under equality of circumstances for all classes of concessions and for all employment, positions, or Councils of the government in which the status of citizenship is not indispensable."

Mexico was on the way to becoming an isolationist country. However, a peasant revolution needed a professional class to develop the economy, and foreigners had proven to do that better than the nationals. The challenge was keeping the foreigners in check.

The immigration laws could just have hung a sign out stating "Foreigners Not Welcome," and in smaller print, "Unless We Need You." The exceptions were tourists, which Mexico desperately required as a source of hard currency.

Though there is evidence that immigrants are a benefit to the development of a modern nation, Mexico bucked the trend. Mexico's unwillingness to welcome immigrants is not hard to understand when we realize that conquest, along with military and economic foreign intervention, was a bitter part of Mexican history that the country was not willing to forget. Without saying so, Mexico never felt it could compete with foreign work ethics, advanced technologies, and money. Added to this, there was malinchismo to contend with. Despite Mexico's anti-immigration stance, there were groups that immigrated to Mexico with some success.

Inter-Cooperation and Utopian Socialism

Albert Kinsey Owen of the Utopia Socialist Colony of New Harmony, Indiana, arrived on the west coast of Mexico in 1880. He surveyed a town at Topolobampo harbor* and concluded there was an opportunity to build a railroad that would eventually connect with Kansas City. Besides the railroad, there also existed the possibility of building a colony based on utopian socialism. He organized the colony as a corporate entity where all property and productivity of its residents belonged to the corporation. With that in mind, the first colonists arrived from the United States in 1886.

In 1881 Owen received a concession from Porfirio Díaz to build the first leg of a railroad connecting Topolobampo to the inland city of Los Mochis, then crossing the sierras heading east into the northern state of Chihuahua. The completion of his dream was left to others. The railroad is known as the Chihuahua al Pacífico Railway, nicknamed the ChP or Chepe. The railroad is famous for taking tourists through the Canyón del Cobre (Copper Canyon— Mexico's Grand Canyon). While his vision only lasted a mere thirty years, most of Owen's contribution to the area is preserved in a library at the University of California at Berkeley and in his home in Los Mochis, which Mexico has preserved as a historic site and museum.

In the early 1890s, many colonists favored individual land ownership rather than the communal corporate ideas of Owen's utopian world. Many of these American settlers left and moved inland. They successfully farmed in the Valle del Fuerte, which is today one of the largest producers of vegetables and fruit in Mexico.

The Mormons

Because the Mormons were being persecuted in the state of New York, Brigham Young led his people into the wastelands of the west beyond the reach of the United States, which considered the practice of polygamy morally abhorrent. Settling in today's Salt Lake City in 1847, the Mormons found themselves in a territory claimed by Mexico and annexed by the United States six months later in the Treaty of Guadalupe/Hidalgo of 1848 at the end of the Mexican War.

By 1885 the Mormons were once more on the run from the U.S. government. To keep their religion alive, the church renounced polygamy. Those that did not agree moved south, eventually settling near the Sierra Madre Mountain range in northern Mexico. In their newfound home they were free to practice

---

* Topolobampo is a harbor next to Los Mochis on the west coast of Mexico (Sea of Cortés) in the northern part of the state of Sinaloa.

their polygamous lifestyle. They settled in eight towns in the states of Chihuahua and Sonora, fairly close to the U.S. border.

In 1907 two of these Mormons, Gaskell Romney and Anna Amelia Pratt, had a son in the town of Galeana in the state of Chihuahua. They named him George. In 1912 many Mormons left Mexico after being under attack by roving bands of revolutionary militia foraging for food during the Revolution of 1910.

George Romney went on to become chairman of American Motors, governor of Michigan (1963–1969), and Republican presidential candidate nominee in 1968, eventually losing to Richard M. Nixon in the Republican primaries. According to the American constitution, he was legally prohibited from becoming president for not having been born in the United States. He was also the father of Mitt Romney, a successful businessman, former governor of Massachusetts, and the Republican candidate in the 2012 presidential elections. There is still a Mormon presence in northern Mexico dedicated to successful farming and, supposedly, single-spouse marriages.

The Mennonites and Amish

Two other groups that immigrated to Mexico were the Mennonites and Amish, who came from Canada in 1922 under an agreement with Mexico that they desist from ever getting involved in the affairs of state of their adopted country.

In 2003 there were approximately 80,000 Mennonites living in and around Arroyo Coquille de Pates in the state of Durango, near the city of Cuauhtémoc in the state of Chihuahua. They became successful communal farmers, a goal the Mexican campesino never achieved under the ejido program of the Agrarian Reform Laws. Of German descent, the Mennonites are largely farmers, producing cheese and other dairy products. One can find them selling their wares on many street corners in the major Mexican cities, dressed in overalls usually topped by a straw hat. They also stand out for their light skin and blond Germanic looks. Once more, the addition of immigrants on Mexican soil proved beneficial to the country.

The Jewish Community

The first Jews arrived in Mexico with Hernán Cortés. Most became victims of the Spanish Inquisition. Those who were not executed were known as converses and forced to embrace the Roman Catholic religion.

In the 1880s many Ashkenazi Jews fled the pogroms in Russia and Romania and came to Mexico. Another large wave of Jewish immigration occurred as the Ottoman Empire collapsed after World War I, leading many Sephardic Jews, mostly from Turkey and Morocco, to also make a new home in Mexico.

On November 9, 1938, due to the rise of Adolf Hitler and the unfolding anti-Semitic laws directed against the Jews in Europe, the Jewish Central Committee of Mexico (JCCM) was founded. Some years later, an analysis and opinion agency was created called the Tribuna Israelita (Israeli Tribunal). The primary purpose of this group was to promote good relations with the Mexican community and the government and to protect the rights of the Jewish population. The organization was similar to the Jewish Anti-Defamation League in the United States.

Mexico opened its doors to a wave of immigrants fleeing increased Nazi anti-Semitism prior to World War II. With the winds of war gathering in Europe, this was one of the few times Mexico allowed the victims of political persecution to enter the country. The other such notable influx was the Spanish Republican sympathizers who fled the Spanish Civil War (1936–1939).

The census bureau estimates that there are approximately 80,000 Jews living in Mexico City, which contains a network of synagogues, schools, and other community institutions. There are over thirty synagogues, most of them Orthodox. The majority of Mexico City's Jews send their children to Jewish schools. The Jewish Community Center, known as the Centro Deportivo Israelita, is the largest of its kind in the Jewish diaspora and includes both sports and social activities. Most members of the Jewish community live in two neighborhoods of the city. It is precisely this ghetto mentality separating them from the Mexican community that has created a resentment towards this ethnic group. They have never assimilated in the country that gave them a refuge from persecution, nor do they seem the least bit inclined to do so. Yet at least two foreign ministers were of Jewish descent, and others have reached prominence in many professions.

◆

The one thing these various immigrant groups had in common was the inability to integrate into the Mexican culture, unlike in the United States where assimilation was the road to a successful new life. Possibly, the reason had something to do with the pronounced religious differences that separated many of these immigrants from the majority of Roman Catholics living in Mexico. More realistically, Mexico, unlike the United States, never lived up to their expectations.

Whatever the reasons, integration into Mexican society was not a problem with the Spanish who came to Mexico before, during, and after their civil war of 1936.

The Spaniards

The first Spaniards hardly came as immigrants; they came as conquerors. After the Hernán Cortés conquest in 1521, they continued coming, their number one objective being the exploitation of Mexico's mineral wealth.

As pointed out, most of the Spaniards were known as gachupines and criollos, those born in Spain and Mexico untainted by indigenous blood. Eventually, through a lack of available women, they intermingled with the Indians to create the mestizo nation of today.

The real Spanish immigrants were those fleeing Francisco Franco's fascist regime during and after the Spanish Civil War. They were seeking political asylum in any Spanish-speaking country that would have them. Despite creating their own clubs, societies, retirement centers, and hospitals, they managed to assimilate into Mexico's mainstream culture. They became shopkeepers, small- and medium-sized business owners, and even founded some of the largest corporations, such as the international beer giant Grupo Modelo.

The Mexican Census Bureau calculates there are between nine and fifteen million Mexicans who have managed to maintain their criollo bloodlines without any cross-breeding with the indigenous population. This is quite an achievement when talking about two and three, or even more, generations.

The American and Canadian Invasion

Up until the latter part of the twentieth century Mexico maintained very strict rules for those who wanted to relocate to Mexico, especially if they wanted to work. The rules were simple. If the job could be done by a Mexican, the best one could do was get the status of a resident without permission to work, known as an FM 3. If sponsored, the government allowed you to work for a specific company in a specific job for a period not to exceed one year. This document was similar to a temporary guest worker visa in the United States.

The more difficult status to acquire was the FM 2. This status classified you as an *imigrante* (immigrant), similar to the green card issued in the United States, and allowed you to work, but only if you were being sponsored by a specific employer for a specific job that could not be done by a Mexican. This opened up a whole new industry for lawyers specializing in immigration, a nice title for those middlemen who personally knew the immigration bureaucrats whose palms had to be greased to evade the strict interpretation of the law.

◆

While most countries divide the year into four seasons, Mexico has a dry season, covering most of the winter months, and a rainy season that keeps the hot summer months cool. To make sure there will always be a sun in the sky shining on Mexico, the gods made sure the rains come in late afternoon and at night. The interior of Mexico's high plateau, between 5,000 and 7,000 feet above sea level, is known as the land of eternal spring.

Like migrating birds heading south to the more temperate climates of Mexico in the winter, temporary residents became known as snowbirds. They live in Mexico during the pleasant winter months and returned to their northern nests in the summer. During the spring-like summer months on the high plateau, the snowbirds are replaced by those fleeing the uncomfortable temperatures of the southwest. The cry, "The Texans are coming," could be heard across the land. After all, who could play golf after 9 a.m. in Houston, not to mention places like Phoenix and Tucson?

For those seasonal visitors who chose to enter by car as a tourist and not confront the labyrinth of red tape when applying for an FM 3, there was the alternative of obtaining a tourist card and facing the vultures lurking on the border. At the discretion of the immigration officer, a visitor might be issued a tourist card for 30, 60, 90, or 180 days. This system also opened the door for another form of discretionary behavior known as the bribe, or *la mordida* (the bite). The savvy tourist would become adept at negotiating his term of stay with immigration officers inclined to give him a thirty-day permit as the basis for renegotiating with those whose intent was to stay longer. When you became proficient at this game, you could also smuggle much of the electronics and other household goods for your second home. While the situation along the border has gotten much better in recent years, these customs stations and immigration offices were excellent classrooms as an introduction to Mexico's national sport of institutionalized corruption.

Of all the places Americans chose to live, San Miguel de Allende, at 6,000 feet above sea level on the high plateau of central Mexico, and the Riviera de Chapala, on Lake Chapala near the city of Guadalajara, became the destinations of preference for a growing number of ex-pats. These two traditional destinations have more recently been joined by the growing town of Alamos, in the northern state of Sonora and many beach resorts that are best known as tourist destinations.

NAFTA

With the advent of NAFTA in 1994, U.S. and Canadian immigration, whether looking for temporary or permanent residency in Mexico, discovered that the welcome mat beckoned. Along the border, the surly on-the-take immigration and customs officials were soon flashing "Amigo Country" smiles. The federal government realized how much these border vultures had damaged the image of their country. They established closer supervision by officials sent from Mexico City. After all, the border had always had a life of its own. Corruption and fleecing the tourist were just two of their bad habits. The time to open the border had finally arrived.

With the passing of NAFTA, Mexico became a facilitator rather than the obstructionist of the past. Getting FM 3 residency documentation became routine. The only real requirement was ensuring the applicants could monetarily sustain themselves without becoming wards of the state.

To make relocating to Mexico more attractive, the new residents were allowed to import their personal cars and, in a one-time-only deal, all their personal household furnishings and appliances. The rush to Mexico was on, fueled by the events of 9/11, great weather conditions, early retirement, and a much lower cost of living. Not only did the traditional destinations in Mexico's interior benefit, but also much of the western coastline and the Baja California peninsula.

On the Gulf of Mexico, a corridor of continuous beachfront developments became known as the Riviera Maya (Mayan Riviera). Stretching from Punta Brava just south of Cancun International Airport to Punta Allen, it covered a distance of a little over a hundred miles.

According to statistics put out by American Citizens Abroad, there are over one million Americans who are permanent or temporary residents of Mexico.

From the United States alone that comprises nearly 25 percent of all Americans living outside the country. With the advent of the financial meltdown of 2008–2009, many Americans are looking to relocate to places like Mexico, which offer a better lifestyle at a more reasonable cost.

Mexico is also allowing many Americans and Canadians who qualify the right to acquire Mexican citizenship; a policy that was unheard of in the past unless you were married to a Mexican or had Mexican children.

A Mexican friend of mine recently returned from Cuba with a tour group of Americans living in Mexico. She was amazed to see how many were lined up at the Mexico City International Airport immigration arrival gate for Mexican citizens.

"What the hell!" she exclaimed. "Most of them can't even speak Spanish."

◆

If Mexico is to succeed as a haven for ex-pats, it will have to address some key problems. At the center of these problems is the issue of security. The drug war along the border has now spread to parts of the interior of the country. While foreigners are rarely targeted by narcos, unless they are involved with drugs, crimes against foreigners do happen. The U.S. government does not take lightly to their citizens being attacked abroad. Embassies complain, and Mexican law enforcement, which normally does not take crimes against its own citizens very seriously, suddenly finds itself under pressure to take action. The bad guys know this. They will usually stay away from using foreigners as targets. Unfortunately, the perception promoted by the U.S. media would have you believe it is dangerous to walk the streets, and insist most of Mexico has become a war zone. Mexico definitely needs to better its public relations efforts. What has become infinitely more dangerous are the organized crime gangs that are involved with kidnapping, extortion, theft, muggings, and other criminal activities. They have names like the Zetas, La Familia, Los Caballeros Templares (The Knights Templar), to name a few.

Americans will also have to make a greater effort to assimilate into the cultural mores and language of their newly adopted country. Americans have never been very good at this, yet they complain when Mexicans do not assimilate in the United States, especially when it comes to learning English. Canadians and Europeans don't seem to have the same problem, as they are more adept at learning the language.

The Mexican Lebanese

I have left this for last because the Lebanese are by far the most interesting group to immigrate to Mexico. Starting in 1892, when Lebanon was part of the Ottoman Empire, and during and after the Israel-Lebanon War (1948) and the Six Day War, they immigrated to the American continent. Most came from four small towns in south Lebanon. The main diaspora on the American continent includes the United States, Mexico, and Argentina.

The most prominent member of this group is Carlos Slim, the wealthiest man in the world, since 2010, with corporate holding of $69 billion. Two other notable Mexicans in non-business professions are Salma Hayek, a film star nominated for an Oscar as Best Actress for her role of Frida in the film *Frida Kahlo*, and José Sulaimán Chagnón, president of the World Boxing Council. There are many others.

Nobody really knows how many Lebanese live in Mexico, but figures run from 1 to 5 million. Not only have these Caucasians (Arab Christians) mostly maintained their racial purity, but also their ethnicity as best described in the following encounter.

My wife and I were having brunch at one of the most fashionable boutique hotels in our hometown of San Miguel de Allende. Adjoining our table were some two dozen men and women chatting away in Spanish; they stood out for their designer clothes, expensive watches and fashionably dressed women bedecked in expensive jewelry.

"Those couples at the adjoining table are interesting, wouldn't you say?"

My wife shrugged. "If you ask me they are just loud-speaking Mexicans eating breakfast and having a good time." Being a woman, she also observed, "The men are good looking, and as a woman I can tell many of the ladies have had a nip and tuck here and there, especially around the nose and eyes."

"If you observe closely they are all Caucasians and not one of them has a single drop of mestizo indio blood."

"So what?"

"You don't find that unusual when over 90 percent of Mexicans are at least part mestizos?"

"I really hadn't noticed."

"Well, dear, meet the affluent Lebanese Mexicans. Well integrated into Mexican society, they still maintain their Caucasian looks and ethnicity."

28

The Cross-Culture Revolution

WHEN I GIVE LECTURES ON CROSS-CULTURE to newly arrived foreigners, I always caution them that if they plan to visit Mexico City, they better look four ways before crossing a street or avenue. And don't trust the green light to indicate that it is safe for pedestrians. If you rely on stop signs and red lights, there are certain corners where your life expectancy will be about fifteen seconds. And, of course, cars blocking crosswalks and intersections seem at times to be a national pastime, as is the car honking the nanosecond the light turns green.

In places like San Miguel de Allende, with a large population of ex-pats, the effects of the cultural invasion are obvious just watching the interaction between traffic and pedestrians. Cars, including taxicabs, give the pedestrian the right-of-way, at times giving the impression this is California and not Mexico. At crosswalks, most cars wait to take their proper turn. When outsiders visit from places like Mexico City and don't know the rules, all sorts of hand and arm gesturing quickly bring them in line. There is also a total absence of honking. I'm happy to say that this relationship of pedestrians and cars has now spread to many towns and cities of Mexico.

I use the evolving change in driving habits in many parts of Mexico, including the use of seatbelts, as an example of U.S. cultural influence that is easily captured by the discerning eye. But there are many other changes taking place because of the American cultural invasion that began in the 1980s and really got legs with the signing of NAFTA in 1994.

One of these areas is the narrowing gender gap. Mexican women have left the confines of the home and family and have entered into the world traditionally reserved for men.

When I first came to Mexico back in the 1960s, Mexican women were described as generally ordinary in looks. Women did not exercise except when they went shopping. Maids did most of the work inside the home, including cleaning, cooking, and taking care of the children. I recently asked a Mexican housewife why she had so few modern kitchen appliances.

"My maid does the work of those electrical appliances," she answered rather smugly.

Men got up early and came back late from the office and other social diversions. They never explained what they were up to during these fourteen to sixteen hours a day away from home. Women never asked as long as their husbands lived up to their responsibilities. If this working relationship broke down and the husband was not complying as a good provider, the wife's family stepped in and negotiated a solution with the wayward male. Take care of your wife and family first, or suffer the consequences. After that problem is taken care of, do as you like. There was no need to see a marriage counselor or a therapist, much less a divorce lawyer. In fact, all three were practically nonexistent.

Today we would consider the social conduct between men and women back in the 1960s and 1970s rather primitive. Yet divorce was nearly unheard of. When a divorce took place, both participants were considered to have failed the system. There were other aspects of the relationship between men and women that an outsider might have a hard time believing.

Back in the 1970s, I had a girlfriend who insisted on coming to my apartment rather than being seen together in public. She normally stayed three or four hours, then left, much like Cinderella's disappearance, at the stroke of midnight.

A Mexican woman friend of mine took me aside one day and explained that the frequent visitor to my apartment was the mistress of a powerful politician who could easily have me disposed of if he were to find out.

"You're a foreigner in this country and under Article 33* he could even have you thrown out of the country."

On her next visit to my apartment I brought up this subject, assured that she would deny the accusations.

"Of course he knows about us," she explained. "Not only that, but he encourages our relationship."

---

* Article 33: see appendix 3, "Mexican Constitution of 1917: Xenophobia toward Foreigners."

"You must be out of your mind to submit me to this kind of risk."

"Look, I have been his mistress since the age of fifteen. He takes care of my family and me. Now I'm a grown woman and he feels I should have a relationship with someone my age.

"And what is supposed to be the outcome of this normal relationship of ours?"

"Hopefully we will marry and settle down."

"Why's that?"

"Come on . . . Mexican macho men only want to marry virgins . . . surely you know that."

"And what about Mr. Big?"

"What about him?" She was indignant I should ask.

"Will he just disappear?"

"Of course not. I'll see him from time to time and he'll continue to take care of my family and be most generous toward the two of us . . . you should know it's not all about sex."

"I suppose he can be godfather to our children?"

"Yes, if you want to assure their future."

Americans have a hard time believing this sort of behavior goes on. American women are especially outraged to think Mexican women are abused in this way. Mexican women have a different point of view. If they're not entirely happy with this sort of arrangement, that's not the impression I had from her and other women sharing a similar story. Much of that seems to have changed, but to tell the truth I can't be sure.

◆

By the late 1980s, as the Mexican economy opened and U.S. investment flooded Mexico on a large scale, American social mores and customs soon followed. The most affected was the macho Mexican male attempting to cope with the onslaught of equal rights for women.

Mexican women discovered the concept of equality of the sexes. They wanted out of the home; they wanted to look like the women in the imported fashion magazines—some were now being published in Spanish. *Cosmopolitan* magazine in Spanish depicted what every young Mexican woman now aspired to. Get in shape, watch your diet, and share the domestic responsibilities. What was most important was to get out of the home. Adulterous behavior became a two-way street. Divorce became as easy to come by for the new Mexican woman as it was for her northern cousins.

Mexican men suddenly found themselves out on the street with nowhere to go. Most of them had never even bothered to learn how to boil water; forget about boiling an egg. The only recourse for men in their forties and fifties was to move back in with their *señora madre*, hardly the macho image of maleness they were so accustomed to. Returning to the bedroom you had lived in as a child was demeaning, if not cause for suicide.

Psychiatry soon became a popular profession as Mexican men found much of the ethical behavior they believed in crashing down on their perfect world. They needed help. Their parents were too anchored in the past to be relied on for good advice.

The storm of change blowing in from the north with the signing of NAFTA was wreaking havoc with Mexican social values. Mexican marriage vows, as set out in the epistle of Melchior O'Campo such as, "The woman, whose principal talents are self-sacrifice, beauty, compassion, keen insight and tenderness should, and will, give her husband obedience, pleasure, assistance, consolation and advice. She should always treat him with delicacy and with the respect due to the one who supports and defends her," were as obsolete as the notion that Agrarian Reform could remedy poverty in rural Mexico. Eventually, by the twenty-first century, these marriage vows were relegated to the archives of Mexico's past.

Not only were women attending universities in great numbers, but they were also becoming bilingual and bicultural in the process. The traditional Mexican machismo became as extinct as the dinosaur. Mexico was once more being invaded from the north, not by economic exploitation and military inter-vention, but by American culture, this time without firing a shot. With the new generation malinchismo was dying at the same pace as machismo.

The close-knit Mexican family had always been the mainstay against out-side forces of moral corruption and vice. Based on the social values of the past, the United States was looked upon as a decadent society; its family values had no place in Mexico. The leading sign of moral decay in the United States was anchored in parents' permissiveness toward their children and the use of mari-juana, heroin, cocaine, and all sorts of mind-altering drugs. Drug use was unheard of in Mexico, largely relegated to the artistic segment of actors, painters, writers, and musicians.

If Mexico had been a major trafficker in drugs, it had never been a consumer. That was about to change. The war on drugs, which had always been a gringo problem, now became a Mexican problem.

The American influence in lifestyle, as evidenced by McDonald's, Subway, Chili's, and other U.S. fast food chains, became commonplace across the Mexican landscape. Mexico was challenging their northern neighbor for first place among the world's most obese nations.

Mexico was even experimenting with adopting some of the legal practices of common law in contrast to the Mexican Napoleonic Codes originally established by Benito Juárez in 1870. A constitutional change now allows for oral arguments in trials, unheard of under Mexico's system of Napoleonic Codes.

When state legislatures in the United States started banning smoking as a major cause of cancer, Mexico, traditionally a country of smokers, soon followed. Smoking bans now exist in most states and include bars, restaurants, and public buildings.

Mexico City even went as far as to legalize abortion in 2009, totally ignoring the country's overwhelming Catholic majority. Mexicans have even started showing some concern for the environment.

If the older generations of Mexicans were holding on to their national pride and the old ways, the younger generations were on the fast track to becoming citizens of the world, absorbing many ideas associated with their neighbor to the north.

One of the areas of change felt most was in politics. The PRI, which governed Mexico for seven decades, now became two parties inside of one. There are the "dinosaurs," in reference to the old guard, versus the up-and-coming younger generation, who scorn the practices of the past.

But there is also a reverse cultural invasion underway.

Mexico is exporting tequila, beer, Mexican cuisine, and even the celebration of Cinco de Mayo, which many Americans believe, erroneously, marks Mexico's independence from Spain. Probably the largest Mexican influence on the United States will be felt in present and future elections. There are between 14 and 18 million registered Hispanic voters, mostly of Mexican descent, out of a total Hispanic population of 39 million who will change the political landscape in the future. To this add on 12 million–plus undocumented Mexican workers and undocumented immigrants, many of whom may someday become U.S. citizens.

To understand just how powerful this emerging voter block is today, here are some interesting statistics. Hispanic voters make up 37.5 percent of the registered voters in New Mexico, 22.9 percent in California, and 16.9 percent in Arizona. While the Hispanic community is demanding comprehensive immigration reform, Washington lawmakers claim they are concerned but have yet to come up with a general outline of a comprehensive immigration bill. How long the Hispanic community will tolerate this indifference is hard to tell. I expect we will see them put forth candidates in all the districts and states with a strong Hispanic population. Hispanics already hold political positions at every level of government, including a Supreme Court justice, though some might argue that Puerto Ricans are not Hispanics in the true sense of the meaning.*

The lack of concern in Washington to the needs of the Mexican population resulted in a series of massive protests. On April 10, 2006, the Hispanic community held a national protest in 102 cities across the United States. Some of the largest demonstrations were in Los Angeles, with an estimated crowd of about 500,000; 350,000 to 500,000 in Dallas; and around 300,000 in Chicago. Waving American and Mexican flags, in many cases parading the image of the Virgin of Guadalupe and backed by Spanish-language media outlets, in particular Univision, Telemundo, Azteca America, and various Spanish-language radio stations across the country, the demonstrators left the United States in shock. Many traditional Anglo-Americans suddenly felt the country was being invaded by some alien force.

The protests would not end there. Two years later Julia Preston accurately described what was happening in an article that appeared in the *New York Times* on February 5, 2008: "Spurred by the widespread crackdown on illegal immigration and by the contentious tone of the national immigration debate, Latinos are gearing up for Tuesday's primary voting with an eye toward making Hispanics a decisive voting bloc nationwide in November."

The largest Latino protest was held in May 2008. While the word Latino implies all of Latin America, the overwhelming majority are undoubtedly of Mexican origin. This was never made clearer than by the resentment of most

---

* Hispanics are usually considered to be those people who emigrated to the United States from a Spanish-speaking country on this continent. Puerto Rico was never a country.

Americans to the constant display of the Mexican flag accompanied by the Virgin of Guadalupe. If there is some sympathy with the Mexican cause, there is no sympathy for flying a flag that is not the stars and stripes. In the politically correct United States, parading religious icons is frowned upon.

There are other negative factors that bother the American people. Spanish is fast becoming America's second language. In some states, written exams for taking out a driver's license can be taken in Spanish. Undocumented Mexicans are putting a strain on many public institutions, such as schools and free medical services. Mexican street gangs are going regional and sometimes even national. Most of these gangs operate out of federal prisons and are, in one way or another, tied into the traffic of narcotics.

Mexican organized crime currently makes the Sicilian and Colombian mafias look like pickpocketing street gangs. Traditional American biker gangs such as the Hells Angels are better off getting a haircut and a shave and trading their hogs for a Honda. Some of these leading Mexican gangs have names like Mara Salvatierra, Zetas, Norteños, Sureños, and Nuestra Familia. Many were soon joining up with their American counterparts.

The wrong answer to the cross-culture influences both countries place on each other is for the United States to ignore Mexico as it has done in the past. Mexico is not the poor cousin next door; the two countries constitute a marriage that needs constant attention.

Only time will tell how these changes will influence relations between both countries. One trend is inevitable—the two cultures are slowly coming together. This alone behooves us to pay more attention to each other. The easiest way is to understand each other's past and cultural differences as the engine that will move both ships of state, side by side into the future.

Epilogue

DENG XIAOPING, THE CHINESE LEADER responsible for his country's "great leap forward" in revamping the economy, made this statement in 1978 after making a trip to Singapore and other emerging Asian economic powerhouses: "I do not care if the cat is black or white. As long as it catches mice, it is a good cat." He was seventy-four at the time. Using this as an example, on April 18, 2010, two-time president of Costa Rica and Nobel Peace Prize-winner Óscar Arias Sánchez followed up Deng's famous statement with a warning to a gathering of Latin American presidents in a speech at the Summit of the Americas he called "Algo Hicimos Mal (We Did Something Wrong)": "Looking around at all you presidents, I don't see anyone near 74 years of age. Let's not wait until we reach that age before making the much overdue necessary changes." Mexico and the rest of Latin America, as well as the United States, were, in his opinion, too involved in fighting over "isms." Among the many were communism, socialism, capitalism, liberalism, conservatism, nationalism, neoliberalism, populism, Catholicism, evangelism, and even most religions for that matter. The Chinese and the Asian Tigers, he claimed, had gotten it right. "Pragmatism" was the obvious solution. Unfortunately, few were listening, Mexico and the United States among them.

What has shocked many Mexicans is the resurgence of the PRI, the one-party dictatorship that ruled Mexico from 1929 to 2000. There is no better example than the presidential election results announced by the IFE in July 2012, that Enrique Peña Nieto of the PRI party was the winner and, if ratified after scrutinizing the results for anomalies and fraud in the voting process, will be declared the new constitutionally elected president for the next six years. Fears that Mexico, like many countries in Latin America, is on a populist track (led by Andrés López Obrador, the Mexican Messiah), have been allayed for the time being. For many Mexicans, the PRI of today has a different face from the one made up of the so-called dinosaurs. They see little resemblance to the past. It is now Mexico's centrist party, with a slight leaning to the left.

However, many Mexican political pundits feel differently about the new PRI. To them, it's the same old party of the past. Their methods of doing business have not changed—only some of the faces of those who make up the leadership. As an example, they point out that the most essential problem facing Mexican lawmakers is a complete overhaul of the tax system, known for years as La Reforma Fiscal (Fiscal Reform). The PRI has made it clear that this is not going to happen now that they have a majority over the PAN and PRD parties. It does seem the tax codes will not be reformed. Business as usual, despite the dire need for change. To have a clear understanding of the problem, Miguel Savastano, economist for the IMF in Latin America, said, "An improved tax system has been on Mexico's agenda for many years. Now might be the time to carry out a structural fiscal reform." Savastano added, "This would amplify the tax base and develop more capacity to generate resources, not just in time of crisis, but also in normal times."

Turning to Pemex, we have already discussed that Mexico has one of the lowest tax collection percentages in terms of GDP. To make up for the shortfall in the yearly federal budget, Pemex pays approximately 33 percent of the federal taxes collected by the government. It is important to review the problem and the solution.

On March 20, 2012, Sergio Sarmiento, a well-known Mexican political commentator, wrote an op-ed in the newspaper *Reforma* titled "Refinado (Refined)" that said, "Instead of the federal government continuing to plunder Pemex's financial assets, all these assets should be used for the exploration and exploitation of crude. We also have to open private investment in refining and the transportation of crude in pipelines. This state owned company does not have to be the strongbox for the government's use of its funds for lack of fiscal reform."

The good news is that the newly elected president has vowed to do much of what Sarmiento suggests. He has promised a constitutional reform allowing Pemex to open its doors to foreign investment and "production sharing." He can count on a majority in the legislative branch of government to make this happen. Mexico has one of the largest untapped oil reserves in the world. The

press has announced that Exxon and Pemex are already negotiating in anticipation of new opportunities in Mexico's oil industry.

While nationalistic fervor still rears its ugly head, pragmatism seems to be
on the rise. The fear that the new president-elect is a throwback to the era of PRI
revolutionary zealots is not at all clear. Unlike most presidents of Mexico who
attended UNAM, the national university known for being the breeding ground
of most Mexican politicians with a leftist/socialist bent, Peña Nieto graduated
from the Universidad Panamericana. He also has a MBA from the Tecnológico
de Monterrey, considered one of the top universities in Mexico that strongly
supports the private sector as the road to Mexico's economic future. Aside of
starting Pemex on the road to privatization, there are also indications, now that
Peña Nieto has been elected president, that he is in the process of replacing
some of his old guard supporters with people professing more pragmatic solutions to many of Mexico's historic post-revolution sacred cows. The new president-elect is young, charismatic, and good-looking, hardly what one might
expect as being representative of the old guard.

One of the major problems is the future of populism in Latin America and
Mexico. There are mixed signals of where this is heading. Venezuela, the populist leader on this continent, is showing some serious cracks. Unemployment
is on the increase, and the currency is being devaluated, which will eventually
result in an upward spiral of inflation. Productivity is on a downward slide, and
the grumbling of discontent increases daily. Hugo Chávez is no longer the same
dynamic leader of the past. His public outbursts generally reflect his hatred for
the United States with absolutely no vision to the future he once so eloquently
talked about.

The Mexican populist politician Andrés López Obrador (AMLO) once
more ran for president, but this time moderated many of his extremist populist
views, among them those concerning elections. He once made the statement
that change did not result from elections but from massive demonstrations in the
streets. This time he vowed to respect the electoral process, unlike the 2006
elections where he lost by a mere .5 percent. But, as the saying goes, "Leopards
can't change their spots." He lost by 6.6 percent of the vote to the winner, which
brought on the following comments in the July 9 edition of the newspaper
Reforma in an op-ed titled "Templo Mayor": "SAY IT ISN'T SO. Every time
they asked him, he would even get more indignant. Nevertheless, Andrés

Manuel López Obrador made the prophecy by his critics come true: he does not respect the electoral results. Everything indicates that the country is going straight into another political crisis by not recognizing Enrique Peña Nieto's triumph." The prophecy is partially true when we view the riots at the new president's inauguration.

Trade

In July 2009, ambassador-designate Carlos Pascual had this to say at his confirmation hearing in front of the U.S. Senate Foreign Relations Committee. "Nothing is more important than the recovery of both our economies. Our common challenge is to make North America [Canada, United States, Mexico] the most important provider of technology, goods and services in the world." He did not explain how this was to be accomplished. What he said, which is a direct reference to NAFTA and its future, is an indication that the Obama administration, while taking an anti-NAFTA bent during his campaign for the presidency, has had a change of heart. When President Obama visited Mexico in August of 2009, he insisted that NAFTA should be expanded and not restricted. This hardly sits well with the liberal wing of his party.

Immigration

When it comes to immigration reform, Senator Charles "Chuck" Schumer promised there would be an immigration bill on the Senate floor by Labor Day 2009. My original assessment was: good luck. This assurance was followed by a promise from President Obama that there definitely would be an immigration bill passed in 2010. It did not turn out to be true. Will the future be any better?

In the August 29, 2010, issue of the *New York Times*, the op-ed titled "Massacre in Tamaulipas," made this succinct commentary.

> The American response to Mexico's agonies has mostly been a heightened fixation on militarizing the border. . . . Enforcement without any overhaul of legal migration creates only the illusion of control. Without a system tied to labor demand, illegality, disorder and death proliferate.
>
> Current temporary-worker programs are so cumbersome and bureaucratic they are almost unusable by employers.

Where have we heard this before?

As of 2012 there was no immigration bill in sight, nor is there anyone in the media who has brought the president and Schumer to task for these empty promises. When it comes to immigration reform, it's business as usual. But the big lie continues. Obama is once more promising that if reelected he will pass a comprehensive immigration reform bill. When will rhetoric become more than just empty promises? Getting votes has always been more important with his presidency than actually trying to get something done.

It is worth mentioning that, instead of concentrating on immigration reform nobody has a stomach for, passing a Temporary Guest Worker Visa Reform Act could correct some of the more immediate problems. Unfortunately neither liberals nor conservatives seem to have a clue about pragmatism.

Narcotraffic

As for the war on drugs in Mexico there could be some end in sight. Many Mexican luminaries such as ex-president Ernesto Zedillo, now a professor at Yale, and writer and social commentator Carlos Fuentes have both reached the conclusion that the United States and Mexico must seriously start down the legalization road. That is never going to happen if the conservatives have their way.

However, the prevailing political opinion seems to be that when the PRI takes over the presidency in 2012, there will be an accommodation with the drug cartels. The most important of these is the Sinaloa cartel under the control of Joaquín "El Chapo" Guzmán. Political opinion was right for a change. As president-elect Peña Nieto has already stated, he will not continue the war against the drug cartels. Instead he has vowed to go after organized crime, which in some cases are the enforcers in the drug war, but also are involved in extortion, murder, torture, kidnapping, hijacking, rape, and robbery, among their many crimes. The most wanted has to refer to the Zetas as heading the list of these organized thugs.

In my opinion, the president-elect has a point. Why should Mexican law enforcement agencies and the military fight a drug war on Mexican soil when the United States drives the conflict by providing the financial resources and much of the weapons to the Mexican cartels? The United States needs to either fight the war on drugs, and shoulder the resulting human casualties, on its own soil; legalize; or stop the demand. A top priority is to bring a halt to the smuggling of arms into Mexico from along the border. The United States seems incapable of doing this.* Stop blaming the Mexicans who have already given far too much of their own citizens' blood. And, for once and for all, stop moralizing on human rights abuses by Mexican law enforcement and the military. The new words in the U.S. lexicon, "collateral damage, enhanced interrogation, extreme measures and renditions" hardly qualify for pointing the finger at anyone but themselves.

The Economy

Keeping in mind that I am not an economist, I shall defer to two qualified sources. The first is Joseph Stiglitz, a 2001 Nobel Prizewinner in economics, and the second is the analysis for 2010 prepared by the American Chamber of Commerce in Mexico.

At a presentation made to Mexican business leaders on November 19, 2009, Stiglitz summarized Mexico's future:

> The new fiscal laws [tax increases] that Mexico put in place starting in 2010 will not stimulate a much needed recovery of the economy.
>
> The solution for Mexico is to reach out to new markets. The only real possibility of real growth is in conjunction with Asia.

Second, the American Chamber of Commerce had some additional comments on the future panorama in "Mexico 2010" as reported in the newspaper *El Universal*:

> Mexico will lose foreign investment due to the fiscal *parche* [patch] law approved by Congress. Capital will be diverted to other countries in Latin America, such as Brazil.
>
> The future vision of the Mexican legislature was "totally mistaken." They should have reduced taxes, not increased them.

At least in the short run, both were proven wrong. In terms of GDP, Mexico's economic growth turned out to be 5.5 percent in 2010 (after a –6.5 percent in 2009), 3.8 percent in 2011, and somewhere around a 3.5 to 4.5 percent prognosis for 2012, according to the economic soothsayers. This growth is largely being

---

* See "Mexico's Gun Traffic," *Washington Post* editorial, September 13, 2010.

driven by a 65 percent increase in automobiles for export. When I asked a leading financial analyst to explain this phenomenon, since car sales in the United States were in a deep slump, he explained, "Sales to China and Brazil are booming." Mexico seems to have heeded Stiglitz's recommendations.

In economic terms, the old refrain that when the United States sneezes, Mexico has pneumonia seems outdated. As of 2012 that saying does not ring true with the dismal prognosis that the GNP in the U.S. might run under 2 percent. This reversal of fortunes may be a historical first.

U.S.-Mexican Relations

In part VI I talked about the positive measures and initiatives being taken in two areas of the Troika of American Foreign Policy: NAFTA and the drug war along the border. However, that still leaves the dismal record of any attempts to give a positive solution to the immigration problem that will only get worse, as it will not go away. At the same time, it is interesting to see how the United States officially views what Ambassador Pascual calls "Mexico at a Crossroads" in a speech he made at Stanford University on October 20, 2010.

> At one of these crossroads we find Mexico at the cusp of a global economy – a G20 partner, yet still with over 40% of its population considered poor. At another crossroads there is Mexico's internal security, where there is terrible violence inflicted by transnational organized crime, but also Mexico's new initiatives to assert the rule of law over criminal activity. And yet a third crossroad, we see the intersection between economies and security – whether the virtues of jobs and competitiveness are a weapon against insecurity, or whether insecurity will drive away economic opportunity.

As of 2012, economic opportunity seems to have healthy prospects, according to George Friedman, founder and CEO of Stratfor Global Intelligence: "A few years ago I wrote about Mexico possibly becoming a failed state because of the effect of the cartels on the country. . . . but it stabilized itself and took a different course instead—one of impressive economic growth in the face of instability."[*]

---

[*] George Friedman, "Mexico's Strategy," Geopolitical Weekly, *Stratfor Global Intelligence*, August 21, 2012.

An unfortunate piece of news was the resigning of Ambassador Carlos Pascual in March 2011 over Wikileaks disclosures between him and the State Department that infuriated President Felipe Calderón. The ambassador criticized the Mexican president for not being aggressive enough on curtailing the activities of the drug cartels. The president was also upset that the divorced ambassador was seeing the daughter of a politician high up in the ranks of the PRI—the main party of opposition. Criticism of Mexico by a foreigner is not acceptable. Anti-malinchismo is very much alive.

When I first introduced the foreign policy of the United States towards Mexico, I used the words "benign neglect." On November 1, 2011, retired secretary of state Condoleezza Rice was being interviewed by Sean Hannity on Fox News when she was asked what she considered one of the important failures during her tenure. She answered, "I think it was our neglect of Mexico. We missed the opportunity with President Vicente Fox to address some of the important issues such as immigration. Unfortunately other events [read: 9/11] distracted us."

When it comes to global politics, the United States always seems to be distracted at the expense of paying closer attention to this hemisphere, and that includes its two neighbors, Mexico and Canada. They seem to have forgotten that the Monroe Doctrine of 1823 got it right. The natural sphere of influence of the United States is this continent first, then Europe, then the Middle East and Asia. The question is: Will this benign neglect ever change?

Appendix 1
Mexican Constitution of 1917:
Introduction

Please note that I am not citing the entire Mexican Constitution, only those sections I feel pertinent to this book.

ARTICLE 3

But as regards elementary, secondary, and normal education (and that of any kind or grade designed for laborers and farm workers) they must previously obtain, in every case, the express authorization of the public power. Such authorization may be refused or revoked by decisions against which there can be no judicial proceedings or recourse.

In effect, the state was now in control of the primary and secondary education of its people, including the official government interpretation of all social sciences and history. The interpretation of history could be managed through the *Texto Únicos*.* In July 2010 the government recalled over one million official history text books, claiming much of the information had to be revised.

ARTICLE 4

All people, men and women, are equal under the law. [However, the] "development" of the family is placed under the responsibility of the woman.

---

* *Texto Único* refers to the standardization of history into only one text book.

If we think about it, this is a modern concept. What it strongly suggests is that Mexico is a matriarchal country, a statement that would raise eyebrows among the ever-present macho population. But similar to the United States, the responsibility for raising children has also become a shared experience as more and more married women and single mothers enter the workplace.

ARTICLE 9

The right to assemble or associate peaceably for any lawful purpose cannot be restricted; but only citizens of the Republic may do so to take part in the political affairs of the country. No armed deliberative meeting is authorized.

This article has been used excessively by organizations large and small to publicly express their grievances in demonstrations that tie up public transit, close off streets and highways, and result in the loss of literally millions of productive work hours. This tactic is especially true when employed by populists groups, leftist political activists, and all forms of organizations in discord with the government. These so-called popular demonstrations are usually concentrated in Mexico City.

ARTICLE 10

The inhabitants of the United Mexican States are entitled to have arms of any kind in their possession for their protection and legitimate defense, except such as are expressly forbidden by law, or which the nation may reserve for the exclusive use of the Army, Navy, or National Guard; but they may not carry arms within inhabited places without complying with police regulations.

The right-to-bear-arms law is interesting when compared to the Second Amendment of the U.S. Constitution. American lawmakers might take note. Let's take a look.

Gun licensing and legislation for Mexican citizens

Federal Law of Firearms and Explosives

Generally, citizens are restricted by law to:
- *pistolas (handguns) of .380 Auto or .38 Special revolvers or smaller in either case,*
- *escopetas (shotguns) of 12 gauge or smaller, with barrels longer than 25 inches, and*
- *rifles (rifles) bolt action and semi-auto.*

The transportation of a weapon can only be done with the express approval of SEDENA, La Secretaría de la Defensa Nacional [Ministry of National Defense].

Handguns in calibers bigger than those mentioned above are forbidden from private ownership.

Appendix 2
Mexican Constitution of 1917: Agrarian Reform, Public and Private Property

ARTICLE 27

The property of all land and water within national territory is originally owned by the Nation, who has the right to transfer this ownership to particulars. Hence, private property is a privilege created by the Nation.

This article became the basis for the Agrarian Reform, another term for the redistribution of land taken from privately owned farms and haciendas and given to the campesinos, and created the Mexican equivalent of the future Soviet Union's communes, known in Mexico as el ejido. Americans would shudder at the suggestion of the redistribution of private property.

The State will also regulate the exploitation of natural resources based on social benefits and the equal distribution of wealth. All natural resources in national territory are property of the nation, and private exploitation may only be carried out through concessions.

At that time the Mexican government very much wanted the United States to recognize the new revolutionary government. As a result, they toned down the expropriation of private property, considering how much of it was in the hands of Americans. The redistribution of land to the campesino was kept in check until the presidency of Lázaro Cárdenas (1934–1940) and Luis Echeverría (1970–1976). Economists know that the equal distribution of wealth always has disastrous consequences.

The right to land ownership and to exploit the subsoil may therefore only be granted by the Nation. Land may also be expropriated whenever deemed necessary.

This interpretation of Article 27 that appears in the Texto Únicos taught in public schools made it possible to control the activities of mining and oil companies and to redistribute the land of large estates among the peasants.

ARTICLE 27 (ON RELIGION)

Religious institutions known as churches, regardless of creed, may in no case acquire, hold, or administer real property or hold mortgages thereon; such property held at present either directly or through an intermediary shall revert to the Nation, any person whosoever being authorized to denounce any property so held. Presumptive evidence shall be sufficient to declare the denunciation well founded. Places of public worship are the property of the Nation, as represented by the Federal Government, which shall determine which of them may continue to be devoted to their present purposes. Bishoprics, rectories, seminaries, asylums, and schools belonging to religious orders, convents, or any other buildings built or intended for the administration, propagation, or teaching of a religious creed shall at once become the property of the Nation by inherent right, to be used exclusively for the public services of the Federal or State Governments, within their respective jurisdictions. All places of public worship hereafter erected shall be the property of the Nation.

ARTICLE 130

The federal powers shall exercise the supervision required by law in matters relating to religious worship and outward ecclesiastical forms.

Articles 130 and 27, dealing with the Catholic Church, when taken in their entirety brought the clergy totally under the control of the state. It ratifies the anti-clerical laws, and Catholic Church property expropriation, initiated in the Reforma during the presidency of Benito Juárez.

President Plutarco Calles (1924–1928), a confirmed atheist, would strictly apply them in a witch-hunt that became known as the Rebellión Cristero (1926–1929).

Appendix 3
Mexican Constitution of 1917:
Xenophobia toward Foreigners

ARTICLE 32

Mexicans shall have priority over foreigners under equality of circumstances for all classes of concessions and for employment, positions, or commissions of the Government in which the status of citizenship is not indispensable.

This article forms the basis of the immigration laws pertaining to foreigners. Simply put, the office of immigration could refuse a work permit to any foreigner if a national could perform the job. This gave the government carte blanche to turn down just about everyone trying to immigrate to Mexico and acquire the right to work. There is no clearer example of the national xenophobia towards foreigners.

ARTICLE 33

The Federal Executive shall have the exclusive power to compel any foreigner whose remaining he may deem inexpedient to abandon the national territory immediately and without the necessity of previous legal action. . . . Foreigners may not in any way participate in the political affairs of the country.

In short, the Mexican government has the right to do just about anything it wishes with foreigners. Here we have the clear manifestation of a national xenophobia towards foreign influence. It clearly brings into focus the malinchismo from the time of the conquest of Mexico (1519–1521).

This article was applied to one of my partners back in the 1970s when he was denounced to the immigration authorities over a minor business difference. My American partner was legally in the country and had a temporary work permit that he was required to renew every six months.

The immigration inspectors came to his apartment and whisked him off to the Mexico City airport where he was placed on the first plane leaving the country, which happened to be to San Antonio, even though he was from Florida. After he was placed in the back of the plane prior to the regular passengers boarding, one of the stewardesses approached him.

"So what did you do wrong to get you deported?"

"You know, believe it or not, I don't know," he answered shaking his head.

"Yeah, that's what they all say," the knowing stewardess answered as she excused herself to tend to her duties.

This article has since been modified by the Supreme Court and allows foreigners to legally defend themselves before having to leave the country.

Appendix 4
Mexican Constitution of 1917:
Non-Reelection Clauses

ARTICLE 59

Senators and deputies to the Congress of the Union cannot be reelected for the immediately following term.

This article also applied to Municipal presidents (city mayors).

ARTICLE 83

The President shall assume the duties of office on the first of December for a term of six years. A citizen who has held the office of President of the Republic, by popular election or by appointment as ad interim, provisional, or substitute President, can in no case and for no reason again hold that office.

This article also applied to state governors.

While both Article 59 and 83 were intended to prevent the rise of dictatorial rule, the effect was quite different. These two articles also removed any pretense of any kind of political initiative based on performance and accomplishment in representing the electorate since no one was permitted to stand for reelection. It in effect gave free rein for politicians to engage in corruption and theft. What other reason could there be for holding an elected office? Since Mexico for all intents was a one-party system until the year 2000,* incoming

---

* The year 2000 was the first open presidential election where the outgoing president did not name his successor.

elected officials generally agreed to not prosecute the outgoing official. This cozy relationship could be very effective in stripping the wealth of a nation and confirmed that famous political Mexican saying, "A politician who is poor, is a poor politician."*

* *"Un político pobre es un pobre político."*—Hank González, ex-governor of the state of México.

Appendix 5
The History of Land Reform:
1910–1934

During the Álvaro Obregón presidency, Mexico began to concentrate on land reform. After the revolution, land was redistributed to Mexicans as part of a process of nationalization and "Mexicanization." Land distribution began almost immediately and affected both foreign and large domestic landowners (Hacendados); however, this process was generally slow. Between the years of 1915 and 1928, 5.3 million hectares were distributed to over a half million recipients in some 1,500 communities. By 1930, though, ejidos constituted only 6.3 percent of national agricultural property by area, or 9.4 percent by value.

CARDENISTA LAND REFORM, 1934–1940

President Lázaro Cárdenas passed the 1934 Agrarian Code and accelerated the pace of land reform. Agrarian reform had come close to extinction in the early 1930s. Cárdenas distributed more land than all his revolutionary predecessors put together, a 400 percent increase. He also accelerated the process and greatly promoted the collective ejido in order to justify the expropriation of large commercial haciendas.

STEP BACK, 1940–1970

Starting with the government of Miguel Alemán (1946–1952), land reform steps made in previous governments were rolled back. Alemán's government allowed capitalist entrepreneurs to rent peasant land. This created phenomenon known as neolatifundismo, where landowners build up large-scale private farms on the basis of controlling land that remains ejidal but is not sown by the peasants to whom it is assigned.

1970 AND STATIZATION

In 1970 President Luis Echeverría began his term by declaring land reform dead. In the face of peasant revolt he was forced to eat his words and embarked on the biggest land reform program since Cárdenas. Echeverría legalized land invasions of huge foreign-owned private farms, which were turned into new collective ejidos.

LAND REFORM FROM 1991 TO PRESENT

In 1988 President Salinas de Gortari was elected. In December 1991 he amended Article 27 of the Constitutional to make it legal to sell ejido land and allow peasants to put up their land as collateral for a loan.

Appendix 6
NAFTA: Preamble and Article 102

PREAMBLE

The Government of Canada, the Government of the United Mexican States and the Government of the United States of America resolved to:

- STRENGTHEN the special bonds of friendship and cooperation among their nations.

- CONTRIBUTE to the harmonious development and expansion of world trade and provide a catalyst to broader international cooperation.

- CREATE an expanded and secure market for the goods and services produced in their territories.

- REDUCE distortions to trade.

- ESTABLISH clear and mutual advantageous rules governing their trade.

- ENSURE a predictable commercial framework for business planning and investment

- BUILD on their respective rights and obligations under the *General Agreement on Tariffs and Trade* and other multilateral and bilateral instruments of cooperation.

- ENHANCE the competitiveness of their firms in global markets.

- FOSTER creativity and innovation, and promote trade in goods and services that are subject of intellectual property rights.

- CREATE new employment opportunities and improve working conditions and living standards in their respective territories.

- UNDERTAKE each of the preceding in a manner consistent with environmental protection and conservation.

- PRESERVE their flexibility to safe guard the public welfare.

- PROMOTE sustainable development

- STRENGHTHEN the development and enforcement of environmental laws and regulations.

- PROTECT, enhance and enforce basic workers' rights.

ARTICLE 102

- Grant favored nation status to the signatures.

- Eliminate barriers to trade and facilitate the cross-border movement of goods and services.

- Promote conditions of fair competition.

- Increase investment opportunities.

- Provide protection and enforcement of intellectual property rights.

- Create procedures for the resolution of trade disputes.

- Establish a framework for further trilateral, regional and multilateral cooperation to expand NAFTA's benefits.

Selected Bibliography

BOOKS

Albertazzi, Daniele, and Duncan McDonnell, ed. *Twenty-First Century Populism: The Spectre of Western European Democracy.* New York: Palgrave Macmillan, 2008.

Baker, Eugene C. *The Life of Stephen F. Austin, Founder Of Texas, 1793–1836; A Chapter of the Westward Movement by the Anglo-American People.* New York: Da Capo Press, 1968.

Blancornelas, Jesús. *El Cártel: Los Arellano Félix, la Mafia más Poderosa en la Historia de América Latina.* Barcelona: Random House Mondadori, 2002.

Braddy, Haldeen. *Cock of the Walk, Qui-Qui-Ri-Quí! The Legend of Pancho Villa.* Albuquerque: University of New Mexico Press, 1955.

Brading, D. A. *Mexican Phoenix: Our Lady Of Guadalupe: Image and Tradition Across Five Centuries.* New York: Cambridge University Press, 2001.

Crosby, Harry. *The Cave Paintings of Baja California: Discovering the Great Murals of an Unknown People.* San Diego: Sunbelt Publications, 1997.

Davidow, Jeffrey. *The Bear and the Porcupine: The U.S. and Mexico.* Princeton, NJ: Markus Wiener Publishers, 2007.

Davis, Margaret L. *Dark Side of Fortune: Triumph and Scandal in the Life of Oil Tycoon Edward L. Doheny.* Berkeley: University of California Press, 1998.

De Mente, Boyé Lafayette. *There's a Word for it in Mexico.* Lincolnwood, IL: NTC Pub. Group, 1998.

Díaz del Castillo, Bernal. *The Conquest of New Spain.* Translated by J. M. Cohen. London: Penguin Books, 1963.

Fernández Menéndez, Jorge. *El Otro Poder: Las Redes del Narcotráfico, la Política y la Violencia en México.* Mexico: Editorial Alfaguaro, 2001 (in Spanish).

Fox Quesada, Vicente, and Rob Allyn. *Revolution of Hope: The Life, Faith, and Dreams of a Mexican President.* New York: Viking, 2007.

González de la Garza, Mauricio. *Ultima Llamada* [Last call]. Mexico: Editores Asociados Mexicanos, 1981(in Spanish).

Grayson, George. *Mexican Messiah: Andrés López Obrador.* University Park: Pennsylvania State Press, 2007.

James, Daniel. *Mexico and The Americans*. New York: Praeger, 1963.

Katz, Friedrich. *Life & Times of Pancho Villa*. Stanford, CA: Stanford University Press, 1998.

King, Nicholas. *George Bush, a Biography*. New York: Dodd, Mead, 1980.

Krauze, Enrique. *Biografía del Poder: Caudillos de la Revolución Mexicana, 1910–1940*. TusQuets, 2002 (in Spanish).

———. *Mexico: Biography of Power: A History of Modern Mexico, 1810–1996*. New York: Harper Perennial, 1998.

Lewis, Oscar. *The Children of Sánchez: Autobiography of a Mexican Family*. New York: Random House, 1979.

———. *Five Families: Mexican Case Studies in the Culture of Poverty*. New York: Basic Books, 1975.

Martín Moreno, Francisco. *México Acribillado: Una Novela Histórica en Cuatro Actos*. Mexico: Editorial Alfaguaro, 2008 (in Spanish).

———. *México Mutilado: La Raza Maldita*. Mexico: Editorial Alfaguaro, 2004 (in Spanish).

McLynn, Frank. *Villa and Zapata: A History of the Mexican Revolution*. New York: Carroll & Graf, 2002.

Oppenheimer, Andrés. *Bordering on Chaos: Mexico's Roller-Coaster Journey toward Prosperity*. Boston: Little, Brown, 1998.

———. *Cuentos Chinos: El Engaño de Washington, la Mentira Populista y la Esperanza de América Latina*. Barcelona: Random House Mondadori, 2006 (in Spanish).

Pastor, Robert A., and Jorge Castañeda. *Limits to Friendship: The United States and Mexico*. New York: Knopf, 1988.

Paz, Octavio. *The Labyrinth of Solitude: Life and Thought in Mexico*. New York: Grove Press, 1962.

Pazos, Luis. *Porque Chiapas?* Mexico: Editorial Diana, 1994 (in Spanish).

Peter, Laurence J., and Raymond Hull. *The Peter Principle*. New York: William Morrow, 1969.

Poniatowska, Elena. *Massacre in Mexico*. Translated by Helen R. Lane. New York: Viking Press, 1975.

Prescott, William H. *History of the Conquest of Mexico*. Philadelphia: J. B. Lippincott, 1891.

Preston, Julia, and Samuel Dillon. *Opening Mexico: The Making of a Democracy*. New York: Farrar, Strauss, Giroux, 2004.

Riding, Alan. *Distant Neighbors: A Portrait of the Mexicans*. New York: Knopf, 1984.

Salinas de Gortari, Carlos. *México: Un Paso Difícil a la Modernidad* [México: A hard step into modern times]. Barcelona: Plaza & Janés Editores, 2002.

Santayana, Jorge. *Reason In Common Sense*. Vol. I. New York: Scribner's, 1905.

Taibo, Paco Ignacio. *68*. New York: Seven Story Press, 2003.

Ulloa Bornemann, Alberto. *Surviving Mexico's Dirty War: A Political Prisoner's Memoir*. Edited and translated by Arthur Schmidt and Aurora Camacho de Schmidt. Philadelphia: Temple University Press, 2007.

Weintraub, Sidney. *Unequal Partners: The United States and Mexico*. Pittsburgh: University of Pittsburgh Press, 2010.

Wilson, Henry Lane. *Diplomatic Episodes in Mexico, Belgium, and Chile*. Garden City, NY: Doubleday, 1927.

Wornat, Olga. *Crónicas Malditas Desde un México Desolado* [Cursed chronicles from a desolate Mexico]. Barcelona: Random House Mondadori, 2003.

ARTICLES

Agren, David. "The Legend of Jesus Malverde." *World Politics Review*, June 28, 2007.

Associated Press. "Remittances Sent Home by Mexican Migrant Workers." February 1, 2011.

BBC News. "Mexico Suffers Devastating Earthquake." September 19, 1985.

BusinessWeek. "Pemex May Be Turning From Gusher To Black Hole." December 13, 2004.

Cabildo, Miguel. "La Brigada Blanca." *Proceso* magazine, October 29, 2000.

Cave, Damian, and Ginger Thomson. "Ambassador Carlos Pascual Resignation." *New York Times*, March 25, 2011.

Crosby, H. W. "Immigration Protests." Center for Strategic & International Studies, May 1, 2008.

Doyle, Kate. "Prelude to Disaster: José López Portillo and the Crash of 1976." National Security Archive, Washington, DC, March 14, 2004.

Dresser, Denise. "Va pa'tras (Going Backwards)." *Grupo Reforma* editorial, May 17, 2010.

El Universal. "Empresas Gastan el 10% de sus Ingresos en Mordidas" [Mexican companies pay 10% of their incomes in bribes]. April 12, 2010.

Forbes. "World's Richest Man." August 6, 2007.

Friedman, Milton. "Prohibition and Drugs." *Newsweek*, May 1, 1972.

Harman, Greg. "Lawsuit Blames Mex. Gov. for Juarez Femecides." *San Antonio Current*, May 5, 2009.

Houston Business Journal. "Zapata Petroleum Drilling in the Gulf of Mexico." April 23, 2003.

Immigration Policy Center. "The Dream Act 2010." American Immigration Council.

International Forum of Intelligence and Security Specialists, December 5–7, 2008, Mexico City.

News, The (Mexico City). "U.S. Mexico Gunrunning." December 28, 2010.

New York Times. "Massacre in Tamualipas." August 29, 2010.

———. "Pemex Case Sentencing." May 8, 1987.

———. "Porfirio Diaz Dies." July 3, 1915.

Preston, Julia. "Rush to Vote by Hispanics." New York Times, February 5, 2008.

Sullivan, Kevin, and Mary Jordan. "Benjamin Arellano Félix Interview." *Washington Post,* October 31, 2002.

Storrs, Larry K. "Drug Certification Issues." Congressional Research Service, 1986–2001.

Time. "The Domino Player." September 14, 1953.

———. "Don't Panic: Here Comes Bailout Bill." February 13, 1995.

———."The Paycheck Revolution." December 8, 1958.

MOTION PICTURES

Juárez. Directed by William Dieterle. Burbank, CA: Warner Bros., 1939.

Presumed Guilty (documentary). Directed by Roberto Hernández and Geoffrey Smith. Mexico: Cinépolis Distribución, 2011.

Viva Villa! Directed by Jack Conway. Beverly Hills, CA: MGM, 1934.

Viva Zapata! Directed by Elia Kazan. Los Angeles: Twentieth Century Fox Film Corporation, 1952.

Wild Bunch, The. Directed by Sam Peckinpah. Burbank, CA: Warner Bros., 1969.

Index

About the Author

BELDON BUTTERFIELD WAS BORN AND RAISED in Buenos Aires, Argentina. At the age of fifteen he was sent away to school in the United States. Months later his parents fled Argentina due to the persecution by the Peronistas under the Juan and Evita Perón dictatorship for his father's contribution of identifying Argentine companies doing business with the Axis powers during World War II. They spent the rest of their lives exiled in Montevideo, Uruguay. This traumatic incident of government overreach awakened the author's interest in global politics and led him to pursue a college degree in history and political theory from Washington & Lee University.

At the age of twenty-six he was posted to Mexico City by Time Life International (TLI). He returned to New York after his disillusionment upon seeing the Mexican government putting down a student uprising, known as the Tlatelolco Massacre, which left the 1968 Mexico Olympics in shambles. Four years later he was back in Mexico and has lived in his adopted country ever since as a media representative working with such prestigious publications as the *Financial Times* and *BusinessWeek*.

After years of giving lectures on cross-border culture and Mexican history to newly arrived ex-pats, as well as competing in equestrian jumping events in central Mexico, he self-published two novels: *The Crystal Bull* and *The Line/La Línea*, based on the traffic of drugs between Mexico and the United States. He is also an avid croquet player and kayaker.

He and his wife, Kate, live in San Miguel de Allende, located in the central highlands of Mexico. He has three daughters, two living in the United States and one in Mexico, and an older brother who has spent most of his life in Brazil as a cattle rancher and soybean farmer.